# MARK

# MARK

*Storyteller, Interpreter, Evangelist*

FRANCIS J. MOLONEY, SDB

Mark: Storyteller, Interpreter, Evangelist
© 2004 by Francis J. Moloney, SDB

Hendrickson Publishers, Inc.
P. O. Box 3473
Peabody, Massachusetts 01961-3473

ISBN-13: 978-1-56563-513-5
ISBN-10: 1-56563-513-2

*Printed in the United States of America*

*Second Printing — June 2006*

Cover Art: Makoto Fujimura. "Between Two Waves." Mineral pigments on Kumohada paper over canvas. With the courtesy of Kristen Fredrickson Contemporary. Photograph by Ed Gorn.

"Between Two Waves" is one of a series of paintings by Makoto Fujimura based on verses from T. S. Eliot's *Four Quartets*. The title of Fujimura's work comes from the following passage from "Little Gidding":

> Not known, because not looked for
> But heard, half-heard, in the stillness
> Between two waves of the sea.

This artwork was chosen for the way the image of "the stillness between two waves of the sea" evokes the presence of God and the limits of human ability to perceive him, as Jesus is surrounded by the tumultuous events recorded in Mark.

### Library of Congress Cataloging-in-Publication Data

Moloney, Francis J.
    Mark : storyteller, interpreter, evangelist / Francis J. Moloney.
      p. cm.
    Includes bibliographical references and indexes.
    ISBN-13: 978-1-56563-513-5 (alk. paper)
    ISBN-10: 1-56563-513-2 (alk. paper)
    1. Bible. N.T. Mark—Criticism, interpretation, etc.  I. Title.
    BS2585.52.M65 2004
    226.3'06—dc22
                                  2003027730

For
Suzanne Marie Schwarz

Χαῖρε, κεχαριτωμένη, ὁ κύριος μετὰ σοῦ

# Contents

## Part 3: Mark the Interpreter

## Part 4: Mark the Evangelist

# Preface

The Gospel of Mark was, for many centuries, one of the best-guarded secrets of the Christian church. The everyday life and practice of the church was dominated by the use of the Gospel of Matthew (for example, the Sermon on the Mount [Matt 5–7], the Lord's Prayer [6:9–13], Peter, the "rock" upon which the church was founded [16:16–18], the Virgin Birth [1:18–25], the Trinity [28:16–20]). The Gospel of Luke provided the church, its preachers and its artistic imagination, with memorable events and parables from the life of Jesus (for example, our Christmas pageantry [Luke 1–2], the Good Samaritan [10:25–37], Martha and Mary [10:38–42], the father and his two sons [15:11–32], the Pharisee and the tax collector [18:9–14], Zacchaeus [19:1–9], the journey to Emmaus [24:13–35]). The Gospel of John stood alone, the soaring eagle of the four gospel traditions, with its remarkable prologue (1:1–18), the lengthy and profound encounters between Jesus and other characters in the story (for example, Nicodemus [John 3:1–21], the Samaritan woman [4:1–30], the man born blind [9:1–38], Martha and Mary and the raising of Lazarus [11:1–44], Mary Magdalene at the tomb [20:11–18]), the unrestrained presentation of Jesus as the Son, the incarnation of the divine (see, for example, 1:14; 10:30, 38), and the witness of the Beloved Disciple (see 19:35; 21:20–24). Among such illustrious company, the Gospel according to Mark was the Cinderella of the Four Gospels, regularly left at home when it came to major celebrations.

Yet the Gospel of Mark was known and respected in the early church, accepted as "Scripture" as early as Tatian's *Diatessaron,* a now-lost Greek or Syriac harmonization of all four gospels (*circa* 170 C.E.). Saint Athanasius had no hesitation, in the second half of the fourth century (367 C.E.), in listing it among the books that we have come to know as "the New Testament." It belonged to that selection made by the early Christian church when it came to decide what should be regarded as the work of "those who, moved by the Holy Spirit, spoke from God" (2 Peter 1:20). However, as almost all of Mark's story is found in the Gospel of Matthew, and there is more from the life of Jesus in Matthew (twenty-eight chapters) than in Mark (sixteen chapters), it is understandable that Mark fell into disuse. Anything in Mark that would be useful for preaching, for exhortation, for discipline, and especially for the establishment of an emerging body of doctrine in the early church, could be found in Matthew.

The birth of what was called higher criticism in the middle of the nineteenth century reversed this situation. The earliest reasons for interest in Mark were historical. This interest remains, but others have been added. The study of the Gospel of Mark that follows will not ignore the historical questions, but its main concern is to trace many of the more literary and theological issues that have made the Gospel of Mark one of the most studied texts in contemporary New Testament scholarship. In English alone, at least ten significant commentaries on Mark have appeared in English in the past three years (J. Donahue and D. Harrington; S. E. Dowd; J. R. Edwards Jr.; C. A. Evans [the second of two volumes]; R. T. France; E. LaVerdiere; J. Marcus [the first of two volumes]; F. J. Moloney; B. B. Thurston; B. Witherington III). The secret of the Gospel of Mark can still be elusive, but it is being increasingly pondered as we enter the third Christian millennium.

Reading scholarly and illuminating commentaries, both classical works and more recent studies, warns one against rushing to conclusions about Mark as a storyteller, an interpreter, and an evangelist. The briefest of the gospels, written in crude Greek, it has been shown to have many layers of meaning, and each new study attempts to peel back yet another layer. The following book does not pretend to lead its reader down every avenue of interpretation emerging from classical lack of interest to the present-day fascination with the Gospel of Mark. I will maintain a conversation with some of that scholarship, largely for the instruction of my readers who may be approaching the Gospel of Mark in a systematic fashion for the first time. However, my main interest is to focus upon the four elements that form the title of this book.

I will first trace how this gospel was attributed to a shadowy figure named Mark, and how much of this historical figure can be gleaned from the gospel itself, and from the early witnesses that refer to "Mark" as the author of this story of Jesus. Given the lack of conclusive data on the person and personality of Mark, I will then investigate Mark's contribution as a historian and as a theologian (Part 1: Mark). To the best of our knowledge, Mark gave the Christian tradition the first coherent written account of the life, teaching, death, and resurrection of Jesus. The second part of the following study will trace, in three chapters, his skills as a storyteller. An initial chapter, investigating the plot of the gospel, will indicate that the story can be read as two major narrative sections, with a turning point at the confession of Jesus as the Christ at Caesarea Philippi (8:29–30). Two further chapters will follow Mark's story from the beginning of the gospel to its midpoint (1:1–8:30), and from its midpoint to its surprising ending (8:31–16:8) (Part 2: Mark the Storyteller). By means of this carefully plotted story, Mark offered a unique interpretation of the primitive Christian tradition that he received. This section is necessarily selective. Mark's contribution to the interpretation of the emerging phenomenon of a community based on faith in Jesus as the Christ and the Son of God is larger than we can hope to cover here. However, the third section of the study will trace the fundamental questions of Mark's interpretation of Jesus of Nazareth, and his interpretation of the Christian community. Again to the best of our knowledge (although the Letter of James and perhaps 1 Peter may have appeared about the same time), Mark is the Christian interpreter who follows close on the heels of Paul in an attempt to interpret the significance of the life, teaching, death, and resurrection of Jesus (Part 3: Mark the Interpreter). The Gospel of Mark has not only become a source of interest and research among scholars; it has also held its place as one of the church's fundamental texts, and is increasingly read in liturgical, group, and private settings. The final section of the book assesses the ongoing relevance of Mark's contribution to the life of the Christian church (Part 4: Mark the Evangelist).

I have written this book for students of religious studies and theology, be they M.A. or M.Div. students. However, I trust that the following reflections may also contribute to Markan studies as such, and thus offer something of value to professional scholars. Technical language will be largely avoided, or further explained when its use is unavoidable. Some consideration will be given to the different methods that have been used in the study of the gospels, from the birth of higher criticism to the present. But every effort will be made to keep these considerations as simple as possible. Occasionally important words will be found in a transliteration of the Greek.

I am grateful to Dr. James Ernest, former Associate Editorial Director at Hendrickson Publishers. He has patiently shepherded this work to a conclusion, after my long digression into a major commentary on Mark, also under Dr. Ernest's expert and careful direction (*The Gospel of Mark: A Commentary* [Peabody: Hendrickson, 2002]). I trust that the preparatory work of the commentary will enrich the very different Markan book that follows. The latter depends heavily on the former. Nevertheless, it was the agreement to write *this book* for Hendrickson that led to my writing of the commentary! After some months of work on a study of Mark, storyteller, theologian, and evangelist, it became increasingly obvious that I could not do justice to these questions without first deciding on the literary and theological designs of the gospel of Mark *as a whole*. Now that my work on a commentary on the gospel is completed and available, I can turn to a study of Mark as a storyteller, theologian, and evangelist.

It is dedicated to Suzanne Marie Schwarz, VHM, in gratitude for her warm and supportive friendship over my years in the United States of America. My rendition of Luke 1:28, cited in Luke's original Greek in the dedication, and addressed to Suzanne, is: "Rejoice, O you in whom God has rejoiced. The Lord is with you." I began the process of writing a first draft of this book at the Pacem in Terris Retreat Center in Saint Francis, Minnesota, where Suzanne was working as a volunteer in the early summer of 2002. The draft was completed while in my native Australia late in that same summer. There, Nerina Zanardo, FSP, read the draft as each chapter emerged.

That first draft was polished and completed and available during the fall semester of 2002 in Washington, D.C., with the invaluable help of the staff of the Mullen Library at the Catholic University of America, and at the Woodstock Library at Georgetown University, in Washington, D.C. I shared a great deal of what follows with the members of my PhD seminar on the Gospel of Mark at the Catholic University of America in that fall semester. Over the period of Christmas and New Year in Australia, Nerina Zanardo again read and further improved what I had thought was the finished script. I can never thank her enough for her tireless dedication to my writing. My research assistant at the Catholic University, Rekha Chennattu, RA, assisted me at every turn and rendered invaluable support in the preparation of the indexes. I am grateful to all, close friends, family, students, and professional colleagues, who have lent their support in Saint Francis, Minnesota; Melbourne, Australia; and Washington, D.C.

Francis J. Moloney, SDB
The Katharine Drexel Professor of Religious Studies
The Catholic University of America
Washington, D.C. 20064

# Abbreviations

| | |
|---|---|
| AB | Anchor Bible |
| *ABD* | *Anchor Bible Dictionary.* Edited by D. N. Freedman. 6 vols. New York: Doubleday, 1992. |
| ABRL | Anchor Bible Reference Library |
| AnBib | Analecta biblica |
| BETL | Bibliotheca ephemeridum theologicarum lovaniensium |
| *Bib* | *Biblica* |
| BNTC | Black's New Testament Commentaries |
| *BScRel* | *Biblioteca di Scienze Religiose* |
| *BTB* | *Biblical Theology Bulletin* |
| *BZ* | *Biblische Zeitscrift* |
| *CBQ* | *Catholic Biblical Quarterly* |
| *DRev* | *Downside Review* |
| *EBib* | *Etudes bibliques* |
| EKKNT | Evangelisch-katholischer Kommentar zum Neuen Testament |
| FB | Forschung zur Bibel |
| FRLANT | Forschungen zur Religion und Literatur des Alten und Neuen Testaments |
| *GNS* | *Good News Studies* |
| HNT | Handbuch zum Neuen Testament |
| HTKNT | Herders theologischer Kommentar zum Neuen Testament |
| *HTR* | *Harvard Theological Review* |
| ICC | International Critical Commentary |
| IRT | Issues in Religion and Theology |

| | |
|---|---|
| *JBL* | *Journal of Biblical Literature* |
| *JR* | *Journal of Religion* |
| *JSNT* | *Journal for the Study of the New Testament* |
| JSNTSup | Journal for the Study of the New Testament: Supplement Series |
| LD | Lectio divina |
| LXX | Septuagint |
| NF | Neue Folge |
| NICNT | New International Commentary on the New Testament |
| *NovT* | *Novum Testamentum* |
| NTA | Neutestamentliche Abhandlungen |
| *NTS* | *New Testament Studies* |
| PL | Patrologiae cursus completes: Series latina. Edited by J.-P. Migne. 217 vols. Paris. 1844–1864. |
| PNTC | Pelican New Testament Commentaries |
| RNT | Regensburger Neues Testament |
| *RSR* | *Recherches de science religieuse* |
| SBLDS | Society of Biblical Literature Dissertation Series |
| SBT | Studies in Biblical Theology |
| *Semeia* | *Semeia* |
| SNTSMS | Society for New Testament Studies Monograph Series |
| SP | Sacra pagina |
| *TDNT* | *Theological Dictionary of the New Testament.* Edited by G. Kittel and G. Friedrich. Translated by G. W. Bromiley. 10 vols. Grand Rapids: Eerdmans, 1964–1976. |
| WBC | Word Biblical Commentary |
| WUNT | Wissenschaftliche Untersuchungen zum Neuen Testament |
| ZNW | *Zeitschrift für die neutestamentliche Wissenschaft und die Kunde der älteren Kirche* |

# PART ONE

# MARK

# CHAPTER 1

# The Author of Mark in History

For many centuries each of the four gospels has been known as "the Gospel according to . . . Matthew, Mark, Luke or John." Only the Fourth Gospel identifies its author as the Beloved Disciple, one of the important characters in the story of Jesus. This disciple is anonymous insofar as he is never given a name. But John 21:24 says of him: "This is the disciple who is bearing witness to these things, and who has written these things; and we know that his testimony is true" (see also 13:23; 18:15, 16; 19:25–27; 20:2–10; 21:7, 20–23). However, even with the Fourth Gospel, not until late in the second century was this story of Jesus associated with one of the Twelve, John, the son of Zebedee.[1] The Gospels of Matthew, Mark and Luke never allude to the authors,[2] and like the Gospel of John, probably had the names "Matthew," "Mark," and "Luke" added to them late in the second century.[3]

## Which Mark?

If there are no indications within the gospel itself of the identity of a figure named "Mark," one must look to other places where such evidence might be found. Minor characters from the early days of the Christian mission with the name "Mark" are found elsewhere in the New Testament. Especially important is a disciple called "John Mark" who accompanied Paul and Barnabas on their first missionary journey. He first appears as a son of a certain Mary in Jerusalem (Acts 12:12). Peter returned to the home of John Mark in Jerusalem, after he was miraculously delivered from prison during the persecution of King Herod

that led to the slaying of James (12:12–17). The spread of further persecution led Barnabas and Saul (as he is called at that stage of the story) to
go back to Antioch, and they took John Mark with them (12:25). However, during that first missionary journey, after preaching in Cyprus,
Paul and Barnabas set sail to Perga in Pamphylia (modern southern
Turkey), but John Mark left them and returned to Jerusalem (13:13).

The so-called Council of Jerusalem decided that the gospel was to
be preached to the Gentiles (15:1–29). After the council, Paul and Barnabas returned to Antioch (vv. 30–35) and prepared for their second
missionary journey (vv. 36–41). However, Paul and Barnabas could not
agree over John Mark. Paul was unwilling to associate him with the mission, as he was dissatisfied with his departure from the group during the
first missionary journey (see 13:13). Thus the two original apostles to
the Gentiles (Paul and Barnabas) separated:

> And Barnabas wanted to take with them John called Mark. But Paul
> thought best not to take with them one who had withdrawn from
> them in Pamphylia, and had not gone with them to the work. And
> there arose a sharp contention, so that they separated from each
> other; Barnabas took Mark with him and sailed away to Cyprus, but
> Paul chose Silas and departed (Acts 15:37–40).

This is not an impressive start to the career of John Mark. It is possible that nothing more is heard of that particular character from the
earliest years of the Christian communities.[4] Nevertheless, the name
"Mark" continues to appear in letters of Paul, or in letters that came
from the period shortly after Paul that looked back to his authority:

> Epaphras, my fellow prisoner in Christ Jesus, sends greetings to
> you, and so do Mark, Aristarchus, Demas, and Luke, my fellow
> workers. (Phlm 23–24)

> Aristarchus my fellow prisoner greets you, and Mark the cousin of
> Barnabas (concerning whom you have received instructions—if
> he comes to you, receive him), and Jesus who is called Justus. These
> are the only men of the circumcision among my fellow workers
> for the kingdom of God, and they have been a comfort to me.
> (Col 4:10–11)

> Do your best to come to me soon. For Demas, in love with this pres-
> ent world, has deserted me and gone to Thessalonica; Crescens
> has gone to Galatia, Titus to Dalmatia. Luke alone is with me. Get
> Mark and bring him with you; for he is very useful in serving me.
> (2 Tim 4:9–11)

There is an immediacy about these passages, with their references to people associated with the life and work of Paul. A certain homogeneity also exists across these three references to Mark, the coworker of Paul in his mission to various places in Asia Minor.[5]

However, there is a dissonance between the role of John Mark in the life of Paul as it is reported in the Acts of the Apostles, and the activities and associates of Paul, as they are found in his letters.[6] It is not obvious that the John Mark of Acts is the same Mark mentioned in the Pauline letters. It is also important to know that the name "Mark" (Latin: Marcus) was a very common name in the Roman world, something like John or William in our own time.[7] Nevertheless, these traces of a Mark in the early years of the Christian mission should be kept in mind.

## Why Mark?

There is no obvious religious, traditional, political, or even ecclesiastical reason why the Mark mentioned elsewhere in the New Testament, or any other Mark, for that matter, should have been associated with one of the gospels in the second century. However, the Christian church of the second century, which had begun to establish itself as a worldwide institution, and was developing its own sacred book as part of its religious identity, looked back to apostolic figures to give authority to its scriptures. Judaism, which had produced Christianity, was inspired and governed by its unique sacred scriptures, known to us as the Old Testament, much of which, according to Jewish tradition, went back to the figures of Moses, King David, and the great prophets.[8] Likewise, the early church turned readily to Matthew, John, and Luke. A gospel story gained authority through its attachment to members of the twelve apostles, as is the case with Matthew and John (see Mark 3:13–19; Matt 10:1–4; Luke 6:12–16). The association made between the Gospel of Luke and the Acts of the Apostles has a New Testament motivation. Paul mentions Luke as his faithful traveling companion (see Phlm 24; Col 4:14; 2 Tim 4:11), and at a certain stage in the text of the Acts of the Apostles, a type of travel diary emerges, written by a firsthand witness to the events who associates himself with the action. These are called "we passages" (see Acts 16:10–17; 20:5–15; 21:1–18; 27:1–28:16). The church fathers were quick to make the link between the Luke of the Pauline letters and Paul's fellow-traveler in the Acts of the Apostles. Modern scholars have strengthened this association by highlighting the presence of a theme of traveling in both the gospel (see especially Luke 9:51–19:44) and Acts (see especially Acts 13–26).

No such connection can be made between any Mark and the life of Jesus within the New Testament. But we do have a supposedly firsthand witness of an association between Peter, one of the Twelve, and Mark, in 1 Peter. This letter from "Peter, an apostle of Jesus Christ," written to "the twelve tribes in the Dispersion" (1 Pet 1:1), signs off:

> By Silvanus, a faithful brother as I regard him, I have written briefly to you, exhorting and declaring that this is the true grace of God; stand fast in it. She who is at Babylon, who is likewise chosen, sends you greetings; *and so does my son Mark.* (5:12–13)

The second-century church quickly accepted 1 Peter into its official list of inspired Scriptures, and regarded the Peter of 1:1 as Simon Peter from the Gospels and Acts. Tradition associated Peter with Rome, and his eventual martyrdom there. The use of the name Babylon to refer to Rome in the Book of Revelation (see, especially, Rev 18:1–24) further strengthened the impression that 1 Peter was a letter written from Rome by Peter, the "rock" of Matt 16:16–18. Precisely these beliefs led to the rapid acceptance of 1 Peter into the Christian canon. This letter, therefore, associated Mark with Peter in Rome, and Mark is described as "my son," a term of endearment that indicated a close relationship.[9]

The earliest historian of the Christian church, Eusebius of Caesarea (born about 260 C.E.) drew on a number of written documents that existed prior to the writing of his *Ecclesiastical History.* Eusebius' *History* runs from the beginnings down to the victory of the Emperor Constantine over Licinius in 324. He disclaimed any originality, and his history (as well as his other works) is at times little more than a string of quotations. This practice, while not producing gripping prose, has nevertheless preserved for us many writings that would otherwise not be in existence. One such document that Eusebius quotes in his *History* is the work of Papias, the Bishop of Hierapolis who, about 130 C.E., wrote a five-volume work titled *Exposition of the Oracles of the Lord.*[10] Papias wrote of the relationship between Peter and Mark, and the production of the Gospel of Mark. As cited by Eusebius, he wrote as follows, in his own turn citing the authority of "the elder" (John), and then taking over the narrative to make his own remarks:[11]

> This also the elder *[John]* used to say. When Mark became Peter's interpreter [ἑρμηνευτής; *hermēneutēs*], he wrote down accurately [ἀκριβῶς; *akribōs*], though by no means in order [οὐ μέντοι τάξει; *ou mentoi taxei*] as much as he remembered of the words and deeds of the Lord; *[what follows is most likely from Papias, who has cited "the elder" thus far, and now makes his own observations on the tradi-*

*tion linking Peter and Mark]* for he had neither heard the Lord nor been in his company, but subsequently joined Peter as I said. Now Peter did not intend to give a complete exposition of the Lord's ministry but delivered his instructions to meet the needs of the moment [or "in anecdotal form": πρὸς τὰς χρείας; *pros tas chreias*] but not making, as it were, a systematic arrangement [συντάξις; *syntaxis*] of the Lord's oracles [λογίων; *logiōn*]. It follows, then, that Mark was guilty of no blunder if he wrote, simply to the best of his recollections, an incomplete account. [Eusebius, *Ecclesiastical History* 3.39.15][12]

The witness of 1 Peter 5:13, and the association of Mark and Peter by Papias,[13] led to the logical step, by later authorities, of locating that association with the city of Rome (Eusebius, *Ecclesiastical History* 6.14.6), Irenaeus (ca. 130–200), and Clement of Alexandria (ca. 150–215).[14] However well or poorly Eusebius may have excerpted it from his source, the evidence of Papias merits consideration. It shows that the tradition of the Gospel of Mark having its origins in the witness of Peter, written in Rome by a person named Mark, was firmly established by the middle of the second century. This tradition may have been received by Papias, and could thus reach back into the last decade of the first century.[15] It remained unquestioned for centuries. One reason for this, apart from general acceptance of tradition concerning these questions, was perhaps because no one was particularly interested in the *personality* of the author of the Gospel of Mark. There was more interest in the authenticity of the Jesus tradition. As Clifton Black has shown, largely following the work of Josef Kürzinger, it is possible that Papias himself was not primarily interested in affirming Markan authorship of a Petrine gospel, but rather in witnessing to the faithful recollection and transmission of the Jesus tradition.[16] Given the widespread acceptance, by the middle of the second century, of Matthew, Mark, and Luke, a lack of interest in the details of the Markan story and the personality of its author is understandable. Because almost all the Gospel of Mark was contained in the Gospels of Matthew and Luke, it fell into disuse. As Morna Hooker remarks: "Since almost all of Mark's material is found in either Mark or Luke, it is remarkable that the Gospel survived."[17]

Yet, it has survived. No doubt the traditional link, made between Mark and Peter, a major figure among the apostles, is a fundamental reason for that survival, despite its being largely ignored by both the Greek and Latin patristic reflections of the third and fourth centuries,[18] and also the lack of its widespread use in the church across the Christian centuries since then. As we will see in the following chapter, the modern and contemporary fascination with the Gospel of Mark devotes little attention to the witness of Papias, and the link between the Apostle Peter and the Mark of 1 Pet 5:13. Although an increasing number of commentators are returning to the traditional links among Mark, Peter, and Rome, they are doing so on somewhat different grounds.

Still the question posed at the beginning of this section remains: Why Mark? We have already seen that there are links with the apostolic tradition that most probably led to the second-century association of the apostles Matthew and John with the two gospels connected with their names. There are also suggestive links within the New Testament that led the second-century church to claim that the Gospel of Luke was the work of the traveling companion of Paul during the account of his journeys in the Acts of the Apostles. Both books seem to come from the same author, and are directed to the same patron (see Luke 1:1–4; Acts 1:1). Our search to discover the link between the name "Mark" and the gospel bearing his name is more tenuous. Why did Papias, Irenaeus, Clement of Alexandria, and Eusebius make that link?

In the end, the two questions posed by this chapter run together: "Which Mark?" and "Why Mark?" cannot be separated. I suspect this is the case because behind the Gospel of Mark lies the memory of a figure, an original storyteller, whose name was indeed Mark. Who he was, what place he occupied in an early Christian community, and whether he was the John Mark of the Acts of the Apostles or the Mark of the Pauline letters is beyond the range of our knowledge. We do not have enough data at our fingertips to be able to claim clear answers to those questions. One fact remains clear: Papias, Clement, Irenaeus, and Eusebius looked to a figure with the name Mark as the author of the gospel. From there arose the further suggestions that linked him with Peter, acting as his secretary, interpreter, or translator in Rome. Whatever one might make of the link with Peter, and the association with Rome, the name Mark might be based in a fact of history. As Clifton Black expressed it:

> The reason for the Second Gospel's attribution to Mark is not in the least bit clear. The Gospel never makes such a claim. Little is explained by the argument that the Gospel was so ascribed because of the presumed author's derivative prominence, through association with Peter and Paul: Why then did not second- and third-century Christians employ a customary expedient and simply assign the book's composition to one of the apostles? . . . Moreover, in almost every early tradition that we know, both within and beyond the New Testament, "Mark" cuts a decidedly second- or third-rate figure. . . . Even if it proves beyond our ability to recover completely, something's afoot in all of this.[19]

Perhaps the best explanation is that there was, in the earliest tradition (prior to 1 Peter and Papias) the memory of a person named Mark who wrote a story that proclaimed the good news that Jesus was the Christ, the Son of God (see Mark 1:1), and that his death and resurrection had changed the way God related to the world (see 16:1–8). In the end, the answer to the question "Why Mark?" may lie in the vague memory, based in fact, that the Gospel of Mark was the story of Jesus written by an otherwise unknown character from the early decades of the Christian story, and his name was Mark.[20] The early Christian church had little interest in the Gospel of Mark. Nor did it have any interest in the history or the personality of its original author.[21]

He would have continued to remain largely unknown and uninvestigated, had it not been for the dramatic turn of events in the nineteenth century that brought the Gospel of Mark to center stage in gospel criticism. This turn of events, generally regarded as the birth of the historical-critical approach to the Bible, will be discussed in the following chapter. Because of this change of approach to biblical texts, a radical change in the type of questions that were being asked of the gospels led to Cinderella's transformation into a princess. Our investigation of "Mark" can now turn from our attempts to trace the identity of this shadowy figure. In the following chapter we will focus our attention more closely on the gospel attributed to him. It is this story that offers best witness to the mind, the heart, and the spirit of its author.[22]

## Where and When?

Is it possible to trace the time when and the place where the Gospel of Mark first saw the light of day? Christian tradition accepted the evidence of Papias, transmitted by other church fathers (especially Eusebius and Clement of Alexandria [ca. 150–215]), that Mark wrote the gospel that bears his name, recording Peter's incomplete exposition of the Lord's ministry. This would mean that the Gospel of Mark appeared some time in the 60s of the first century, as Peter was most probably martyred during the persecutions that took place under Emperor Nero (64–65 C.E.).

Critical scholarship in the first decades of the twentieth century severely questioned this long-standing tradition. As we will see in the following chapter, in 1901 Wilhelm Wrede demonstrated Mark wrote his story for theological rather than historical reasons. In 1906, Albert Schweitzer laid to rest the many nineteenth-century attempts to write a life of Jesus using the Gospel of Mark as the source for the historical outline of Jesus' career. These two epoch-making studies threw into serious question the traditional association of the Gospel of Mark with Rome and Peter, an association that assured a close link with the words and events of the life of Jesus. Yet aspects of the Gospel of Mark have led other scholars, both classical and contemporary, to insist that the gospel was written in Rome and that it betrays a Petrine interest.[23] The earlier critical scholars looked to features like the gospel's inelegant Greek style, the use of Latin loanwords and Mark's seemingly poor knowledge of Palestinian geography as indications of its Roman provenance. More recent scholars comb through the narrative itself to find hints in the apocalyptic nature of the story, to trace the experiences and social location of the community behind the text that can be read between the lines. Against that more general background, they find a relationship between the Christology and the theology of discipleship found in the gospel that may best address a situation of Roman persecution.[24]

It is impossible to be sure about when and where the Gospel of Mark first saw the light of day, but three elements need to be taken into account and held together in these discussions.[25] First, the syntax and loanwords that indicate a Roman setting must be explained. For example, the word "legion" appears in a Greek form in 5:9 (λεγιών; *legion*). The Greek used for "soldier of the guard" or "executioner" in 6:27 (σπεκουλάτωρ; *spekoulatōr*) is a transliteration of a Latin word. In 12:14, the Latin word "census" (κῆνσος; *kēnsos*) is used to refer to the tax that was paid to Rome. Roman coins are mentioned without any explanation in 6:37 and 14:5, δηνάριον; *dēnarion* (a day's salary), and in 12:42, κοδράντης; *kodrantēs* (a penny). As well as these Latin words, Mark's clumsy Greek is sometimes understood as having been influenced by a Latin (and therefore Roman) background.[26] There is much that is Roman in the Gospel of Mark, from words to a form of Greek that may reflect a writer of Greek who was also familiar with Latin, the language of Rome.

Second, there is a concern in the Gospel of Mark for the Gentile mission. Jesus heals a demoniac in Gentile territory, and tells him to go to his hometown to announce what the Lord has done (see 5:1–20). After a bitter encounter with Israel (7:1–23) Jesus journeys outside the borders of Israel to the region of Tyre and Sidon, to bring healing to a Syrophoenician woman (7:24–30). His passage from the region of Tyre and Sidon back to the eastern side of the lake deliberately keeps him in Gentile lands (see 7:31). There he heals a Gentile, and for the first time in the narrative his actions are recognized by Gentiles as the work of the expected Messiah (7:31–37). He nourishes Gentiles, who "have come a long way" (8:1–10). As he defuses anxiety about the end of time, in the midst of many false signs, he tells his disciples: "the gospel must first be preached to all the nations" (13:10). The end will come, however, and at that time the Son of Man "will send out the angels and gather his elect from the four winds, from the ends of the earth to the ends of heaven" (13:27). At his death, in the temple the veil that hid the holy of holies from the rest of the world is rent asunder (15:37–38), and a Roman centurion confesses that Jesus was the Son of God.[27]

Third, the discourse in Mark 13 presupposes that Jerusalem has fallen.[28] Many details *look back* to that dramatic experience for both Israel and the early Christian Church: false prophets (see 13:5–6, 21–22), wars and rumors of wars (see 13:7, 14–20), events that took place at the fall of the temple (13:14). Mark 13 is "rather like a window which allows a close view of Markan circumstances."[29] The final lengthy discourse that Jesus delivers to a group of disciples at the end of his ministry is an important indication of the situation in the life of the Markan community that gave birth to the gospel. In the light of Mark 13, therefore, the gospel must have reached its final shape in the period during or just after 70 C.E., as the horror and significance of the destruction of Jerusalem and its temple made their impact on the Markan community.[30]

These three elements leave us with some hard facts, which can, in turn, lead to a suggestion about the time and place of the Gospel of Mark. I would regard the following details as hard facts:

1. A familiarity with the Roman world, its language, and its mode of government lies behind the Gospel of Mark.

2. Wherever the gospel was written, the author and the community for whom he was writing the Jesus story were concerned about the mission to the Gentiles.

3. The community is exposed to suffering and persecution, and its members are probably being discouraged by the failure of some to commit themselves, unto death, for the gospel of Jesus Christ.[31]

4. Mark's gospel was written shortly after the fall of Jerusalem in 70 C.E.

The traditional location of Rome still deserves consideration, but the background to Mark 13 of the fall of Jerusalem suggests somewhere geographically closer to these events. Were the Roman Christians in need of severe warnings not to heed false prophets who were rising up in the midst of the postwar chaos to declare that the end time had come (see 13:5–6, 21–22)? The Roman Christians may have been suffering persecution, but they lived at the center of the known world. Was it necessary to tell Roman Christians that they must calm their apocalyptic fever, because before the final coming of the Son of Man the gospel had to be preached to all the nations (see 13:10)? How real were *all* the threats of 13:11: "They will deliver you up to councils; and you will be beaten in synagogues; and you will stand before governors and kings for my sake" (13:9)? The Gospel of Mark does not create the impression that the storyteller and the community receiving the gospel had a special interest in Rome or the Romans.[32] Roman characters, even in the passion narrative where they could have been drawn more deeply into the story, remain peripheral. They are present when the story demands it, especially in the passion narrative (15:1–47). Matters Roman, whether they are Latin loanwords or Roman characters, remain extrinsic to the Markan story. The power of Rome, bringing with it coins, soldiers and methods of government, was present all across the Mediterranean basin. Similarly, the suggestion that Mark's rough Greek reflects a Latin background remains to be proven. Mark writes in rough but powerful and readily understandable Greek. There was no need to be in Rome to find such expressions and practices. Without the long-standing *tradition* concerning the Roman origins of the Gospel of Mark, there is little else that forces a reader to think that this is a gospel concerned with matters Roman.[33]

It seems impossible to determine an exact location, a region, or a city where the gospel might first have seen the light of day, and thus I can speculate and suggest only a possible scenario. The might of Rome was felt in many parts of the Mediterranean world, and powerfully so in the recalcitrant states of Syria and Palestine. The traditional location of the origin of Mark in the city of Rome leaves too many questions unresolved, and thus (excluding Rome) I would agree with Morna Hooker:

> All we can say with certainty, therefore, is that the gospel was composed somewhere in the Roman Empire—a conclusion that scarcely narrows the field at all![34]

The field could be narrowed to the extent that the place in the Roman Empire that produced the Gospel of Mark must have been reasonably close to Jerusalem. Reports of "wars and rumors of wars" (see 13:7) are reaching the ears of the Markan Christians. They know what the author means when he writes of "the desolating sacrilege set up where it ought not to be" (v. 14). They are wondering: Is this the moment for the return of the Son of Man (vv. 7, 10, 13)? They are told—not yet, but that day will come. Be ready, and watch (vv. 24–37). For these reasons, the

Markan community may have been located somewhere in a broad area that might be called southern Syria.[35]

The dating of the gospel also plays a part in determining its likely place of origin. A date late in or probably after 70 C.E., yet before 75 C.E., is called for.[36] This date allows time for both Matthew and Luke, who wrote some time between 80 and 90 C.E., to use the Gospel of Mark as one of the sources for their gospels. Almost thirty years after the death of Jesus, wherever the precise location of the Markan community might have been, these early Christians were involved in a mission to the Gentiles. Several places in the gospel provide evidence of this mission (see, for example, 5:1–20; 7:24–8:10; 13:10). This aspect of the Markan narrative may tip the balance in favor of southern Syria,[37] but we cannot be sure of the ethnic mix of Palestine in the 70s of the first Christian century. Northern Palestine may also have provided a missionary setting. However, this would make Mark's vagueness about Palestinian geography difficult to explain.[38]

## Conclusion

This initial exploration of Mark shows the speculative nature of our search for the evangelist. To the question "Which Mark?," the permanence of the name Mark in the tradition *may* point to a person from the early church who both bore that very common name, and also wrote the Gospel of Mark. This suggestion is further strengthened when one answers the question "Why Mark?" From its earliest records down to our own time the Christian tradition has insisted on a figure with the name of Mark. Whether he was one of the several Marks who appear in the pages of the New Testament, or another figure who never appears there, is beyond the range of our knowledge.

However, without certainty, it is possible, and even probable, that someone with the name Mark was the final redactor of this gospel. The expression "final redactor" is important, but so is its association with the term "gospel." To speak of our Mark as a final redactor does not mean that he simply strung traditions together, generating a sequence of reported events without any care for a specific order or without any narrative or even theological design for his story. Mark was not just an editor. He wrote a gospel. That means he was an evangelist: he regarded his task as a proclamation of the good news. The original appearance of the gospel somewhere in northern Palestine or southern Syria may best explain a large number of the features of this gospel. It would have been written at the time of the Jewish War, or at least sometime shortly after

the destruction of Jerusalem and its temple (70 C.E.). In the end, however, it is Mark's understanding of what God did for humankind in and
through Jesus of Nazareth, the Christ, the Son of Man, and the Son of
God, that is transmitted through this story of Jesus. This is what led to
this gospel's immediate inclusion within the Christian canon, and the
ongoing reading and listening to this story that has taken place within
the Christian community for almost two thousand years.

## Notes

1. For a more detailed discussion of this question, see F. J. Moloney, *The
Gospel of John* (SP 4; Collegeville: Liturgical Press, 1998), 6–9.
2. Some interpreters suggest that the young man whom the authorities try
to seize in Gethsemane at the arrest of Jesus, and who runs away naked (see
Mark 14:51–52), was the evangelist. This proposal explains how the details of
Jesus' solitary prayer in Gethsemane were recorded. Mark was there. See, for example, B. Saunderson, "Gethsemane: The Missing Witness," *Bib* 70 (1989):
224–33. However, even if this interpretation were correct, it would only prove
that the evangelist was an eyewitness to the events, not that his name was Mark.
For a full survey of the discussion, see C. A. Evans, *Mark 8:27–16:20* (WBC 34B;
Nashville: Thomas Nelson, 2001), 427–29.
3. For a different opinion, see M. Hengel, *Studies in the Gospel of Mark*
(trans. J. Bowden; Philadelphia: Fortress, 1985), 64–84. Hengel points out that
the author used the Greek expression εὐαγγέλιον *(euangelion)* in an innovative
fashion. The word was already widely used in Greek literature, in the LXX, and
by Paul, prior to the Gospel of Mark. Its basic meaning is "good news." However, it had never been used to describe a "life story." In Mark 1:1 it is used to
describe the book that follows: an account of the ministry, the death, and resurrection of Jesus, Messiah, and Son of God. Hengel claims that this usage introduced a new literary form into early Christian literature, and that it may have
led to the book's being called "the *euangelion* according to Mark" at a very early
stage. The titles given, at a later stage, to Matthew, Luke, and John, imitated the
application of the name "Mark" to a document that did not reveal the name of
its author.
4. See C. Clifton Black, *Mark: Images of an Apostolic Interpreter* (Studies on
Personalities of the New Testament; Minneapolis: Fortress, 2001), 25–49, for a
detailed study of John Mark's role in Acts. While not discounting a historical
John Mark, Black rightly sees the figure as a foil to Luke's presentation of the
principal characters. The presence of Mark in the story "subtly discloses or con-
firms the values and purposes of Barnabas, Paul, and even God, who through
the Holy Spirit initiates and sustains their missionary program" (p. 43).
5. See Black, *Mark*, 50–60, on these references to Mark. Black concludes
that there is a "coherence of the figure of Mark in the Pauline tradition" (p. 60).
6. A few critical problems emerge here. The Gospel of Luke and the Acts of
the Apostles form a two-volume work by the same author, known to us as Luke,
and was sent to a "reader" (who may or may not be a fictitious creation of the
author) named Theophilus (see Luke 1:1–4; Acts 1:1–2). These books have an

*what Gospel/(Biblical Book) doesn't?*

important theological program driving the narrative. Through them, the author traces a relentless journey (not without its difficulties and suffering) fulfilling the Old Testament world of Zechariah and Elizabeth, Simeon and Anna (Luke 1–2), from Galilee to Jerusalem, to Jesus' ascension to heaven, via the cross and the resurrection (Luke 3–24). Acts continues the story into the world of the apostles and the first disciples. They receive the Holy Spirit (Acts 1–2), and are witnesses to Jesus as the Christ, first in Jerusalem, then in all Judea and Samaria, and finally (especially by means of the journeys of Paul) to the ends of the earth (Acts 3–28. See Luke 24:44–49; Acts 1:8). Acts closes with Paul preaching the kingdom and the Lord Jesus Christ boldly in Rome (Acts 28:30–31). The author certainly had good information, but—given the theological program determining much of the story—when it comes to rediscovering the historical events that surrounded Paul's life, it is better to use the material that can be gleaned from Paul's letters, rather than Acts. Second, all accept that Paul wrote Philemon. Many (including myself) would say the same for Colossians (but not Ephesians), and a good case can be made for the authentic Pauline character of the personal notes in 2 Timothy, one of the so-called Pastoral Epistles. On this, see M. Prior, *Paul the Letter-Writer and the Second Letter to Timothy* (JSNTSup 23; Sheffield: JSOT Press, 1989); L. T. Johnson, *The First and Second Letters to Timothy: A New Translation with Introduction and Commentary* (AB 35A; New York: Doubleday, 2001), 438–51.

7. See, among many, B. B. Thurston, *Preaching Mark* (Fortress Resources for Preaching; Minneapolis: Fortress, 2002), 4: "It was one of the most common names in the Empire."

8. I will consistently use the traditional nomenclature "Old Testament" and "New Testament." For some, the use of "Old Testament" is problematic, but no less so than other designations such as "Hebrew Bible" or "First Testament." I retain the use of "Old Testament" in this study, but the adjective is used in the sense of "ancient" rather than superseded.

9. Contemporary scholarship is reacting against earlier historical criticism that sometimes claimed that 1 Peter was a pseudonymous letter, possibly to be dated in the second century, without any association with Rome or Peter. It is nowadays increasingly suggested that 1 Peter, although not written by the historical Peter, was probably written in Rome ("Babylon") after the death of Peter in the mid-60s, by an author or authors who reflected the Petrine tradition (a Petrine circle). For excellent treatments of these questions, see P. Achtemeier, *1 Peter* (Hermeneia; Minneapolis: Fortress, 1999), 1–50; J. Elliott, *1 Peter. A New Translation with Introduction and Commentary* (AB 37B; New York: Doubleday, 2000) 118–38, and the summary in Black, *Mark,* 60–66.

10. Eusebius, like most authors, had his own prejudices and cited sources that suited them best. It is also likely that he modified them according to his agenda. There is, therefore, some concern over the accuracy of his use of Papias, or at least concerning the way he may have edited Papias's original work. See Black, *Mark,* 84–86.

11. The sequence of the passage is not always clear. I will add some clarifying comments in italics and in brackets. For a thorough and up-to-date study of the witness of Papias, see Black, *Mark,* 82–94.

12. The translation is my own, guided by the interpretative suggestions of S. Kealy, *Mark's Gospel: A History of Its Interpretation* (New York: Paulist, 1982), 12, and Black, *Mark,* 83.

13. The exact nature of that association is debated, as the Greek word *hermēneutēs* is open to a number of interpretations: secretary, interpreter, translator.

14. Unique to the patristic witness to Markan authorship, however, is that there is little or no interest in the references to the possible New Testament associations with John Mark or the Pauline Mark, not even to 1 Pet 5:13. See, on this, Black, *Mark,* 77.

15. See Black, *Mark,* 87–88.

16. See Black, *Mark,* 89–93. Kürzinger (followed, with some reservations, by Black) suggests that this collection of sayings of the Lord may not have indicated (for Papias, whatever Eusebius made of it) the Gospel of Mark. Much depends on what one makes of the expression πρὸς τὰς χρείας *(pros tas chreias).* Recent interest in the literary form of the *chreia* stresses the use in Greco-Roman literature, to refer to synthetic anecdotes. Much is made of their formative influence in the development of the Christian tradition. See R. C. Tannehill, ed., *Varieties of Synoptic Pronouncement Stories (Semeia* 20 [1981]: 1–141), and V. K. Robbins, ed., *The Rhetoric of Pronouncement (Semeia* 64 [1994]: i-xvii, 1–301). Thus the idea of Mark gathering Peter's reminiscences "to meet the needs of the time" as the only possible meaning for πρὸς τὰς χρείας *(pros tas chreias),* can be questioned. A definitive collection of Kürzinger's voluminous work on Papias can be found in J. Kürzinger, *Papias von Hierapolis und die Evangelien des Neuen Testaments: Gesammelte Aufsätze, Neuausgabe und Übersetzung der Fragmente, Kommentierte Bibliographie* (Eichstätter Materialen 4; Regensburg: Pustet, 1983). The collected and annotated bibliography is the work of E. König and M. Vinzent.

17. M. D. Hooker, *The Gospel according to St. Mark* (BNTC; Peabody: Hendrickson, 1991), 7. See also R. H. Lightfoot, *The Gospel Message of St. Mark* (Oxford: Clarendon Press, 1950), 1–14; Kealy, *Mark's Gospel,* 7–57; E. Masseaux, *The Influence of the Gospel of Saint Matthew on Christian Literature before Saint Irenaeus* (trans. N. J. Belval and S. Hecht; ed. A. J. Bellinzoni; New Gospel Studies 5; Macon: Mercer, 1993); B. D. Schildgen, *Power and Prejudice: The Reception of the Gospel of Mark* (Detroit: Wayne State University Press, 1999).

18. See the excellent sifting and summarizing of the evidence in Black, *Mark,* 114–91, especially the perceptive pages on "a Patristic conspectus" (pp. 183–91). Perhaps the most celebrated and most cited patristic evaluation of the Gospel of Mark (discussing the relationship between Mark and Matthew) comes from Augustine: "Mark appears only as his follower and abbreviator" *(De consensu evangelistarum* 1.2 [PL 34:1044]: "Marcus eum subsecutus tamquam pedisequus et breviator eius videtur").

19. Black, *Mark,* 11–12.

20. See Black, *Mark,* 224–50. He states, as one of his conclusions: "The Second Gospel bespeaks the handiwork of a creative traditionist, arguably a stylist and religious thinker of merit, who may have been named Mark. Nevertheless, the author's identity is irrecoverable, and the historicity of that ascription cannot be verified" (p. 239).

21. The third edition of *The Oxford Dictionary of the Christian Church* (eds. F. L. Cross and E. A. Livingstone; Oxford: Clarendon Press, 1997), 1038, suggests (on the basis of Eusebius, *Ecclesiastical History* 2.14.1; 16.1) that Mark went from Rome to Alexandria and became its first bishop, and points to the close association between Mark and Venice.

22. As we shall see in the following chapter (see below, pp. 19–43), literary theory distinguishes between a "real author" who actually took writing implements in hand and wrote a text, and an "implied author" whose voice can be heard throughout the text. See further W. Carter, *Matthew: Storyteller, Interpreter, Evangelist* (Peabody: Hendrickson, 1996), 278–80.

23. Among the important older commentators who made this claim, see V. Taylor, *The Gospel according to St. Mark* (2d ed; New York: St. Martin's, 1966), 26–31; W. L. Lane, *Commentary on the Gospel of Mark* (NICNT; Grand Rapids: Eerdmans, 1974), 21–23. Among more recent scholars see, for example, Hengel, *Studies in the Gospel of Mark*, 1–30; J. Gnilka, *Das Evangelium nach Markus* (5th ed.; EKKNT II/1–2; 2 vols.; Zürich/Nerkirchen-Vluyn: Benziger Verlag/ Neukirchener Verlag, 1998–1999), 1:34–35; J. R. Donahue and D. J. Harrington, *The Gospel of Mark* (SP 2; Collegeville: Liturgical Press, 2002), 41–46.

24. It is important to recognize that the recent return to interest in Rome as the origin of the Gospel of Mark does not simply repeat the patristic and older presentation of this argument. On this, see Donahue and Harrington, *Mark*, 41–46. For a more complete survey, see Black, *Mark*, 224–50. After a thorough review of the question, Black concludes, "In any case, the association between Mark's Gospel and Rome, drawn by most patristic interpreters and perpetuated by some of their modern counterparts, is, if not proven, then at least not improbable" (p. 238).

25. These issues must be raised, as they are neglected by some reader-oriented studies. See, for example, B. van Iersel, *Reading Mark* (trans. W. H. Bisscheroux; Collegeville: Liturgical Press, 1988), 15: "The fact that the author time and time again warns his audience so seriously of the danger of persecutions says much about their situation but little or nothing about the time when the book was written." As one element among several, it may be a very helpful indicator of when the book was written.

26. See J. Marcus, "The Jewish War and the *Sitz im Leben* of Mark," *JBL* 111 (1992): 441–46.

27. See Marcus, "The Jewish War," 453–54; R. Pesch, *Das Markusevangelium* (HTKNT II/1–2; 2 vols.; Freiburg: Herder, 1976–1977), 1:10–11.

28. See Marcus, "The Jewish War," 446–48. As Pesch, *Markusevangelium*, 1:14, remarks: "Thus, the dating of the Gospel of Mark depends upon the interpretation of Mark 13." (Here and throughout I have translated into English quotations from French and German works.) Not all would agree that Mark 13 reflects the destruction of Jerusalem, and most suggest it reflects Israel's prophetic tradition. See, for example, G. R. Beasley-Murray, *Jesus and the Last Days: The Interpretation of the Olivet Discourse* (Peabody: Hendrickson, 1993), and Hengel, *Studies in the Gospel of Mark*, 14–28. For R. A. Horsley, *Hearing the Whole Story: The Politics of Plot in Mark's Gospel* (Louisville: Westminster John Knox, 2001), 129–36, the discourse has no connection with the destruction of Jerusalem and its temple. It is built on Israel's prophetic tradition, and focuses on the struggle of Jesus' freedom movement against the repressive violence of the Roman rule.

29. W. Kelber, *The Kingdom in Mark: A New Place and a New Time* (Philadelphia: Fortress, 1974), 110.

30. On the importance of 13:14 ("the desolating sacrilege where it [he] ought not to be"), see the fine study of W. A. Such, *The Abomination of Desolation in*

the Gospel of Mark: Its Historical Reference in Mark 13:14 and Its Impact in the Gospel (Lanham: University Press of America, 1999).

31. See J. Marcus, Mark 1–8 (AB 27; New York: Doubleday, 2000), 28–29.

32. For a strong case, arguing that Markan Christology is a direct response to the divine claims made by the Roman imperial tradition, see Evans, Mark, lxxx–xciii.

33. Horsley, Hearing the Whole Story, 121–48, argues that the so-called apocalyptic elements and the exorcisms, especially the expulsion of Legion in 5:1–20, are directed to peasant people subjected to Roman imperial power, and are aimed at arousing a renewal movement among the people in Galilean village situations. Even if Horsley is correct, his theory would locate the origins of the Markan gospel(s) in Galilee, not Rome. On the naming of demons with military terms, insisting that Legion has nothing to do with the occupying power, see the perceptive remarks of K. Berger, Identity and Experience in the New Testament: A Historical Psychology (trans. C. Muenchow; Minneapolis: Fortress, 2003), 49–51.

34. Hooker, St Mark, 8. See also D. Lürhmann, Das Markusevangelium (HNT 3; Tübingen: J. C. B. Mohr [Paul Siebeck], 1987), 7: "Mark and his reader may have lived anywhere close to or distant from Palestine, perhaps in Syria. However, this cannot be proved. It may have been anywhere from the Mediterranean as far into the East as the Iran and Iraq of today."

35. See Marcus, Mark, 33–37. See also, R. I. Rohrbach, "The Social Location of the Markan Audience," BTB 23 (1993): 114–27.

36. See also Marcus, Mark, 37–39, who suggests a time not earlier than 69 C.E. and not later than 74 C.E. For Evans, Mark, lxii–lxiii, it was written during the Jewish War, and not after the destruction of Jerusalem and the temple.

37. Marcus, "The Jewish War," 460–62, suggests "one of the Hellenistic cities" (perhaps even Pella) on the basis of the Gentile mission. As he says elsewhere, "A provenance close to Palestine, but not in it, is thus an attractive possibility" (J. Marcus, The Mystery of the Kingdom [SBLDS 90; Atlanta: Scholars Press, 1986], 10). On literary grounds (reader-response), M. A. Beavis, Mark's Audience: The Literary and Social Setting of Mark 4:11–12 (JSNTSup 33; Sheffield: Sheffield Academic Press, 1989), suggests a Greco-Roman missionary context for the Markan community. See especially pp. 157–76.

38. See Marcus, The Mystery, 10.

FJM leans heavily on Block & Marcus in this 1st chap w almost no challenge to this work(s). FB challenges/critiques extensively Block.

It seems that FJB finds the FC paradigm handy for his study of Mark (or rather the community of Mark. I suspect that FB's paradigm is going to render this book obsolete... the emperor has no clothes & FJM has not realized it!

7/27/08

# CHAPTER 2

# History and Theology

Mark did not insert his name into his story of Jesus, and may not have played an apostolic role during the life and ministry of Jesus. Nevertheless, subsequent reflection on the author of the Gospel of Mark by later generations settled very quickly on the identity of Mark as the evangelist. This treatment by the early and patristic church reflected the fact that the text of the Gospel of Mark was only rarely used, and hardly commented on. No commentary on Mark appeared until the sixth century, and from 650 to 1000 C.E. thirteen major commentaries were written on Matthew, but only four on Mark. This neglect continued down to the end of the eighteenth century.[1] Paradoxically, it was the post-Enlightenment attack on the Bible that led to a scholarly focus on the Gospel of Mark, placing this story of Jesus at the center of the stage of gospel criticism. It has not left that privileged position since then.

## The Historian

The Renaissance of the fifteenth and sixteenth century led to a rebirth of interest in the great achievements of the classical world. In its turn it produced a Reformation of the European church in the sixteenth century, and the birth of a new spirit of freedom and confidence in the limitless capacity of the human mind. The philosophical systems of the seventeenth century generated a period across the seventeenth and eighteenth centuries that celebrated this new spirit and freedom, the Age of Enlightenment. Along with serious, inquiring minds and exciting scientific experimentation that produced some spectacular inventions, European culture came to accept that claims to truth had to withstand the critique of the human mind. Unless an affirmation could be shown to be true by means of experimentation and the strict application of logical principles, then it should be regarded as uncertain and unprovable. Such affirmations were increasingly regarded as irrelevant for the progress of humanity. Many positive aspects of contemporary culture flow from this period: humanitarian concerns, toleration of differences, better legal systems and their administration, education, social welfare, critical scholarship in all areas of learning, and the rapid development of serious and objective scientific experimentation. However, there were also some damaging results, especially the overestimation of the intellect, and the underestimation of that which could not be proved as true by rational processes. Religions based on a book that received its authority from an unprovable affirmation that it was divinely inspired were soon to come under fire.

This new spirit led to a movement, beginning among the so-called English Deists (e.g., Lord Herbert of Cherbury, John Toland, and Matthew Tindal), and spreading to France (e.g., Voltaire, Jean-Jacques Rousseau, and Denis Diderot), Germany (e.g., King Frederick II and Gotthold Lessing), and the United States (e.g., Benjamin Franklin and Thomas Jefferson). These influential figures were either skeptical of a biblically revealed religion, or condemned it completely. This critical, scholarly generation found unacceptable the many imaginative narratives of the Bible, the logical non sequiturs, the repetitions, and especially many of the doctrines and ethical principles that flowed from a literal reading of the Bible.[2] In general, they did not reject the need for some form of religion, but it was to flow from the identifiable principles that directed nature and was to be articulated according to the principles of human reason.

There is a close connection between this post-Enlightenment age and the birth of what was called, at that time, "higher criticism," and has since come to be known as historical-critical biblical scholarship.[3] The Christian religion, especially as it was understood and practiced in the Protestant traditions in Germany at that time, was deeply dependent on the Bible. The catchphrase of Martin Luther, *sola Scriptura* (Scripture alone), was taken very seriously. The attack on the religious value of the Bible had to be challenged; an enduring sense of the Bible as a revealed Word of God, despite its obvious oddities, had to be pursued. Thus, it needs to be kept in mind that the critical approach to the Bible, which led to so much turmoil in nineteenth-century Europe, was born from a desire *to defend the biblical basis of the Christian religion*. To do so, the tools of the post-Enlightenment age had to be taken up and applied to the Bible. A closer analysis of the relationships between the various biblical texts (source criticism), a deeper study of the original languages and the worlds that lie behind the Bible (historical criticism), and eventually a comparative study of the religion of the Bible and the religions of other ancient Near-Eastern cultures (history of religions), were the major tools of the first century of higher criticism.[4] Many of the early scholars fell away from mainstream religious traditions and practice as they exposed the biblical text to severe historical criticism. Many aggressively anti-Christian scholars joined the fray, and the Christian churches and their beliefs were subjected to severe rationalist criticism, much to the dismay, fear, and pain of religious leaders and believers.[5] But this criticism should not distract us from recognizing the Christian motivation that led to the desire among many of the original historical critics to defend the biblical basis of the European religious traditions.

An important feature of burgeoning critical biblical scholarship during the nineteenth century was an attempt to show that the books of the Bible did not drop out of the skies, directly handed to an author by God or by some inspiring angel. They may have been the word of God, but they were products of human experiences, and eventually written down in the words of men and women.[6] Thus, it became increasingly clear that the books had their sources. This was most obvious in the first five books of the Old Testament: the Pentateuch of Genesis, Exodus, Leviticus, Numbers, and Deuteronomy. This collection of books was regarded by Israel, and subsequently by Christianity, as writings left by Moses. Even before the rise of critical biblical scholarship, scholars had searched for the different popular traditions lying behind this collection of authoritative texts. They were seen as a blend of narratives (some of them telling the same story twice, but in different ways [most famously, the account of the creation in seven days Gen 1:1–2:4, and the second, more imaginative, account of Gen 2:5–3:24, highlighted by the creation of Adam and Eve and the beginning of sin]), folktales, liturgical settings (Jewish feasts), laws, genealogies, exhortations to faithfulness, and much other material. Scholars of the Old Testament had long questioned the possibility that Moses had written all five books personally, and entirely from his own experience.[7]

The same questions were simultaneously asked of the gospels by an emerging group of New Testament scholars. One of the problems generated by the Gospels of Matthew, Mark, and Luke was the acceptable repetition of the same stories (they were, after all, about the same man), but the unacceptable differences found in the three accounts of the same episode. For example, at Caesarea Philippi, did the encounter between Jesus and Peter run as it was reported in Matt 16:16–20, with Peter's complete understanding of Jesus' person, followed by Jesus' blessing of

Peter before his warning not to speak of his messianic status? Or was it a briefer recognition on the part of Peter that Jesus was the Christ followed by Jesus' warning not to make this truth known, as is found in Mark 8:27–30? Maybe the encounter happened in an unnamed place, after Jesus had prayed alone, where Peter simply answers Jesus' question about the disciples' understanding of his identity with the words: "You are the Christ of God," as Luke reports (Luke 9:18–20). Did Jesus deliver the Beatitudes to his disciples on a mountain (Matt 5:1–11), or did he speak them to a large crowd that included Gentiles, on a level place after he had come down from a mountain where he had chosen the twelve apostles (Luke 6:12–26)? Close analysis of the Gospels of Matthew, Mark, and Luke soon showed that these issues emerged in almost every episode reported by all three (Matthew-Mark-Luke), or by any two of the evangelists (Mark-Matthew, Mark-Luke, Matthew-Luke [Q material][8]).

Nineteenth-century post-Enlightenment criticism wanted to know what had actually happened so that the "real Jesus" could be identified. The best way to discover that information was to trace the source of the three so-called Synoptic Gospels. Thus, early gospel criticism developed what came to be known as source criticism. It did not take long to decide that Mark, the shortest and least used of the gospels, was the major source for Matthew and Luke. Ongoing work on the three Synoptic Gospels continues to lead most contemporary scholars to agree with the majority position from the nineteenth century: Mark was the first of all the gospels. Not all agreed then, and there are still several vocal scholars who regard the theory of Markan priority a scholarly imposition that does not resolve all the problems. It is certainly true that Markan priority does not resolve *all the problems*. Thus theories concerning the relationships among the three Synoptic Gospels have become more complex, with greater attention given not only to the antiquity of the Markan material, but also to the material that is found only in Matthew (sometimes called "M"), the material found only in Luke (sometimes called "L"), and a large amount of material common to Matthew and Luke that does not appear in Mark, generally called "Q" (after the German word for source [*Quelle*]). Most problematic are the so-called minor agreements: those passages where Matthew and Luke should be depending on Mark (in the classical theory of Markan priority), but which agree almost word for word with one another, over against the Markan rendition of the same episode or words of Jesus.

The majority of contemporary scholars adopt what is called the two-source theory. They accept that Mark was the first to write a gospel, one of the sources used by Matthew and Luke, who also used a second source: Q. A number of contemporary scholars question what is, after all, a theory that still leaves a number of questions unresolved.[9] The probable solution to these difficulties, especially the minor agreements, is the dynamic and ongoing nature of the oral tradition. Writing in the second half of the second century, Papias (as cited by Eusebius) can still rate oral traditions about Jesus more important than written books (see Eusebius, *Ecclesiastical History* 3.39.3–15). These oral traditions must have played an important part in the development of the synoptic tradition, independent of the strictly literary dependence of Matthew and Luke upon Mark and Q, and they necessarily generate a fluidity that scholarly accuracy finds difficult to catalog.[10]

The underlying concern of the source critics, however, was not primarily the literary question, but the historical question. Their primary aim was not simply to trace the use of one literary text by another (although they did that), or the way the Christian tradition developed from source to source (the literary question), but to establish which gospel was the earliest (the historical question).[11] Once the historical issue was resolved, they suggested they discerned a bedrock account of the life of Jesus. They claimed that the authentic source for all subsequent lives of Jesus, including those of Matthew, Luke, and (to a lesser extent) John, had been found.[12] The source critics, especially (but not only) H. J. Holtzmann, argued that the Gospel of Mark, the most primitive of all the gospels, took us back to a reliable historical framework for the life of Jesus. On the basis of the Gospel of Mark, one could be certain that Jesus' life story evolved as follows: Jesus' messianic consciousness developed over a period of preaching in Galilee, and reached its high point at Caesarea Philippi. There he made known to his followers his belief that he was the expected Jewish Messiah. His journey to Jerusalem and his end there were the result of the Jewish leadership's rejection of his claim.[13] Thus, it could be concluded that the evangelist Mark, on the basis of the gospel that bears his name, was the first to write *a history of Jesus*. Mark, whoever he may have been, was *a historian*.

This conclusion has been thoroughly demolished since the time of Holzmann and his optimistic supporters. At the turn of the twentieth century, two scholars, independently, produced epoch-making studies indicating that the Gospel of Mark could not be used to provide information about *history*. The first of these studies, William Wrede's *The Messianic Secret in the Gospels*, addressed the thesis of those who, like Holtzmann, regarded the Gospel of Mark as a fundamentally faithful record of a framework for the life of Jesus.[14] The study looked at all the gospels, but devoted particular attention to the many occasions in the Gospel of Mark where Jesus commands his disciples to silence. These commands generally follow an event (see, for example, Mark 1:40–45 [the cure of a leper]; 3:7–12 [the curing of the ailments of all who come to him]; 5:21–43 [the cure of the woman with a flow of blood and the raising of the daughter of Jairus]) or a confession of faith (see especially 8:27–30 [the confession of Peter at Caesarea Philippi]) that reveals the messianic status of Jesus. Wrede developed his theory of the "messianic secret" from these commands to silence. He claimed that they did not come from the life of Jesus, but from a later stage in the history of the early church when there were two traditions about Jesus at large. Some people had no knowledge of Jesus' messianic status, and did not regard him as the Messiah, while others did. The Gospel of Mark was the product of the latter group, and the messianic secret was a literary and theological technique they used to draw the two traditions together.

According to Wrede, the Markan story of Jesus was not primarily a reliable *history*, and had never been intended to be such. It had been written out of a *theological* conviction, and for a *theological* and evangelical purpose: to prove that Jesus is the Christ, the Son of God (Mark 1:1). To explain why many early Christians did not know this truth, Wrede claimed that Mark inserted commands to silence into his gospel, whenever Jesus performed messianic gestures, or whenever anyone rightly saw that Jesus was the Messiah and confessed that truth. The end product was a story during which Jesus insisted that the truth of his messianic status be kept a secret. This explained why many early Christians did not know that Jesus was the Messiah. For Wrede, whether Jesus of Nazareth was *historically* the long-expected Messiah was not the issue. The Gospel of Mark, however, had a *theological* agenda: to proclaim that Jesus was the Christ, the Son of God.

Wrede rightly focused on an important feature in the Gospel of Mark: It is primarily a story of Jesus driven by a *theological* rather than a *historical* agenda. However, the major difficulty with the theory, to which we will return when we consider the Markan presentation of Jesus as the Christ and the Son of God,[15] is Wrede's attempt to find a *single* explanation for *all* the commands to silence. It is possible that some may have come from Jesus, some may have come to Mark in the traditions that existed prior to his recording them in a written form, while others may be Markan creations. All need to be studied in their own immediate context first, and then set within an overall understanding of the gospel. However, Wrede opened a new era in the study of the gospels, and Mark in particular. He was the first to point to the truth that even Mark, the earliest of the gospels, is not primarily *a history book*, but above all the proclamation of the faith of the early church. Reflecting the spirit of the era, he wrote: "The Gospel of Mark belongs to the history of dogma."[16] More aptly, it should be said: The Gospel of Mark, like all the literature of the New Testament, including that which is expressed in a narrative form (the gospels), professes the faith of the early church.

In this sense the Gospel of Mark is one of the sources for later Christian dogma, but it is hardly correct to claim that Mark was writing "dogma." Rather, he was confessing the belief that Jesus was the Christ, the Son of God, and that God had transformed the human situation because of the life, teaching, death, and resurrection of Jesus. Wrede was correct in claiming that one should not look to the Gospel of Mark for the framework of the life of Jesus. The opening verse and the presentation of John the Baptist and Jesus' baptism (1:1–13), followed by the ministry of Jesus in Galilee (1:14–9:50), his journey to Jerusalem (10:1–11:11), and his last days, death, and resurrection in Jerusalem (11:12–16:8) are the result of the creative activity of the evangelist, or the tradition he received. For Mark (and Matthew and Luke who follow him) there is only one journey to Jerusalem, and the story heads dramatically toward that place, where the death and resurrection occur. Interestingly, although often regarded as the least historical of the gospels, the Gospel of John probably reflects more accurately Jesus' regular presence in Jerusalem for the celebration of the Jewish feasts (Passover [2:13; 11:55–57; 12:12–18], Tabernacles [7:2], Dedication [10:22]), and much of his description of Jesus' passion is more historically probable.[17]

Shortly after Wrede's epoch-making study, Albert Schweitzer's *The Quest of the Historical Jesus* reviewed the portrayal of the historical Jesus by nineteenth-century scholars.[18] Schweitzer's study was not dedicated to any one of the gospels, but to a thorough critique of the major attempts to reconstruct the life of Jesus. As these reconstructions made use of the framework provided by the Gospel of Mark, Schweitzer laid bare the shortcomings of any such approach. With remarkable clarity and knowledge of the numerous publications that appeared, especially in Germany, associated with the burst of interest in the life of Jesus that had blossomed with the birth of the historical and critical approach to the gospels, he laid bare a fundamental problem of all interpretation. Each life of Jesus across the nineteenth century reflected more the mind, heart, and setting of a nineteenth-century scholar than a first-century Palestinian Jew. In his own inimitable prose (even in translation) Schweitzer describes the accepted Christian understanding of the person of Jesus, Messiah and Savior, as follows:

> The Jesus of Nazareth who came forth publicly as the Messiah, who preached the ethic of the kingdom of God, who founded the

kingdom of heaven on earth, and died to give His work its final con-
secration, *never existed.* He is a figure designed by rationalism, en-
dowed with life by liberalism, and clothed by modern theology in a
historical garb.[19]

In the end, Schweitzer was iconoclastic when it came to the development of his own portrait of Jesus. He viewed the gospels as
highly prejudiced sources, most unreliable as historical documents. For
Schweitzer, the preaching of the kingdom of God marked Jesus out as a
figure who preached the imminent end of time. As such, as a historical
character, he had to be judged a failure. Jesus believed, taught, and died
because he understood his God-ordained mission as the proclamation
of the end of time. The failure of these eschatological hopes of the historical Jesus, however, did not render Christianity irrelevant. It was
overcome in the growing Christian church and its understanding and
preaching of Jesus. The four gospels and the rapid development of a
Christian people and culture reinterpreted his person and message.
Thus, largely as the result of the work of Wrede and Schweitzer, the role
of Mark as a *historian* was discredited once and for all.

These studies, however, were not limited to the libraries and lecture
halls of German universities. As already mentioned, the critical study of
the Bible began in the nineteenth century in an attempt to put the study
of the sacred text on the same footing as the many other scholarly pur-
suits of the post-Enlightenment period. As biblical scholarship became
increasingly obsessed with the rediscovery of historical issues, it lost
touch with the narratives themselves.[20] The problem was accentuated by
a turn toward the other religions of the time, and a fascination to classify
the documents of the New Testament, and the constituent parts of those
documents, by finding parallels with other religions.[21] Between World
War I and World War II, Karl Ludwig Schmidt, Martin Dibelius, and
Rudolf Bultmann founded a new approach to the Synoptic Gospels that
focused upon the identifiable prehistory of each individual passage in
the gospels.[22] These passages, carefully divided into smaller literary
units called "pericopes," were subjected to intense scrutiny, compared
with parallel literature from other ancient religions, and classified. The
early so-called form critics had different names for the various "forms"
of pericopes in the gospels, but parallel or similar forms could be identified in the literatures of other religions and cultures. Certain common
forms and structures could be found in miracle stories, conflict stories,
legends, pronouncement stories, parables, and so on. Once each passage
had been classified according to its literary form, then its history was
sought. Did this passage come from a setting in the life of Jesus *(Sitz im*

*Leben Jesu),* or from a setting in the emerging Christian church as it developed its founding narratives *(Sitz im Leben der Kirche)*?

During a period of some fifty years, Mark had been regarded as the
first and most important *historian* to provide a framework for the life of
Jesus (Holtzmann). Further reflection on this now crucial text led to the
conclusion that Mark was an author who devoted little attention to history, but creatively developed a narrative to communicate a theological
message concerning Jesus' messianic status (Wrede, Schweitzer). The
form critics took the process one step further, and came to regard him as
an editor who assembled pieces of material that came from the historical Jesus (very little) and from the creativity of the early church (a great
deal). As Rudolf Bultmann commented in 1921:

> In Mark we can still see clearly, and most easily in comparison with
> Luke, that the most ancient tradition consisted of individual sec-
> tions, and that the connecting together is secondary.... Mark is not
> sufficiently master of his material to be able to venture on a system-
> atic construction himself.[23]

Not only had the historian par excellence been reduced to an editor,
but—if Bultmann's assessment was correct—to a rather poor editor at
that! However, something of lasting value emerged over those years,
hand in hand with the shifts of direction in the study of the Gospel of
Mark. Wrede correctly pointed to the theological creativity of Mark, and
the form critics (Schmidt, Dibelius, and Bultmann) showed that, as an
author, he received much of his material from prior traditions, shaping
them to form his story of Jesus.

The form critics, however, have not won the day in the assessment
of Mark as "not sufficiently master of his material to be able to venture
on a systematic construction himself."[24] While Wrede has been remembered as the scholar who destroyed any suggestion that Mark was a reliable historian, he also insisted that the writing of the Gospel of Mark
was not driven by a desire to write history, but by a desire to communicate a theological point of view. But even here we must be wary. The
post-Enlightenment era, of which Wrede was a product, assessed good
or bad history by judging, according to its own criteria, whether the historian under scrutiny reported the past exactly as it had happened. This
is not the only responsibility of a historian. Modern historiography insists that good history is *at least as concerned* to report not only a well-
researched order of events, but also to provide some interpretation of
*what these events meant.*[25] Wrede correctly insisted that Mark was primarily interested in theology, not a correct sequence of events that

might serve as a framework for the rediscovery of the life of Jesus. But perhaps Mark, in his compilation of a narrative guided by a theological agenda, did make an honest attempt to pass on to later generations *what the events of the life, teaching, death, and resurrection of Jesus meant*.[26]

# The Theologian

After World War II (1939–1945) Wrede's often forgotten insistence that Mark was primarily a theologian became increasingly important. Two major moments signaled the deepening scholarly appreciation of Mark the theologian. In a first moment, several scholars, who depended on the work of the form critics and accepted that Mark was an editor of sources, began to ask why he edited his sources in a fashion that produced the work known to the Christian tradition as the Gospel of Mark. This approach to Mark (and the other gospels) has been given the name "redaction criticism."[27] But just as redaction criticism was generated by asking the logical question left unanswered by the form critics (and posed, but not answered, by Wrede), so in a second moment there emerged, in the last decades of the twentieth century and into the twenty-first century, a greater appreciation of Mark as a theologically motivated storyteller. This approach to the gospels has been called "narrative criticism."[28] A survey of the achievements of the redaction critics and the narrative critics will show how, increasingly, Mark is being understood as a very creative theologian. His history of Jesus is not *primarily* concerned with what actually happened during the life of Jesus and at his death and resurrection, but with what these words and events meant and still mean.[29]

## Redaction Criticism

The period across the 1950s and 1960s was marked by an increasing number of scholars who accepted that all four evangelists received many traditions, oral and written, and acted as editors to assemble our present gospels as we have them. But, scholars began to insist, there were further questions to be asked of the activity of the evangelists. Each evangelist assembled the traditions, and rewrote them, in a unique fashion. Once Markan priority was established as a basic working hypothesis, it was relatively easy for scholars to follow how Matthew or Luke had taken words of Jesus, or an account from the life of Jesus they found in Mark, and adapted them for their own ends. The acceptance of a common source called Q also enabled them to trace the different use of the same material that is common to Matthew and Luke, even though not found in Mark. This process was bound to be speculative, as Q is reconstructed on the basis of the common material (generally supposing that the Lukan version is older). The project has been well described by Hans Conzelmann, whose work on the theology of the Gospel of Luke is widely regarded as a founding study in the development of redaction criticism:

> Our aim is to elucidate Luke's work in its present form, not to enquire into possible sources or into the historical facts which provided the material. A variety of sources does not necessarily imply a similar variety in the thought and composition of the author. *How did it come about that he brought together these particular materials? Was he able to imprint on them his own views?* It is here that the analysis of the sources renders the *necessary service* of helping to distinguish *what comes from the source and what belongs to the author.*[30]

The stressed passages highlight Conzelmann's programmatic statement, originally published in German in 1957, for all subsequent redaction critics. The form critics had determined that the authors of the gospels worked with sources, and worked largely as editors. The redaction critics asked further: "How did it come about that he brought together these particular materials?" It must be taken for granted that Matthew, Mark, Luke, and John had a great deal of material, some oral, some written, some perhaps embedded in the community's Christian rituals (e.g., hymns, prayers), and each evangelist *made a selection* from these sources. What were the overarching literary and theological agendas that drove such a selection? This important question, however, depended on the work of the form critics. It is not as if the redaction critics ignored the sources that had been uncovered by the form critics, but "the analysis renders the *necessary service* of helping to distinguish what comes from the source from what belongs to the author." The methods and the conclusions of the form critics were essential for the redaction critical approach to the gospels.

But it proved to be more difficult to apply the principles of redaction criticism to the Gospel of Mark than to Matthew and Luke. With the latter, the critic could be sure that Matthew and Luke had Mark and probably Q in front of them. It was easier, by the simple use of a *synopsis,* a book that printed the texts of the three Synoptic Gospels side by side, to see the alterations made to their sources, Mark and (although more speculative) Q.[31] This was not possible with Mark, as we have no literary text on which Mark might depend that was in existence prior to Mark. The absence of a source that may have been redacted by Mark, however, has not stopped the redaction critics. Starting from the *correct insight* that Mark was primarily a theologian and not a historian, the critics have developed methods to determine what passages in Mark are clearly non-Markan, and what are clearly Markan.

Some passages through the gospel summarize the action thus far, and move the reader from one episode to another (see, for example, 1:14–15; 3:7–12; 6:6b). These certainly are the work of the editor, moving the story along according to his agenda. Other passages, if Wrede was correct, display the overarching theological agenda of the author (for example, all the commands to secrecy). But one cannot be certain of this. It is perfectly possible that some summaries may have come to Mark in his tradition, and that he created others. Similarly, perhaps the major problem with Wrede's solution to the so-called messianic secret was his unwarranted conclusion that all the commands to secrecy have to be given the same explanation: They are there to serve the evangelist's purpose of explaining the two traditions about Jesus' messianic status. An even more circuitous method is the search for obviously Markan words and turns of phrase across the gospel. In an analysis of a particular pericope, such expressions can be regarded as Markan, and the critic can credit them to the evangelist, and thus lay bare the remains of the passage under consideration as its non-Markan original source. But how reliable is it to decide what is Markan, eliminate it, and finish up with a non-Markan source? Often critics bring their own agenda to the excision of Markan material, and thus the redactional activity of Mark looks just as they suspected it might be.[32]

Indeed, the redaction-critical approach to the Gospel of Mark is fraught with difficulty.[33] Nevertheless, the last three decades of the twentieth century saw a proliferation of redaction-critical studies of Mark. By using the methods briefly described above, scholars investigated theological issues that are doubtless central to the message of Mark. Some major themes visited and revisited many times since Willi Marxsen published the first genuine redactional study of Mark in 1956[34] are: Jesus' family, the disciples of Jesus, the journeys back and forth across the lake in a boat, his miracle working activity, his conflicts with the Jewish leaders, his use of christological titles, the messianic secret, the trial narrative, the passion narrative, the resurrection of Jesus, and the roles of women.[35]

The work of the redaction critics, because of the difficulties in determining Mark's sources objectively and with precision, can often be confusing. Different scholars come up with quite different assessments of the same literary and theological theme.[36] Despite these difficulties, the redaction critics have uncovered a rich understanding of Mark's theological contribution to the life and development of the early Christian church. The evangelist Mark has emerged as one of the foundational and formative theological thinkers and authors in the Christian tradition.[37] The shadowy figure of Mark has created a gospel, as a new literary form within the early church, by developing a story of Jesus to proclaim his theological message. It is becoming increasingly clear that, however little we can rediscover of his person, we are gradually uncovering his rich theological agenda.

## Narrative Criticism

Contemporary narrative criticism has its roots in the study of narrative literature in general. Rather than tracing various sources, and seeing how each storyteller has arranged these sources to develop a certain point of view, narrative criticism insists that the narrative must be understood as a whole. An author writes a narrative from beginning to end, and it must be approached as a *unified utterance*. The narrative critics continue the process of the redaction critics as they look for an author's point of view. But they pay less attention to the work of the form critics, who worked hard to discover the history of the elements that were edited to generate the story. The narrative critics' main concentration is on "the world in the text." They attempt to show how the story has been designed and told in order to influence "the world in front of the text." Biblical scholarship has gradually come to appreciate more fully that there are more than two "worlds" involved in the interpretation of an ancient text. Historical-critical scholarship has devoted almost two hundred years to the rediscovery of "the world behind the text," so that there would be no modern agenda imposed on the world in the text. Redaction critics focused more intensely on "the world in the text." Contemporary narrative critics are devoting more attention to "the world in front of the text," as there is now a greater interest in approaching each single document, however limited and flawed it might be, as a work of art.[38]

There are many extended narratives in the Old Testament. Old Testament scholars were the first to use techniques developed by literary theorists to analyze these narratives. New Testament critics were not slow to follow.[39] Their reasoning is that behind each "story" there is a "real author" who has a definite person or group of people in mind as he or she tells the story. Thus, there is an intended "real reader" for whom the story was originally written. Neither of these figures can be found *in* the story itself. One produces it and the other takes it in hand to read it, or listen to it. The Gospel of Mark is one such writing, but it is something more. The real author, whoever he might have been, is long since dead, as are the original recipients of the book. However, the gospel still has a widespread readership. There is something about this book that has generated interested readers for almost two thousand years, however little we may know of the original author and readers.

Although the real author and the real reader(s) do not play an active role in the events of the narrative, they leave their traces. Narratives have deliberately contrived plots and characters that interact throughout the story along a certain time line, through a sequence of events. An author devises certain rhetorical features to hold plot and character together so that the reader will not miss the author's point of view. These rhetorical features are *in* the narrative. One can broadly claim that the communication between a real author and a real reader who are *outside* the text takes place through an implied author, a narrator, and an implied reader who are *inside* the text. The details of the concrete situations of the original real author and the original real reader(s) may be obscure. We know nothing about the "historical Mark," the original author who penned these pages (the real author). We can only speculate, in the light of the evidence of the Gospel of Mark, on the concrete situation of the people for whom the gospel was originally written (the real readers). Nevertheless, *we have the text*, and much can be gleaned from it. However theoretical this description may appear to be, it reflects everyone's reading experience. The following example of a possible reading experience may throw light on the above.

A lost letter picked up by a disinterested third party quickly tells the reader something of the person writing the letter. The rhetoric of the letter also reveals something of the author's understanding of and approach to the reader. The person who has found the letter knows neither the real author nor the original intended reader, but the real reader—the person who picked up the letter from the pavement—is able to identify the communication attempted by the letter. The person who found the letter traces an author "implied" and a reader "implied" by the letter. Indeed, a very beautiful letter may even move the eavesdropper. When that happens, mutuality is established between the reader implied by the letter and the real reader of the letter. One does not have to be part of the original communication process between the original writer of the letter and its original reader to be moved and inspired by the power of the emotions expressed by the letter. The literary form of a letter is very different from the sometimes complex literary shape of a narrative, espe-

cially one (like the Gospel of Mark) that was written almost two
thousand years ago. However, the process of communication between
an author and a reader takes place in both. Contemporary narrative approaches to the gospels attempt to enter into the process of communication between an author and a reader whom we do not know, and who
are long since dead, so that today's reader might be moved and inspired
by the passionate convictions of the author.

Narrative critics focus on the literary features found in the narrative
of the Gospel of Mark. Much attention is given to the literary shape of
each section of the story; the way each section follows logically from
what went before and leads directly into what follows; the roles of the
various characters in the story; the passing of time; unresolved puzzles
that emerge, forcing the reader to look further into the narrative to tie
these puzzles together; the consistency of the underlying point of view
of an author who has shaped and told a story of the life of Jesus in a way
unparalleled by any other early Christian writing. Like the reader who
eavesdropped on the letter found on the pavement, and was moved by
the sincerity and power of the emotions communicated by the letter, we
are eavesdropping on an ancient story of Jesus. Eavesdropping on this
particular story, however, has been going on for some time, and it has
served as an inspiration for Christians from all walks of life for almost
two thousand years.

We can allow ourselves to be seduced by the perspective of the author—but which author? It is possible for an author to write a narrative
that communicates a point of view that is not a reflection of his or her
own situation in life, humor, personality, or personal experience. There
is, therefore, an author *in the text* of the Gospel of Mark, just as there was
an author *in the text* of the letter described above. Whatever the perspective of a historical flesh-and-blood author may have been, we can claim
to trace the theological point of view of an author only in the text itself.
Such an author is generally called *the implied author*. This feature of any
narrative is not a historical person, however well the point of view may
or may not reflect the choices of that figure from the past who should be
called *the real author*. Unlike some contemporary narratives, it can generally be assumed (but never proved) that the real author *of* and the implied author *in* New Testament narratives speak with the same voice. It
is difficult to imagine that such a passionate book as the Gospel of Mark
is anything but the communication of a historical person's deeply held
and passionate belief in what God has done in and through Jesus.[40]

Like the historical author of the book, now long since dead, the
flesh-and-blood historical first real readers are beyond our knowledge.
We cannot be sure of the reception that this passionate story of Jesus

received. The ongoing existence of the gospel—and the many manuscripts that contain it—demonstrates that it was received, treasured, and passed on. Already in the second century, later generations of Christians had, in their own turn, both received it and honored it. How I might respond to a narrative in any of the gospels may vary from day to day, depending on a number of circumstances. We are well aware of the numerous circumstances that affect, for better or worse, the reading process. Yet, *within the narrative* there is a reader addressed by the implied author, as there was an identifiable reader implied by the letter described above. As the narrative unfolds, the implied reader is gradually provided with information and experiences that such a reader cannot avoid. This reader is shaped by the desires of the author and emerges as the text unfolds. This reader does not suffer from the vagaries that can impinge on the reading process. Critics speak of a literary construct within the narrative itself, an implied reader whose responses are totally controlled by the implied author. The implied reader is not a historical person. Historically there are only real readers.

By tracing the developing knowledge and experience of the implied reader as each page of the text is opened, I am better able to appreciate the temporal flow of the narrative and grow in my appreciation of the unfolding narrative. Stanley Fish has described the use of the implied reader by a narrative critic as follows:

> The basis of the method is a consideration of the *temporal* flow of the reading experience, and it is assumed that the reader responds in terms of that flow and not to the whole utterance. That is, in an utterance of any length, there is a point at which the reader has taken in only the first word, and then the second, and then the third, and so on, and the report of what happens to the reader is always a report of what happened *to that point*.[41]

As each page of the Gospel of Mark is opened, much is learned about Jesus, his "new teaching" (see Mark 1:27), and his encounters with others, especially the disciples. But there is still more to learn from those parts of the story that lie ahead. The Gospel of Mark, unlike the other gospels, does not even allow the reader a satisfying end to the story. The women hear the Easter message (16:6), and are told to announce the message of Jesus' going before the disciples into Galilee (16:7; see 14:28), but they run away frightened, and say nothing to anyone (16:8).[42]

The ending of the Gospel of Mark will call for more attention in our study of Mark as a storyteller and as an evangelist,[43] but the citation from Fish needs expansion, as it does not fully exhaust the experience of the readers of ancient canonical texts like the Gospel of Mark. The implied reader gradually emerges from the unfolding narrative shaped by the author. The implied reader knows only what has been read so far, with an ability to move backward to recall events already narrated. But it is impossible that the reader of a Christian gospel would have no knowledge or experience of the story of Jesus of Nazareth and Christian life and its practices. The direct importation of literary scholarship into New Testament studies has sometimes presupposed such a virginal reader, but this is unrealistic. The author of the Gospel of Mark takes it for granted that the implied reader knows many things already. The implied reader knows Greek, to start with, and also understands Jewish titles of honor that are applied to Jesus, especially Son of God, the Christ, and the Son of Man. Allusions to the celebration of the Lord's Supper in Mark 6:41–44, 8:6–8, and 14:22–25 show that the original readers were already practicing this ritual. Above all, however, the reader of the Gospel of Mark lived in a believing community, a belief based on the significance of the death and resurrection of Jesus (see 1:1, 11; 9:7; 14:62; 15:29–32, 39). Much more than knowledge of the rough Greek of the text of the Gospel of Mark is presupposed of its reader. The reader in the story of the Gospel of Mark may be credited with a knowledge of the story of Jesus, but its Markan form is being presented to bring the reader (or listener) to accept a particular point of view. The reader knows that Jesus died on a cross, but the author of this gospel insists both that this death is a cruel and humiliating descent into abandon (see 15:33–37), and that Jesus is established as Messiah and Son of God, the rejected cornerstone upon whom a new temple of God will be built (see 12:10–11; 14:58; 15:29–30, 37–38).

But it is dishonest not to recognize that every word of the gospel is historically and culturally conditioned. The fact that it is written in the everyday Greek of Jesus' time *(koinē)* is prima facie evidence of this truth. There is inevitably something strange and foreign about the biblical text that demands that we wrestle with it. First-century history and culture must play a part in interpretation. The Gospel of Mark, like all biblical texts handed down to us by Jewish and Christian tradition, is a foreign text when read in translation in our present cultural context. The original readers of the gospel are an important point of reference in following the interplay between author and reader in the text. Adela Yarbro Collins has rightly insisted that we:

> give more weight to the original historical context of the text. This context cannot and should not totally determine all subsequent meaning and use of the text. But if . . . all meaning is context bound, the original context and meaning have a certain normative character.

I suggest that Biblical theologians are not only mediators between genres. They are also mediators between historical periods. . . . Whatever tension there may be between literary- and historical-critical methods, the two approaches are complementary.[44]

Every narrative generates an implied reader as it unfolds, but the modern scholarly reader must do more than trace the temporal flow of a narrative. The use of such literary techniques will still tell us only how an author achieves an effect. But there are other elements that must be kept in mind for a sound, critical reading of an ancient, normative text. *The world behind the text* (first century) must be respected and studied, in order to understand its distance from our world and our concerns. A narrative approach should also ask: How does the implied reader *in the text* who emerges as this ancient story of Jesus unfolds relate to the knowledge and experience of the twenty-first century Christian reader *of the text*? There is, of course, a context that unites the original and nearly all subsequent readers of the Gospel of Mark: a context generated by Christian faith. Both the original readers and most contemporary readers believe that Jesus is the Christ, the Son of God (1:1).

The secret of the lasting value of a narrative lies in the mutuality that is created between the implied reader *in the text* and the real reader *of the text*; the common context of Christian belief helps this mutuality. A story that tells of Jesus the Christ, the Son of God, should appeal to Christians. Nevertheless, whole libraries of Christian books lack that appeal! What is it in the Gospel of Mark that has generated its ongoing readership? There must be an understanding and respect for the world behind the text, which shaped the reader *in the text,* but there is more. When I read a good novel for the first time, I relate to an implied reader. I become part of the story, caught in its characters, events, time, and places as the pages turn. This is the case with any good book, but in a classic there is an even deeper relationship between the reader in the text and the reader of the text. A classic is not simply a narrative that catches my imagination during my reading, only to be forgotten as I pass on to my next activity. A classic generates a deeper mutuality between the implied reader *in the text* and the real reader *of the text*. As David Tracy has said: "The classic text's real disclosure is its claim to attention on the ground that an event of understanding proper to finite human beings has here found expression."[45] As Honoré de Balzac's narrator informs the reader at the beginning of *Père Goriot:* "You may be certain that this drama is neither fiction nor romance. *All is true,* so true that everyone can recognise the elements of the tragedy in his own household, in his own heart perhaps."[46] For Balzac, the issue was human tragedy, but there are many other profound expressions of experience and belief, "events of understanding proper to finite human beings," that can be communicated by means of classical narrative writing.

The practice of reading and the community of readers that have produced the Bible show that truth. The Gospel of Mark can lay claim to being a Christian classic. As we continue to read this urgent gospel after nearly two thousand years of reading, in a variety of contexts, we can be sure that there has been mutuality between its implied and real readers. The unfolding narrative of the Gospel of Mark raises problems that the reader will solve through the ongoing reading of the story of Jesus. Did these solutions speak to the members of the Markan community, the original intended readers who were part of the world of the narrative of the Gospels in a way that the contemporary real reader can never be? They read Greek, or at least understood it as it was read; they caught the subtleties of references to their suffering Messiah, their own experience of failure and suffering, their celebration of the Lord's Supper, and the ironies found across the story, especially in the Passion Narrative. None of this can to be taken for granted as shared by most of today's readers of the Gospel of Mark. Do the questions raised and the solutions offered by this story of Jesus still speak to real readers at the beginning of the third millennium? Is this text a classic? Our study of Mark the storyteller, interpreter, and evangelist, will attempt to provide a positive answer to these questions.

## Conclusion

A further aspect to the Gospel of Mark needs to be mentioned about contemporary narrative approaches and the reader-response criticism that builds on them. Sometimes, as we read a story, we may have a further response that is independent of the implied reader, and thus outside the control of the author. It is unavoidable that our response, either of empathy or antipathy, will be the result of our privileged position as the recipients of almost two thousand years of the Christian practice of reading the gospels. The Markan story of the life, teaching, death, and resurrection of Jesus is told in a way that touches the reader's experience. The span of Christian history is fair indication that generation after generation of Christian readers have "entered the fictional contract" of the Gospel of Mark; they have identified with the implied reader.[47] There can be no single meaning given to the Gospel of Mark because the response of each one of us to any text is necessarily determined by our own particular context. What results is but one person's attempt to respond to the text of the Gospel of Mark. Yet, while there can be *many* readings of the Gospel of Mark, it is not open to *any* reading.

Enough has been said of these theories. We have met Mark, insofar as it is possible to discover him from ancient sources and from an appreciation of the story of the Gospel. It is time to turn to the text of the Gospel of Mark. We cannot be certain of the precise identity of Mark. Nor can we claim to have determined accurately the time or the place where this story of the life and teaching, death, and resurrection of Jesus first saw the light of day. His claim to importance in and for the Christian tradition lies not so much in who he was, or where and when he wrote, but in what he has written. The following understanding of Mark as a storyteller, interpreter, and evangelist locates itself within the Christian tradition. It is but one attempt among many to respond to the perennial difficulty so well described in Philip's encounter with the Ethiopian eunuch in Acts 8:30–31: "So Philip ran up to him and heard him reading Isaiah the prophet, and asked, 'Do you understand what you are reading?' And he said, 'How can I, unless someone guides me?' "

## Notes

1. See S. P. Kealy, *Mark's Gospel: A History of Its Interpretation* (New York: Paulist, 1982), 6–57; B. D. Schildgen, *Power and Prejudice: The Reception of the Gospel of Mark* (Detroit: Wayne State University Press, 1999), 35–42.

2. See Schildgen, *Power and Prejudice,* 111–23. In assessing this period, one must reject arrogant overconfidence in the achievements of the human being, but one must also remember that many socially accepted evils came from an uncritical reading of the Bible. One that immediately springs to mind is the widespread presence of slaves in the United States (and elsewhere, prior to the Enlightenment). Both sides in the American Civil War of the 1850s were citing biblical texts in support of their positions. The same could be said today (2003) about the debate over the death penalty in the United States, where biblical texts are used uncritically and indiscriminately by both sides.

3. This is not the place for a full-scale history of the development of historical-critical scholarship. Yet, it is interesting to note that one of the major moments in its early years was the posthumous publication, by Lessing, of some fragments that pointed to the unreliable nature of an uncritical reading of the Gospels, written by H. S. Reimarus, rightly regarded as the founder of modern quests for the historical Jesus. He saw Jesus as a failed political messiah who had been reinstated by his followers as a spiritual messiah. They stole his body and announced that he would return in glory as judge. For them, according to Reimarus, Jesus' death was necessary to obtain forgiveness for humankind. See W. Carter, *Matthew: Storyteller, Interpreter, Evangelist* (Peabody: Hendrickson, 1996), 36–37. For an English edition of these famous "fragments," see C. H. Talbert, ed., *Reimarus: Fragments* (Philadelphia: Fortress, 1971).

4. For the period up to the attack of the Deists on the biblical text, see W. Baird, *History of New Testament Research: Volume One: From Deism to Tübingen* (Minneapolis: Fortress, 1992). For a history of the birth and development of scholarly biblical criticism in the nineteenth century, see W. Kümmel, *The New Testament: The History of the Investigation of Its Problems* (Nashville: Abingdon, 1972), 40–193; A. Schweitzer, *The Quest of the Historical Jesus* (ed. J. Bowden; First complete edition; trans. W. Montgomery, J. R. Coates, S. Cupitt, and J. Bowden; Minneapolis: Fortress, 2001); W. Baird, *History of New Testament Research: Volume 2: From Jonathan Edwards to Rudolf Bultmann* (Minneapolis: Fortress, 2002).

5. John Updike, describing the loss of faith of Clarence Arthur Wilmot, a Presbyterian minister and the founding figure of the dynasty traced in his novel, brilliantly caricatures the impact of this radical criticism: "He [Clarence] had plunged into the chilly Baltic Sea of Higher Criticism—all those Germans, Semler and Eichhorn, Baur and Wellhausen, who dared to pick up the Sacred Book without reverence, as one more human volume, more curious and conglomerate than most, but the work of men—of Jews in dirty sheepskins, rotten-toothed desert tribesmen with eyes rolled heavenward, men like flies on flypaper caught fast in a historic time, among myths and conceptions belonging to the childhood of mankind. They called themselves theologians, these Teutonic ravagers of the text that Luther had unchained from the altar and had translated out of Latin, and accepted their bread from the devout sponsors of theological chairs, yet were the opposite of theologians, as in the dank basement of Greek and Aramaic researches they undermined Christianity's ancient supporting walls and beams" (J. Updike, *The Beauty of the Lilies* [New York: Fawcett Columbine, 1996], 15).

6. This is the background to Updike's caricature.

7. Already in the seventeenth and eighteenth centuries, two French scholars, Richard Simon (1638–1712) and Jean Astruc (1684–1766), had proposed sources for the Pentateuch. Simon had also queried the historicity of the gospel narratives, given the many contradictions found there. The quest for these sources and the issue of the historicity of the gospels became the major concerns of the higher criticism of the nineteenth century.

8. See below, pp. 22–23, 28–29, for an explanation of what is meant by "Q material."

9. In contemporary reflection on the Synoptic Question several scholars are returning to the claim made by Augustine, that Mark was an abbreviation of Matthew, or even of both Matthew and Luke. For important surveys, deciding that, despite its weaknesses, the two-source theory best explains all the data, see J. A. Fitzmyer, "The Priority of Mark and the 'Q' Source in Luke," in *To Advance the Gospel: New Testament Studies* (New York: Crossroad, 1981), 3–40; C. M. Tuckett, *Q and the History of Early Christianity: Studies on Q* (Peabody: Hendrickson, 1996), 1–39; J. Marcus, *Mark 1–8* (AB 27; New York: Doubleday, 2000), 40–47; C. A. Evans, *Mark 8:27–16:20* (WBC 34B; Nashville: Thomas Nelson, 2001), xliii–lviii. See also Carter, *Matthew*, 38–41.

10. Worthy of note is the attempt to explain the "minor agreements" on the part of A. Fuchs and U. Schnelle (among others), who suggest that there must have been a *Deuteromark,* a second edition of the canonical Mark, used by Mathew and Luke. The "minor agreements" come from this second edition of Mark. See U. Schnelle, *The History and Theology of the New Testament Writings*

(trans. M. E. Boring; Minneapolis: Fortress, 1998), 170–72. However, if there was a second edition of Mark, what happened to it? It has left no trace in early Christianity, except in the minor agreements. This is unlikely. Recently, R. A. Horsley, *Hearing the Whole Story: The Politics of Plot in Mark's Gospel* (Louisville: Westminster John Knox, 2001), 53–78, argues (following the suggestion of Werner Kelber; see below, p. 57 note 6) that Mark was primarily an oral experience, never told twice in exactly the same way. If this were the case, then the minor agreements may have their source in one of the many oral versions of Mark. In my opinion, however, this is unlikely.

11. As we shall see, the aspect of the "literary question" that traced the development of the use of the *same* literary tradition to address *different* situations in the early Church assumed its importance at a later stage in the history of Gospel criticism, with the development of redaction criticism.

12. The relationship between John and the Synoptic Gospels was a great problem for the early critics, and it has remained a matter of serious study since that time. In the end, most early critics regarded the fourth gospel as a "spiritual gospel," of little or no historical value, possibly coming very late in the theological development of the Christian church (some time in the second century). So much of it appeared to present Jesus as a God striding over the earth, uttering long theological discourses that would not have been possible for a first-century Palestinian Jew. This totally negative assessment of the historical worth of the Gospel of John is nowadays rejected. See below, note 17. For an excellent summary of the discussion of the relationship between the Gospel of John and the Synoptic Gospels, from the beginning of critical scholarship down to the present time, see D. Moody Smith, *John among the Gospels* (2d ed.; Columbia: University of South Carolina Press, 2001).

13. H. J. Holtzmann, *Die synoptischen Evangelien: Ihr Ursprung und geschichtlicher Charakter* (Leipzig: Wilhelm Engelmann, 1863). Other important figures were K. Lachmann, C. H. Weisse, J. Hawkins, and P. Wernle. For a fuller discussion, see Kealy, *Mark's Gospel,* 58–89; Schnelle, *History and Theology,* 162–79.

14. W. Wrede, *Das Messiasgeheimnis in den Evangelien: Zugleich ein Beitrag zum Verständnis des Markusevangeliums* (Göttingen: Vandenhoeck & Ruprecht, 1901). This book has been reprinted four times since then, the last reprint as recent as 1969. It is available in English: W. Wrede, *The Messianic Secret* (trans. J. C. G. Grieg; Cambridge & London: James Clarke, 1971).

15. See Part 3: Mark the Interpreter in this volume.

16. Wrede, *The Messianic Secret,* 131.

17. On this question, see the principles for tracing historical data in the Fourth Gospel, stated by J. P. Meier, *A Marginal Jew: Rethinking the Historical Jesus* (3 vols.; ABRL; New York: Doubleday, 1991–2001), 1:41–45. See also F. J. Moloney, "The Fourth Gospel and the Jesus of History," *NTS* 46 (2000): 42–58.

18. A. Schweitzer, *Von Reimarus zu Wrede: Eine Geschichte der Leben-Jesu-Forschung* (Tübingen: J. C. B. Mohr [Paul Siebeck], 1906). This edition of Schweitzer's work was translated into English as *The Quest of the Historical Jesus* (trans. W. Montgomery; London: A. & C. Black, 1910). A considerably enlarged edition of the German original, titled simply *Geschichte der Leben-Jesu Forschung,* was published in 1913, and a full English edition of this study has recently appeared: *The Quest of the Historical Jesus* (First complete edition; trans. W. Montgomery, J. R. Coates, S. Cupitt, and J. Bowden; ed. J. Bowden; Minne-

apolis: Fortress, 2001). This study retains its freshness and importance, even though it was written almost one hundred years ago.

19. Schweitzer, *The Quest*, 478 (2001 edition). Stress mine.

20. An important study of this loss of contact with the essentially narrative basis of the Christian tradition, and its impact on the interpretation of the Bible, can be found in H. Frei, *The Eclipse of Biblical Narrative: A Study of Eighteenth and Nineteenth Century Hermeneutics* (New Haven: Yale University Press, 1974).

21. This scholarly activity also had its beginnings in the German universities, and was not limited to biblical studies. New archaeological and literary discoveries opened up a world of ancient religions hitherto unknown. There were different methods, but this movement was called The History of Religions School *(Die Religionsgeschichtliche Schule)*.

22. K. L. Schmidt, *Die Rahmen der Geschichte Jesu: Literarkritische Untersuchungen zu ältesten Jesusüberlieferung* (Damstadt: Wissenschaftliche Buchgesellschaft, 1964 [original 1919]); M. Dibelius, *From Tradition to Gospel* (trans. B. L. Woolf; Library of Theological Translations; Cambridge & London: James Clarke, 1971 [original German: 1919]); R. Bultmann, *History of the Synoptic Tradition* (trans. J. Marsh; Oxford: Basil Blackwell, 1968 [original German: 1921]).

23. Bultmann, *History*, 338, 350.

24. Ibid., 350.

25. Much has been written on this topic. For a brief, but first-class, treatment, see E. H. Carr, *What Is History?* (New York: Knopf, 1962). In her Booker Prize-winning novel, *The Blind Assassin* (London: Virago Press, 2001), Margaret Atwood's storyteller pauses in her (fictional) autobiography to catch this question of telling "the truth": "I look back over what I have written and I know it's wrong, not because of what I've set down, but because of what I have omitted. What isn't there has a presence, like the absence of light. You want the truth, of course. You want me to put two and two together. But two and two does not necessarily get you the truth. Two and two equals a voice outside the window. Two and two equals the wind. The living bird is not its labelled bones" (p. 484).

26. I have deliberately used the expression "compile a narrative" to indicate my agreement with the nineteenth- and twentieth-century critics that Mark did not generate his narrative from his own personal memories and literary creativity. As we shall see, he was certainly creative, but he worked with traditions, some of them possibly written, that came to him.

27. For a good survey of the work of the original redaction critics, see J. Rohde, *Rediscovering the Teaching of the Evangelists* (trans. D. M. Barton; Philadelphia: Westminster, 1968). See also N. Perrin, *What Is Redaction Criticism?* (Philadelphia: Fortress, 1969).

28. Narrative criticism, which interprets a story as a whole, and focuses on the many techniques used by an author to generate a "good story," has led to the development of other approaches that focus on the reader of the text. The method followed by this study is limited to narrative criticism, and does not consider other methods that sometimes neglect the text and the world that produced the text to privilege the experience of the reader. For an introduction to narrative criticism, see F. J. Moloney, "Narrative Criticism of the Gospels," in *"A Hard Saying": The Gospel and Culture* (Collegeville: Liturgical Press, 2001), 85–105; M. A. Powell, *What Is Narrative Criticism?* (Minneapolis: Fortress,

1990); and D. Rhoads, J. Dewey, and D. Michie, *Mark as Story: An Introduction to the Narrative of a Gospel* (2d ed.; Minneapolis: Fortress, 1999). For an introduction to a number of reader-focused readings see E. S. Malbon and E. V. McKnight, eds., *The New Literary Criticism and the New Testament* (JSNTSup 109; Sheffield: Academic Press, 1994), and especially, The Bible and Culture Collective, *The Postmodern Bible* (New Haven: Yale University Press, 1995).

29. I have stressed the word "primarily" because I am convinced that many genuine memories from the words and actions of Jesus can be recovered from the Gospel of Mark. The quest for the historical Jesus, still alive and well in contemporary Gospel scholarship, is not the concern of this study. For the best, and most comprehensive, work on the question, see the three-volume work of Meier, *A Marginal Jew*. A proposed fourth volume will complete this magisterial study.

30. H. Conzelmann, *The Theology of St. Luke* (trans G. Buswell; London: Faber & Faber, 1961), 9. The stress is mine, for reasons that (I trust) will become obvious.

31. The problem with using Q as a source comes from the fact that we do not have a document called "Q." It is speculatively reconstructed from the material common to Matthew and Luke, generally supposing that Luke contains the oldest version of Q. Thus, judging how Mathew and Luke may have redacted Q always remains hypothetical. However, this has not discouraged contemporary scholars from developing theories that describe the community (or several communities) that produced Q, theories concerning the redaction history of Q, and even a so-called critical edition of Q. See J. M. Robinson, P. Hoffmann, and J. S. Kloppenborg, eds., *The Critical Edition of Q: Synopsis Including the Gospels of Matthew and Luke, Mark and Thomas with English, German, and French Translations of Q and Thomas* (Hermeneia; Minneapolis: Fortress, 2000).

32. For a fine article that surveys these approaches, see W. R. Telford, "The Pre-Markan Traditions in Recent Research," in *The Four Gospels 1992: Festschrift Frans Neirynck* (eds. F. van Segbroeck, C. M. Tuckett, G. van Belle, and J. Verheyden; BETL 100; 3 vols.; Leuven: Leuven University Press, 1992), 2:695–723. This study contains an excellent bibliography (pp. 713–23). See also R. H. Stein, "The Proper Methodology for Ascertaining a Markan Redaction History," in *The Composition of Mark's Gospel: Selected Studies from Novum Testamentum* (ed. D. Orton; Brill's Readers in Biblical Studies 3; Leiden: Brill, 1999), 34–51.

33. For an early warning, see M. D. Hooker, "In His Own Image?" in *What About the New Testament? Studies in Honour of Christopher Evans* (eds. M. D. Hooker and C. Hickling; London: SCM, 1975), 28–44.

34. W. Marxsen, *Mark the Evangelist: Studies on the Redaction History of the Gospel* (Nashville: Abingdon, 1969 [original German: 1956]).

35. For good surveys of this work, see W. Telford, ed., *The Interpretation of Mark* (IRT 7; Philadelphia: Fortress, 1985), 15–28, and further, W. Telford, *The Theology of the Gospel of Mark* (New Testament Theology; Cambridge: Cambridge University Press, 1999), 29–163.

36. For a study that traces this difficulty by focusing on the way different redaction critics have understood the role of the disciples in Mark, see C. Clifton Black, *The Disciples according to Mark* (JSNTSup 27; Sheffield: Sheffield Academic Press, 1989).

37. On this, see C. Clifton Black, "The Quest of Mark the Redactor: Why Has It Been Pursued, and What Has It Taught Us?" *JSNT* 22 (1989): 19–39.

38. See S. M. Schneiders, *Interpreting the New Testament as Sacred Scripture* (2d ed.; Collegeville: Liturgical Press, 1999). For what follows, see also F. J. Moloney, *The Gospel of John* (SP 4; Collegeville: Liturgical Press, 1998), 13–20.

39. As well as the studies mentioned above (note 28), see the early work on Mark's Gospel by F. Kermode, *The Genesis of Secrecy: On the Interpretation of Narrative* (Cambridge, Mass.: Harvard University Press, 1969), and N. Petersen, *Literary Criticism for New Testament Critics* (Philadelphia: Fortress, 1978). On a narrative critical approach to Mark, see also J. R. Donahue and D. J. Harrington, *The Gospel of Mark* (SP 2; Collegeville: Liturgical Press, 2002), 20–22.

40. See chapter 1 for a discussion of who this figure may have been.

41. S. Fish, *Is There a Text in This Class? The Authority of Interpretative Communities* (Cambridge, Mass.: Harvard University Press, 1988), 26–27.

42. Matthew (28:1–20), Luke (24:1–52), and John (20:1–31) all close with the discovery of an empty tomb by women (only one [Mary Magdalene] in John), the Easter message, the communication of the Easter message to the disciples, appearance(s), and a final commissioning of the disciples. The final three elements are missing in the Markan account (16:1–8).

43. See Parts 2 (Mark the Storyteller) and 4 (Mark the Evangelist) in this volume.

44. A. Yarbro Collins, "Narrative, History and Gospel," *Sem* 43 (1988): 150, 153.

45. D. Tracy, *The Analogical Imagination: Christian Theology and the Culture of Pluralism* (New York: Crossroad, 1981), 102.

46. H. de Balzac, *Old Goriot* (Penguin Classics; Harmondsworth: Penguin Books, 1951), 28. Stress in original.

47. See S. Chatman, *Story and Discourse: Narrative Structure in Fiction and Film* (Ithaca: Cornell University Press, 1978), 150.

*[handwritten note: He doesn't even ref. RB in this entire study! Nor NTW!?]*

# PART TWO

# MARK THE STORYTELLER

# CHAPTER 3

# Mark's Story

It may appear naive to say that a successful story has a good beginning, a good middle, and a good end, but it should be said of the Gospel of Mark. The story begins with a solemn confession concerning the good news of Jesus as the Christ and the Son of God (Mark 1:1). Then follows a gradual introduction of Jesus into the story, by means of God's prophetic word (vv. 2–3), John the Baptist (vv. 4–8), culminating in the witness of God in a voice from heaven (vv. 9–11), and Jesus' victory over Satan (vv. 12–13). In the middle of the gospel, Jesus asks his disciples who they think he is, and Peter confesses: "You are the Christ" (8:29). At the end, the reader finds the spectacular proof that Jesus' story did not end with his death, but that he has been raised. The women see the empty tomb and hear the Easter proclamation from the young man at the tomb. But in an intriguing closure to the story, they do not obey the young man's command to inform the disciples that he is going before them into Galilee. They are so frightened they run away, and say nothing to anyone (16:1–8).

Scholars and commentators almost universally recognize the beginning, the midpoint, and the end of the Gospel of Mark as part of the deliberate literary and theological design of a storyteller. It is possible to trace more hints of a storyteller at work by searching for what have been called "textual markers."[1] Textual markers are places in the story where the hand of the author is most in evidence. They offer the reader clear hints that the storyteller is up to something. The most obvious textual marker in any narrative is a summary, where an author pauses to open a new section in his story, to draw a conclusion, or to pass a critical comment on events just reported. There are many summaries in Mark (see, for example, Mark 1:14–15, 39, 45b; 3:7–12; 4:33–34; 6:6b, 53–56;

9:30–31; 10:1), and they have been regularly used by redaction critics as firsthand evidence of the mind and purpose of the evangelist.[2] Other textual markers may be repeated elements. For example, there are two bread miracles, in Mark 6:31–44 and 8:1–9. The passion predictions are found three times, in 8:31, 9:31, and 10:32–34. Two stories tell of the cure of a blind man (8:22–26; 10:46–52). Other markers may be found when the storyteller shifts the action from one place to another (a change in the geography of the story), from one period of time to another (a change in the time frame of the story), or from one set of characters to another (a change in the author's focus on characters). The Gospel of Mark has many such indications (see, for example, 1:35; 2:1, 23; 3:7; 4:35; 7:24, 31). The suggested plot of the Gospel of Mark that follows will depend on some of the textual markers that indicate a carefully designed story of Jesus.[3]

## The Plot of the Gospel of Mark

The plot of the Gospel of Mark has been devised not only to have emotional and artistic effects (and it certainly does that), but also to convey a message about Jesus, the Christ, the Son of God (see 1:1).[4] "The beginning" of the story is announced in 1:1, and it runs from verse 1 to 13. Jesus' first appearance on the scene, proclaiming the good news of the impinging presence of God as king (1:14–15), also needs to be taken into account. Reporting Jesus' first public appearance, it signals an important moment in the story. The midpoint is highlighted by Peter's confession and Jesus' command to silence (8:29–30). These events close the first half of the gospel and are followed by the first passion prediction (8:31), as Jesus sets off on his journey to Jerusalem. The second half of the gospel has begun. The end of the story reports the morning after the Sabbath, as women go to anoint the body of the crucified Jesus and discover an empty tomb (16:1–4). We can thus suggest that there are four clear textual markers:

1. The gospel begins (1:1).

2. Jesus opens his ministry in Galilee (1:14–15).

3. Jesus announces his journey to Jerusalem and his forthcoming death and resurrection for the first time (8:31)

4. Women discover an empty tomb (16:1–4).

The gospel story has been domesticated to such an extent that we are not sufficiently aware of the dramatic nature of these turning points.

Mark the storyteller wrote his account of the ministry, death, and resurrection of Jesus, following a plot. Due attention must be given to this for a better appreciation of the story of the gospel. This careful ordering of a succession of events in the earliest Christian gospel is a first and important indication that the story as a whole is permeated by a storyteller's desire to proclaim something about God, the Christ, and the followers of Jesus.[5] Whatever the first readers knew of the life story of Jesus of Nazareth was subverted by the Markan story. The account of Jesus' presence in Galilee, his single journey to Jerusalem to be rejected, tried and crucified, the resurrection and the surprising silence of the women at the empty tomb, *told in this way*, was not familiar. The *radical newness of the Markan story must be kept in mind*.[6] It is an original way of telling events from the life of Jesus, and the storyteller must be credited with an equally original understanding of why he thus plotted the story.

On the basis of the four textual markers listed above, one can trace an initial idea of the author's literary design.

1. Mark 1:1–13 serves as a prologue, providing the reader with a great deal of information about God's beloved Son.

2. Through Mark 1:14 to 8:30 the words and deeds of Jesus' ministry increasingly force the question of Jesus' identity (1:27, 45; 2:12; 3:22; 4:41; 5:20; 6:2–3, 48–50; 7:37). Some people accept him, some are indifferent, and many oppose him, but the question behind the story is: Can he be the Messiah? In 8:29 Peter, in the name of the disciples, resolves the problem by confessing: "You are the Messiah." The guessing has come to an end. This section of the gospel can be framed as a question: "Who is Jesus?" In the last verse, however, Jesus warns Peter not to tell anyone of his being the expected Messiah (8:30). The warning from Jesus foreshadows the second half of the story. Peter's confession may not contain the whole truth about Jesus.

3. Mark 8:31–15:47 opens with the first passion prediction (8:31: "And he began to teach them that the Son of Man must suffer many things, and be rejected by the elders and the chief priests and the scribes, and be killed, and after three days rise again"). Jesus is setting out on a journey to Jerusalem. He will suffer, be crucified and rise in that city. One can sense that this part of the story forms a second half of Mark's literary and theological presentation of the story of Jesus. Mark 1:14–8:30 made it clear that Jesus was the Messiah (8:29), but in 8:30 the suggestion emerges that this may not be the whole truth. The second half of the story

shows that Jesus is the Messiah who will be revealed as the Son of God on the cross, a suffering and vindicated Son of Man (8:31; 9:31; 10:32–33; 13:26; 14:61–62; 15:39). In 15:39 a Roman centurion confesses: "Truly this man was God's Son!" The suffering Christ is truly the Son of God. The mystery has come to an end. Mark 8:31–15:47 can be titled "the suffering and vindicated Son of Man: Christ and Son of God."

4. Many questions raised by the story, however, remain unresolved. The disciples have fled (see 14:50) and Jesus has cried out: "My God, my God, why have you forsaken me?" (15:34). His question is resolved in the concluding story of the women visiting the tomb (16:1–4). In 16:1–8 the reader learns that God has not forsaken his Son. He has been raised (see 16:6). But a solution to the problem of failing disciples lies in the future. They are to go into Galilee; there they will see him (v. 7). The women, frightened by all they have seen and heard, flee and say nothing to anyone (v. 8).

These major sections in the narrative have been determined by giving due importance to the textual markers found at 1:1, 1:14–15, 8:31, and 16:1–4. Closer examination shows that other markers indicate that 1:14–8:30 and 8:31–15:47 can be further subdivided. The first half of the gospel (1:14–8:30) establishes relationships, as well as raising questions concerning the person of Jesus. But the Gospel of Mark is not only about Jesus, Christ, and Son of God (see 1:1, 11). It is equally about the challenge of "following" a suffering Son of Man to Jerusalem and beyond, a theme that will dominate the second half of the story (8:31–15:47), but is not altogether absent from 1:14–8:30.

On three occasions across 1:14–8:30 the storyteller slows down his fast moving story to summarize Jesus' ministry at that stage. These summaries of Jesus' activities cannot be easily tied to a time or a place. They offer, in a more general fashion, illustrations of that activity (see 1:14–15; 3:7–12; 6:6b). The Gospel of Mark contains other similar summaries of Jesus' ministry (see, for example, 1:39, 45b; 4:33–34; 6:53–56; 9:30–31; 10:1). What is unique about the general descriptions of Jesus' ministry in 1:14–15, 3:7–12, and 6:6b, however, is that each of these summaries is followed by material that deals with disciples and discipleship (1:16–20; 3:13–19; 6:7–30). The summaries, and the associated report of Jesus' association with his disciples, are followed by a series of episodes during which three different audiences respond to the words and deeds of Jesus. At the end of each episode, a decision is made about Jesus. Two of the decisions are negative (3:6 [the Pharisees and the Herodians]; 6:1–6a [people from "his own country"]), and the third is a misunderstanding (8:29 [Peter, responding on behalf of the disciples]).[7]

The three summaries leading directly into passages that deal with disciples, and concluding with a response to Jesus, indicate Mark's careful writing of 1:14–8:30. The three sections unfold in this way:

1. *Jesus and the leaders of Israel (1:14–3:6)*

    In 1:14–15 we read a summary of the ministry of Jesus: "Now after John was arrested, Jesus came to Galilee, proclaiming the good news of God, and saying, 'The time is fulfilled and the kingdom of God has come near, repent and believe in the good news.'" This summary is followed by the account of the vocation of the first disciples (1:16–20). Jesus then exercises his ministry in Galilee, chiefly at Capernaum (1:21–3:6), until representatives of the Jewish people, the political leaders, and the religious authorities, respond to him: "The Pharisees went out and immediately conspired with the Herodians against him, how to destroy him" (3:6).[8]

2. *Jesus and his new family (3:7–6:6a)*

    In 3:7–12 we find a lengthy general statement about Jesus' Galilean ministry. It concludes with the summary: "He had cured many so that all who had diseases pressed upon him to touch him. Whenever the unclean spirits saw him, they fell down before him and shouted, 'You are the Son of God!' But he sternly ordered them not to make him known" (3:10–12). This summary leads into the account of Jesus' institution of the Twelve (3:13–19). But his ministry meets opposition from his family and from Israel (3:20–30). He establishes new principles for belonging to his family (3:31–35), and teaches through parables (4:1–34) and a stunning series of miracles (4:35–5:43). As Jesus returns to his hometown, his own people reject him: "'Is not this the carpenter, the son of Mary and brother of James and Joses and Judas and Simon, and are not his sisters here with us?' And they took offense at him" (6:3). Jesus was "amazed at their unbelief" (6:6a).

3. *Jesus and his disciples (6:6b–8:30)*

    Following Jesus' rejection in his hometown, we find another brief general summary about his ministry in Galilee: "Then he went about among the villages teaching" (6:6b). Jesus then sends out the Twelve on a mission that parallels his own (6:6b–13). The narrative continues, marked by increasing hostility between Jesus and the Jews, especially in his conflict with the Pharisees (see 7:1–23). His disciples, his new family, also become more deeply involved with his ministry (see 6:7–13, 30–44; 8:1–10). It draws to a close as Jesus broaches the question that has been lurking behind the narrative since 1:14: "Who do people say that I am?" (8:27) "Who do you say that I am?" (v. 28). Peter responds: "You are the Christ" (v. 29). The reader, informed by the storyteller at 1:1, has known from the outset that Jesus is the Christ. The question "Who is Jesus?" has been answered. There is a sense in which Peter is correct, but Jesus' words to the disciples ("them") sounds a warning bell and opens the door to the second part of the gospel: "He charged them to tell no one about him" (8:30).

Jesus' commanding his disciples to silence in 8:30 closes the first half of the story, and points toward the second half, which opens with the first prediction, in 8:31, of his future death and resurrection in Jerusalem. Textual markers across 8:31–15:47 point to a further threefold articulation of the suffering and finally vindicated Son of Man, Messiah, and Son of God. Obvious changes of place, characters, and situations occur across this second half of the story.

1. *Jesus and the disciples journey to Jerusalem (8:31–10:52)*

   Jesus' journey to Jerusalem focuses strongly on his teaching of his oncoming death and resurrection (8:31; 9:31; 10:32–34) and his instruction of increasingly recalcitrant disciples.

2. *Endings in Jerusalem (11:1–13:37)*

   Jesus enters Jerusalem (11:1–11), brings all temple practice to an end (11:12–24), encounters and silences Israel's religious authorities (11:27–12:44), and prophesies the end of the Holy City and the world (13:1–37).

3. *The passion and death of Jesus (14:1–15:47)*

   The ministry is over as Jesus accepts and suffers his passion and death.

It is noticeable that the storyteller designed the first half of his gospel asking the question, "Who is Jesus?"[9] The second half is designed to respond: "the suffering and vindicated Son of Man, the Christ, and Son of God." However, these two halves of the plot overlap. Narrative units are not separated by brick walls. One flows into the other, looks back to issues already mentioned, and hints at themes yet to come.[10] Peter's confession of faith in Mark 8:29 might mark the closure of "The Mystery of the Messiah," but a theme of blindness has emerged in 8:22–26 in the strange story of a blind man at Bethsaida, who has his sight restored in stages. This theme will be resumed in 10:46–52 where a further story of a man coming to sight is reported: the story of blind Bartimaeus. Between these two miracle stories, where blind men are cured, Jesus speaks of the oncoming death and resurrection of the Son of Man (see 8:31; 9:31; 10:32–34), an issue hidden behind the events reported in 1:14–8:30 (see 3:6; 7:14–29; 8:11–15). After each of the passion predictions, Jesus instructs increasingly obtuse disciples, who will not or cannot understand what it means to follow him (see 8:32–33; 9:33–37; 10:36–45). An earlier accusation of blindness also comes into play. After the second multiplication of the loaves and fishes (8:1–9) Jesus asks his dull disciples: "Do you not yet perceive or understand? Are your hearts hardened? *Having eyes do you not see,* and having ears do you not hear?" (8:18).[11] These examples of the overlapping themes of Jesus' destiny and the failure of the disciples also signify textual markers for the reader. Although not as *structurally* important as 1:1, 1:14–15, 8:31, 11:1–11, 14:1–2, and 16:1–4, they are further indications of Mark's skill as a storyteller.

It is now possible to suggest how Mark the storyteller, using traditions that came to him, designed and completed his unique gospel. The above considerations of the plot of the narrative will determine the following overview of Mark the storyteller's activity. He takes readers who are already familiar with the story through a new telling that transforms its well known ending. Mark faced a problem stated some twenty years before the gospel appeared:

> For Jews demand signs and Greeks seek wisdom, but we preach Christ crucified, a stumbling block to Jews and folly to Gentiles, but to those who are called, both Jews and Greeks, Christ the power of God and the wisdom of God. For the foolishness of God is wiser than human wisdom, and the weakness of God is stronger than any human strength. (1 Cor 1:22–25)

Mark also attempts to solve the scandal of the cross by means of a story that begins as "the good news" that Jesus is the Christ, the Son of God (1:1, 11), and ends with a scream from a cross and an agonizing death, an empty tomb, and an Easter message that is not delivered

(15:33–16:8). A story of the Christ and the Son of God that ends in this fashion is a narrative repetition of the Pauline message: "the foolishness of God is wiser than human wisdom, and the weakness of God is stronger than any human strength" (1 Cor 1:25).

Many scholars object to attempts to find divisions and sections in the Gospel of Mark. One of our best commentators, Morna Hooker, remarks as she makes her own first division at 3:7: "Most commentators make a major break at this point, but such divisions are largely arbitrary. There are plenty of links with previous sections."[12] Certainly, there are links with what went before, and pointers to what is yet to come, an indication of the skill of a good storyteller, but there are also sufficient indications in the text itself to show that Mark designed a narrative that unfolds in four identifiable moments.

For the purposes of clarity, the overall structure of the Gospel of Mark follows below. However, this skeleton presentation of the gospel's narrative structure is merely a brief list of the headings that we have already uncovered. The more detailed reading of the text that will follow in Chapters 4 and 5 will nourish a fuller understanding of the way the story unfolds. Nothing is compartmentalized, as Hooker and others have rightly insisted. But there is a carefully articulated story that can, nevertheless, be schematically presented. What follows, therefore, is something of the bare bones of the story of the Gospel of Mark, a type of roadmap that a first-time reader can glance at occasionally, to see where she or he is at any particular time or place during the journey through the story. This roadmap, therefore, suggests that the Gospel of Mark unfolds in the following fashion:[13]

1. Prologue: The beginning (1:1–13)

2. Who is Jesus? (1:14–8:30)

    (a) Jesus and the leaders of Israel (1:14–3:6)
    (b) Jesus and his new family (3:7–6:6a)
    (c) Jesus and the disciples (6:6b–8:30)

3. The suffering and vindicated Son of Man, Christ, and Son of God (8:31–15:47)

    (a) On the way from blindness to sight (8:31–10:52)
    (b) The symbolic end of Israel and the world (11:1–13:37)
    (c) The crucifixion of the Son of Man, Christ, and Son of God (14:1–15:47)

4. Epilogue: A new beginning (16:1–8)

# Conclusion

This chapter concludes with a word of warning. It must not be thought that once the roadmap is discovered, the journey from this point on will be easy. There are places in the Gospel of Mark where a reader finds the logic of the movement from one episode to the next hard to follow. We have become used to stories that flow smoothly, and tend to judge them according to the author's ability to lead the reader gently from one episode to the next. Such an easy passage is not always the case in the Gospel of Mark. One good example of this is found in 9:42–48, where a series of sayings of Jesus, which may have originally been independent, have been placed side by side on the basis of the repetition of the same words in the sayings ("cause to sin" [see vv. 42, 43, 45, 44], and "salt" [vv. 49, 50]). But the link between each saying is hard to trace, and one must strain one's imagination to follow the logic of vv. 42–48. These moments of obscurity in the narrative indicate the respect that the early writers in the Christian church had for the traditions that came to them. Mark was certainly a creative writer, but he respected words and events from the life of Jesus that he received. As the first attempt to write a narrative of the life of Jesus that also proclaimed that Jesus was the Christ, the Son of God, Mark's story must not be judged by the criteria we use to judge an enjoyable novel.

The tensions in the narrative should be resolved by the application of two principles. In the first instance, we need to understand that Mark the storyteller attempted to write an account of the ministry, death, and resurrection of Jesus that coherently communicated what he wanted to say to his original readers. The fact that we are historically, culturally, and even religiously distant from those original readers means that we must allow ourselves to be challenged by the strangeness of this ancient text. Second, every reader strives "even if unconsciously, to fit everything together in a consistent pattern."[14] Inevitably a reader traces literary and theological connections across the gospel that may be judged as the striving of *that particular* reader to impose *her or his* consistent pattern. That is an inevitable and perfectly acceptable part of the reading and listening process. But we must not imagine that we can impose our meanings on the text. It is true that, in some respects, we shape the meaning of what we read in the light of our own experiences and understanding. But the text also shapes us. This is particularly the case when Christians read or listen to the gospel. Respect and admiration for a text that has been read again and again by many Christian individuals and within the life of the Christian church inspire our striving to understand the message of the Gospel of Mark.[15] "Every element in the story is there for a reason, which we will discover only by combing back and forth through the text until it yields its own narrative coherence."[16] To give up on a section of the narrative—or even on the gospel as a whole—because it does not speak to me according to my expectations is to forget that, while we always bring ourselves to our reading, we must also allow this important text to speak to us *in its own terms*. The following two chapters will attempt to take up the challenge of tracing the narrative design and theological message of Mark, a storyteller whose report of the life, teaching, death, and resurrection of Jesus of Nazareth retains its place at the heart of the Christian tradition.

## Notes

1. For a focus on "textual markers" (which he calls "text signals"), see B. van Iersel, *Reading Mark* (trans. W. H. Bisscheroux; Collegeville: Liturgical Press, 1988), 18–30. See also A. Stock, *Call to Discipleship: A Literary Study of Mark's Gospel* (GNS 1; Wilmington: Michael Glazier, 1982), 47–53.

2. Redaction critics use the summaries as the best place to discover the hand of Mark. See C. W. Hedrick, "The Role of 'Summary Statements' in the Composition of the Gospel of Mark: A Dialog with Karl Schmidt and Norman Perrin," in *The Composition of Mark's Gospel: Selected Studies from* Novum Testamentum (ed. D. E. Orton; Brill's Readers in Biblical Studies 3; Leiden: E. J. Brill, 1999), 121–43; E. Best, *The Temptation and the Passion* (2d ed.; SNTSMS 2; Cambridge: Cambridge University Press, 1990), 63–102.

3. No single textual marker in itself indicates an important change of direction in the plot. It requires generally a combination of several. For example, there are many summaries in Mark's gospel, but only 1:14–15, 3:7–12, and 6:6a are *immediately* followed by material dealing with the disciples. For a more detailed presentation of the following, see F. J. Moloney, *The Gospel of Mark: A Commentary* (Peabody: Hendrickson, 2002), 16–22. For some reflections on the lack of due consideration given to Mark's whole story, see R. A. Horsley, *Hearing the Whole Story: The Politics of Plot in Mark's Gospel* (Lousiville: Westminster John Knox, 2001), 1–25.

4. Literary critics have many approaches to the plot of a narrative, but—for our purposes—it is well summed up as follows: "The plot in a dramatic or narrative work is the structure of its actions, as these are rendered and ordered toward achieving particular emotional and artistic effects" (M. H. Abrams, *A Glossary of Literary Terms* [5th ed.; New York: Holt, Rinehart & Winston, 1985], 139). For further ideas on Mark's plot, see D. Rhoads, J. Dewey, and D. Michie, *Mark as Story: An Introduction to the Narrative of a Gospel* (2d ed.; Minneapolis: Fortress, 1999), 73–97.

5. Horsley, *Hearing the Whole Story*, regularly insists on the danger of domesticating Mark's message (see, for example, pp. ix–xii, 1–2, 37, 53, 81–86, 99). His own reading, however, glosses over important exegetical issues to produce yet another domesticated Mark—Jesus the liberator and restorer of original pu-

rity. Horsley unfortunately argues (without sufficient attention to the Markan text) that centuries of Christian reading have mistakenly led us to search the gospel for a message about God, the Christ, and the followers of Jesus.

6. See the important essay by E. Schweizer, "Mark's Theological Achievement," in *The Interpretation of Mark* (ed. W. Telford; IRT 7; Philadelphia: Fortress, 1985), 42–63. W. H. Kelber, *The Oral and Written Gospel: The Hermeneutics of Speaking and Writing in the Synoptic Tradition, Mark, Paul and Q* (Philadelphia: Fortress, 1983), pushes this to the limit. He rightly argues that Mark took a vivid and living oral tradition and created something quite different with his "writing" (see pp. 44–139). But he argues that the movement from oral tradition to written Gospel created a written text that was a betrayal of what went before. The thesis is overstated, but further highlights the radical newness of the Gospel of Mark. See also Horsley, *Hearing the Whole Story*, 53–78. For a critique of this position, see E. S. Malbon, "Texts and Contexts: Interpreting the Disciples in Mark," in *In the Company of Jesus: Characters in Mark's Gospel* (Louisville: Westminster John Knox, 2000), 100–30.

7. For this proposal, which many have followed, see Schweizer, "Mark's Theological Achievement," 46–54. For a more detailed analysis, resulting in the overall structure followed by this study, see A. George and P. Grelot, eds., *Introduction à la Bible. Tome III. Nouveau Testament* (7 vols.; Paris: Desclée, 1976–1986), 2:48–51.

8. Care must be taken with the use of the expressions associated with Israel and Judaism. For Mark, the first part of his story of Jesus' ministry in Galilee is entirely focused on a Jewish region and the Jewish leadership. The geographical locations and the characters involved in the story will be broadened in 5:1 20 and also in later episodes (see 7:24–8:10). Horsley, *Hearing the Whole Story*, 112, objects to the use of the expression "Jewish leaders," but then proceeds to show how corrupt Jewish rulers oppressed the people (pp. 112–17). Their attitude to Jesus is the issue in the Markan story, not whether they actually "led" the people.

9. This paragraph is repeated, with minor changes, from Moloney, *The Gospel of Mark*, 19–20.

10. For extensive consideration of this phenomenon in the Gospel of Mark, see J. Dewey, "Mark as Interwoven Tapestry: Forecasts and Echoes for a Listening Audience," *CBQ* 53 (1991): 225–36; E. S. Malbon, "Echoes and Foreshadowings in Mark 4–8: Reading and Rereading," *JBL* 112 (1993): 211–30. On 8:22–26 as an overlap between the first and the second half of the gospel, see Horsley, *Hearing the Whole Story*, 14–15.

11. See C. Myers, *Binding the Strong Man: A Political Reading of Mark's Story of Jesus* (Maryknoll: Orbis, 1990), 110–11. For a comprehensive study of the two halves of the gospel, showing that the break comes between 8:30 and 8:31, see Q. Quesnell, *The Mind of Mark: Interpretation and Method through the Exegesis of Mark 6,52* (AnBib 38; Rome: Pontifical Biblical Institute, 1969), 126–76. R. E. Watts, *Isaiah's New Exodus and Mark* (WUNT 2. Reihe 88; Tübingen: J. C. B. Mohr [Paul Siebeck], 1997), 124–32, also suggests that 8:22–26 serves as a hinge.

12. M. D. Hooker, *The Gospel according to St. Mark* (BNTC; Peabody: Hendrickson, 1991), 109. She makes parallel remarks on several occasions through her commentary. Dennis Nineham is even more skeptical: "Scholars are looking for something that is not there and attributing to the Evangelist a

higher degree of self-conscious purpose that he in fact possessed" (D. E. Nineham, *The Gospel of St. Mark* [Westminster Pelican Commentaries; Philadelphia: Westminster, 1978], 29). For a survey of the multiplicity of conflicting opinions on the structure of the gospel, see Dewey, "Mark as Interwoven Tapestry," 221–25.

13. There is widespread agreement that the scene at Caesarea Philippi (8:27–30) is something of a watershed at the center of the narrative, and that this event divides the gospel into two even halves. Many scholars, however, influenced by the "inclusion" between 8:22–26 and 10:46–52 (two cures of blind men) end the first half of the gospel at 8:21. See, for example, the important commentaries of R. A. Guelich, *Mark 1–8:26* (WBC 34A; Dallas: Word, 1989), 47; J. Gnilka, *Das Evangelium nach Markus* (5th ed.; 2 vols.; EKKNT II/1–2; Zürich/Neukirchen-Vluyn: Benziger Verlag/Neukirchener Verlag, 1998), 235–36; J. Marcus, *Mark 1–8* (AB 27; New York: Doubleday, 2000), 63–64; and B. B. Thurston, *Preaching Mark* (Fortress Resources for Preaching; Minneapolis: Fortress, 2002), 96–97. Others see the parallel between 8:22–26 and 10:46–52, but make a major break after 8:26. See, for example, J. R. Donahue and D. J. Harrington, *The Gospel of Mark* (SP 2; Collegeville: Liturgical Press, 2002), 48–49, 257–58. The literary shape suggested above understands 1:1–13 as a prologue (widely accepted) and 16:1–8 as a conclusion, reading 16:7, "there you will see him as he said" (see 14:28), as a resumption of the theme of "beginning" from the prologue (see 1:1). See also G. Bilezikian, *The Liberated Gospel: A Comparison between the Gospel of Mark and Greek Tragedy* (Grand Rapids: Baker, 1977), 131–34, and M. A. Beavis, *Mark's Audience: The Literary and Social Setting of Mark 4:11–12* (JSNTSup 33; Sheffield: Sheffield Academic Press, 1989), 128–29.

14. W. Iser, *The Implied Reader: Patterns of Communication in Prose Fiction from Bunyan to Beckett* (Baltimore: Johns Hopkins University Press, 1978), 283.

15. For some hermeneutical reflections on this process, see F. J. Moloney, "Adventure with Nicodemus: An Exercise in Hermeneutics," in *"A Hard Saying:" The Gospel and Culture* (Collegeville: The Liturgical Press, 2001), 259–79.

16. Myers, *Binding the Strong Man,* 109.

# CHAPTER 4

# Mark 1:1–8:30:
# Who Is Jesus?

In the previous chapter we traced some of the literary features of the Gospel of Mark. They provide a guide to the plot and the design of the gospel's unfolding story. We now turn to a closer reading of the text of the gospel, attentively following the movement of the narrative from one episode to another. An appreciation of the way one episode flows into another, at times looking back to what has already been told, and at other times forward to what is yet to come, uncovers more fully the creative literary and theological activity of Mark the storyteller. This chapter will focus on Mark 1:1–8:30: from the beginning to the midpoint.[1] The following chapter (Chapter 5) will read the gospel from the midpoint to the end.[2]

## The Beginning (1:1–13)

The Gospels of Matthew (Matt 1–2) and Luke (Luke 1–2) both begin with birth narratives that unveil to the reader the true nature, and even the mission, of Jesus.[3] The Gospel of John opens with a remarkable christological hymn that performs the same task.[4] These beginnings can rightly be called "prologues," as prologues to any narrative—not just the gospels—introduce a reader to the major personalities of the story that is to follow, and provide hints concerning the role and significance of the hero. A prologue will generally inform the reader about *who* the hero is and *what* the hero does, but the reader must enter the story that follows to discover *how* the hero manifests what has been said in the prologue.[5]

Mark the storyteller introduces his account of the ministry, death, and resurrection of Jesus in 1:1–13, a passage that can also be called a prologue to the Gospel of Mark. It is very different in form from Matt 1–2, Luke 1–2, and John 1:1–18, but it has the same literary and theological function. Significant scholars and commentators have suggested that the Markan beginning runs to v. 15,[6] but vv. 1–13 are bound tightly together by their singular style. The following features that unite vv. 1–13 must be noticed. After the "beginning" (ἀρχή; *archē*) in v. 1, "John the Baptist *came*" (ἐγένετο; *egeneto*) in v. 4. The word "and" (καί; *kai*) unites vv. 6 and 7. In v. 8 "Jesus *came*" (καὶ ἐγένετο; *kai egeneto*). The rest of the passage is held together by the expressions "and immediately" (καὶ εὐθύς; *kai euthys*) in v. 10, "and" (καὶ; *kai*) in v. 11, "and immediately" (καὶ εὐθύς; *kai euthys*) in v. 12, and finally, "and" (καὶ; *kai*) in v. 13. This steady rhythm of seemingly unimaginative link-words, highlighted by "and" (καί; *kai*) along with "immediately" (εὐθύς; *euthys*) is very typical of Mark's writing. It is called parataxis.[7]

This rhythm is broken in v. 14 with the expression "now after" (μετὰ δέ; *meta de*) that introduces a change of time and place, and Jesus' first words in the story. One of the main reasons for suggesting that Mark's beginning runs from v. 1 to v. 15 is the presence of the word "good news" (εὐαγγέλιον; *euangelion*) in v. 1 and vv. 14–15. However, one should also notice that the word "wilderness" (ἔρημος; *erēmos*) appears twice at the beginning of vv. 1–13 (in vv. 3 and 4), and is repeated twice at the end of vv. 1–13 (in vv. 12 and 13). The "good news" (εὐαγγέλιον; *euangelion*) announced in v. 1 opens the Markan beginning, and Jesus' proclamation of the "good news" (εὐαγγέλιον; *euangelion*) in vv. 14–15 opens the first major section of the story itself.[8]

The prologue focuses on five major issues, and as each issue unfolds, an intense presentation of the person and mission of Jesus is developed. Two voices speak in vv. 1–3. The first is the authoritative voice of the storyteller himself, announcing that he is beginning a narrative that will indicate that Jesus of Nazareth is the Christ and the Son of God.[9] The use of the expression "beginning" (αρχή; *archē*) has two meanings. Mark tells his readers that they are at the beginning of a story, while he also looks back to another beginning, the beginning of God's creating presence, recorded in the book of Genesis, which also opened with the word "beginning" (LXX Gen 1:1). There can be no questioning the opinion of the storyteller. It is his story, after all. His confession of faith, that the good news is that Jesus is the Christ and the Son of God, along with the hint that a new creation is at hand, is followed by an even more authoritative voice: the word *of God*, as it was spoken by Isaiah the prophet (vv. 2–3).[10] Speaking in the first person, God announces that he will send a messenger to prepare the way of the Lord. Across vv. 1–3, the most authoritative voices in the story (the storyteller and God) tell a divine message: the good news that follows will have to do with Jesus, Christ, Son of God, and Lord.

The second stage in the prologue belongs entirely to the storyteller (vv. 4–6). He tells of the partial fulfillment of God's promise in the announcement, appearance, and description of the forerunner, the one who is to prepare the way (see vv. 2–3). After his brief introduction, the forerunner moves into action. The Baptist is no longer described, and his words, delivered in the first person, form the third stage of the prologue (vv. 7–8). The Baptist announces the coming of the "stronger one," one before whom the forerunner is totally unworthy. The stronger one "will baptize with the Holy Spirit." He is preparing the way for "the Lord."

The focus of the narrative prologue shifts again as the Baptist continues to be the main actor in the story, but Jesus is introduced (vv. 9–11). Though Jesus does nothing, the promise of the voice of God that the coming of "the Lord" is at hand (see v. 3), is fulfilled. He is baptized by John, and as he comes up out of the water the heavens open. God again enters the story as the firmament that separates the divine and the human spheres is opened, and the Spirit with which Jesus will baptize (see v. 8) descends upon him from above. A divine voice speaks directly to Jesus: "You are my beloved Son; with you I am well pleased" (v. 11). In the fifth and final moment of the prologue (vv. 12–13), the Baptist disappears from the scene and the presence of Jesus dominates, although the design of God directs the action. The divine Spirit drives Jesus into the wilderness (v. 12). While he is present there for forty days, Satan tempts him, and the angels minister to him.

At the end of the prologue the actions of Jesus are mentioned: "He was with the wild beasts" (v. 13). The hint of a new creation in v. 1 ("the beginning") returns in vv. 12–13. In the Genesis story Satan's victory over Adam led to hostility and fear in creation (see Gen 3:14–21; Ps 91:11–13). Our storyteller began the account of the ministry, death, and resurrection of Jesus with a suggestion that this situation has been reversed: he was *with* the wild beasts. Prophetic traditions surrounding the new creation are fulfilled (see Isa 11:6–9; 35:3–10; Ezek 34:23–31). A link with creation themes is also found in the presence of the angels serving Jesus. Exodus, Elijah, and creation motifs gather in this brief statement. Repeatedly throughout the desert experience of Israel angels help and guide the wandering people (see Exod 14:19; 23:20, 23; 32:34; 33:2). During Elijah's experience of hunger and despair in the wilderness, he is served by angels (1 Kgs 19:5–7). Supplementing the biblical account, other Jewish documents speculate that Adam and Eve were fed by the angels in the Garden of Eden.[11]

Only toward the end of the prologue the hint returns of the link with the original creation, provided by the "beginning" of v. 1. Jesus is with the wild beasts and waited on by the angels. His coming restores the original order of God's creation. The promise of the beginning in v. 1 (see Gen 1:1), and the coming of the creating presence of the Spirit of God in v. 10 (see Gen 1:3), indicate that the prologue to the Gospel of Mark is linked to the prologue to the human story, as told in Gen 1–11. God has been the most active figure in Mark 1:1–13. Although appearing only toward the end of the prologue, Jesus has already been *presented* to the reader. He is the Christ, the Son of God (v. 1), the Lord (v. 3), the stronger one (v. 7), one who will baptize with the Holy Spirit (v. 8). God's voice has assured the reader that he is the beloved Son of God, and that God is well pleased with him (v. 11). He is filled with the Spirit (v. 10), and driven into the desert to reverse the tragedy of the Adam and Eve story, to reestablish God's original design (vv. 12–13).

Mark provides a dense prologue for the reader/listener. There should be no doubt in the reader's mind about *who Jesus is*. However, there are hints throughout the prologue that point to a ministry, if he is to baptize with a holy spirit (v. 8). There is perhaps even a hint that he will accept total and unconditional self-sacrifice as God's "beloved" (v. 11).[12] Mark wants the reader to arrive at the end of the prologue well informed about *who* Jesus is, but as yet unaware of *how* Jesus is the Christ, the Son of God, the Lord, the stronger one who baptizes with the Holy Spirit, and *how* in his person God's original creative design is to be restored. All early Christians knew that Jesus of Nazareth was crucified, and they may well have questioned how such an end could be pleasing to God (see v. 11).[13] Mark has written a story that attempts to respond to that question.

By means of his prologue, therefore, Mark sets up a situation where only the reader of (or listener to) the gospel is aware of what has been said in the prologue. The various characters in the story: the Pharisees, the crowds, the Romans, and *especially* the disciples, have not read the prologue. But from the very start of the story, the readers know that Jesus' life ended on a cross. Mark leads them into a story that will tell of Jesus, the Son, responding to God, and how he lives, preaches, and dies in a way that restores God's original design (v. 13) and makes the Father delight in him (v. 11). For most of the narrative of the gospel, Mark does not explicitly direct his words to the readers (see, however, 13:14),[14] who have been the unique focus of the words of 1:1–13. However, at the end of the story (16:1–8), Mark the storyteller will return to focus his attention on the readers and their understanding of the person of Jesus as the vindicated Son of Man, and point to their identification with the experience of the disciples and the women in the story. Mark will subtly ask them where they stand as they hear: "And they went out and fled from the tomb; for trembling and astonishment had come upon them; and they said nothing to anyone, for they were afraid" (16:8). The storyteller behind the Gospel of Mark has designed a narrative with a prologue (1:1–13) and an epilogue (16:1–8), during which he directs his attention to those who read (or listen to) the words and events reported in 1:14–15:47.[15]

## Jesus and the Jews (1:14–3:6)

Mark next leads the reader into the story of Jesus' public ministry by means of the first and perhaps major summary statement of the gospel (1:14–15). As we have seen in the previous chapter, 1:14–3:6 is the first of three parallel sections across the first half of the gospel (1:14–8:30). Each of them opens with a summary statement about the ministry of Jesus (1:14–15; 3:7–12; 6:6b), is followed by an episode where Jesus calls or commissions his disciples (1:16–20; 3:13–19; 6:7–30), and eventually leads to a decision against or for Jesus (3:6; 6:1–6a; 8:29). This first section opens with the most important summary of Jesus' ministry in the gospel: his coming announces the impinging presence of God as king, and calls for repentance (1:14–15). Although he bursts onto the scene alone, he begins his ministry by calling his first disciples (1:16–20). After a series of events from Jesus' ministry in Galilee, during which opposition steadily mounts, representative leaders of Israel make a decision (3:6: the Pharisees and the Herodians). From opposite ends of Jewish leadership, the Pharisees and the Herodians come together (συμβούλιον ἐδίδουν; *symboulion edidoun*). This is a most unlikely union of groups that traditionally despised one another.[16] But together they plan a unified agenda, to destroy him (ὅπως αὐτὸν ἀπολέσωσιν; *hopōs auton apolesōsin*).

The storyteller's carefully designed arrangement of the sequence of events reported in 1:14–3:6 is simple, but very effective.[17] Jesus bursts on the scene in Galilee, proclaiming the gospel and demanding conversion. His presence brings in the urgent reality of the reigning presence of God, among us and yet to come, a presence that demands repentance, "the rectifying power of the impinging future" (1:14–15).[18] Immediately he calls others to follow, and they respond without hesitation, following him down his way (vv. 16–20). Together they go forth. From this point on there are always disciples, the Twelve, or some named members of the Twelve with Jesus, until they separate themselves from him, fleeing in fear in 14:50. Representative powers of evil are overcome: an unclean spirit (vv. 21–28), sickness, and taboo as Jesus touches Simon's mother-in-law, heals her, and is served by her (vv. 29–31). The pace of the story slows down for a moment as Mark summarizes Jesus' healing activity and his power over demons (vv. 32–34), and Jesus goes to a lonely place to pray (v. 35). But Simon and some of the disciples disturb Jesus in his prayer. He accepts this as the design of God, announcing, "for this is why I came out" (v. 38c). He thus resumes his response to God, with whom he has been briefly joined in prayer. He journeys throughout all Galilee, preaching and casting out demons (vv. 36–39). The presence of the power and goodness of the reigning presence of God (see 1:14) again cuts through ritual taboo as Jesus touches a leper and heals him (vv. 39–45).

The reader comes away from these first pages of the gospel with the impression that Jesus' proclamation in v. 15 is bearing fruit. The presence of the kingdom *of God* is rendering powerless the signs of the kingdom *of evil;* sickness, taboo, and unclean spirits evaporate before him, vanquished by his authoritative word (vv. 25, 39, 41) and touch (vv. 31, 41). The mystery of Jesus is already present: "What is this? A new teaching! With authority he commands even the unclean spirits and they obey him" (v. 27). This authority is also seen in the vocation of the first disciples. Without a murmur, they show all the signs of conversion (μετάνοια; *metanoia*), leave their worldly success, and walk after Jesus (vv. 16–20). The time is fulfilled, there is repentance, and the power of the reigning presence of God is at hand. The first moments of the gospel's proclamation by word and deed bear no opposition (v. 15).

This situation, however, does not last. The first moments of Jesus' ministry are directed against *the powers of evil,* and such powers are unable to withstand his presence, but such is not the case in the encounter between the word, works, and person of Jesus and *the leaders of Israel.* As the story proceeds, Jesus continues to work wonders. He cures a paralytic (2:1–12) and a man with a withered hand (3:1–6). He gathers further disciples from the peripheries of Jewish society (2:13–17), and what he says and does arouses wonder: "We never saw anything like this!" (2:12). But opposition increases.

The five episodes in 2:1–3:6 report not only the spread of Jesus' ongoing authority, but also a mounting rejection of this authority, as can be seen in the following scheme.[19]

• *2:1–12*

Jesus *enters* Capernaum *again* (καὶ εἰσελθὼν πάλιν εἰς; *kai eiselthōn palin eis* [see 3:1]), and forgives *the sins* of a paralytic, but "some of the scribes" *in their hearts* question Jesus' authority to forgive *sin* (see also vv. 9, 10). He affirms this authority by *raising* (v. 11; see also vv. 9, 12) the paralytic.

> • *2:13–17*
>
> Jesus calls Levi from his tax office and shares his table and *eats* (v. 16a; see also v. 16b) with similarly situated characters, sinners and tax collectors, along with his disciples. "The scribes of the Pharisees" complain about such behavior *to his disciples.*
>
> > • *2:18–22*
> >
> > At a time when the disciples of the Baptist and the Pharisees are *fasting* (v. 18a; see vv. 18b, 19, 20), "people" *came to him* and asked why he did not fast like other religious people. They will fast when the bridegroom is *taken away* (v. 20) from them.
>
> • *2:23–28*
>
> As Jesus and his disciples pluck grain and eat *on a Sabbath,* "the Pharisees" *question Jesus* on the right observance of the Law, only to be instructed on Abiathar's *eating* the bread of the Presence (v. 26a; see also v. 26b).

• *3:1–6*

On a Sabbath, a man with a withered hand is present as Jesus *enters* the synagogue *again* (καὶ εἰσῆλθεν πάλιν εἰς; *kai eiselthen palin eis* [see 2:1]). But "they" were watching to see what he would do on the holy day so that "*they might accuse him.*" He reduces them to silence, grieves over the *hardness of their hearts* (v. 5), *raises* the maimed man (v. 3), and performs the miracle (v. 5). The Pharisees and the Herodians hold counsel: how to destroy him.

Although I have highlighted the main elements in this outline, this presentation of 2:1–3:6 calls for some clarification, to understand better the skill of Mark the storyteller. The various events reported here, all of which contain some form of conflict between Jesus and leading figures in Israel, were probably part of traditions that were older than Mark, and reached back into the early church's memory of Jesus. Mark has taken them into his story, shaping the reports and juxtaposing them, to make two basic points. In the first place, opposition to Jesus grows. Second, however, the power of the reigning presence of God continues. At the beginning and end of these five episodes (2:1–12 and 3:1–6), Mark reports Jesus' entry into a town and a synagogue. On both occasions— but nowhere in the intervening three episodes (2:13–28)—he works a miracle. Both stories refer to "raising" (see 2:9, 11, 12; 3:3). Mark has framed the five episodes with the episodes that show the power of God's reigning presence, and the authority of Jesus, despite the opposition of the leaders of Israel.

The second and the fourth episodes (2:13–17 and 23–28) both focus on the theme of eating, and in each episode objections from the Jewish leadership are overcome by Jesus' teaching and his affirmation of his authority. At the very center of the five episodes (2:18–22: the third episode), the opposite of eating is fasting. This theme of fasting is dominated by Jesus' statement in 2:20 that the time will come when the bridegroom will be taken away. Then the disciples who are feasting because of his presence, will fast. This is the first hint of Jesus' violent death at the hands of the people who are opposing him, his teaching, and the actions of his disciples. It is the central message of 2:1–3:6, contrasting with the references to "raising" in the first and last episodes (2:1–12; 3:1–6). Mark the storyteller has consciously taken material from the traditions about Jesus that came to him, and shaped them in a way that scholars often refer to as "chiastic."[20] In this literary pattern, episodes are systematically placed side by side to form a unified passage around a central statement. The first passage is picked up and repeated in the final passage, the second restated in the fourth, and the central message is provided for the reader in the third episode. Thus, at the heart of the five originally independent traditions, assembled in this way by Mark, the passage states the main point of this section of the story.

But one must be careful not to be overfascinated by what I have described as a chiasm. Mark also continues his account in an ongoing fashion. Themes are carried further, in a linear fashion, as each episode unfolds a continuing story.[21] The five episodes indicate a *mounting opposition* to Jesus. His opponents initially object "in their hearts" (2:6). They speak to the disciples (v. 16), then to Jesus (v. 18). They next dispute with him over Sabbath law (v. 24). Finally, in silence they watch that they might accuse him (3:2), and plot his destruction (v. 6). There is a similar increase in the people who oppose Jesus. Representatives of Israel are included in descriptions of the opponents: scribes (2:8), scribes of the Pharisees (v. 16),[22] people (v. 18), the Pharisees (v. 24), "they"

(3:2), and the Pharisees and the Herodians (v. 6). But, despite the opposition, there is also an ongoing development of the presentation of the authority of Jesus and his teaching. The first two episodes deal with sin and sinners (2:1–12, 13–17), and in the final two episodes Jesus performs actions that question a traditional understanding of the Sabbath (2:23–28; 3:1–6). The unveiling of Jesus' role and authority also develops from the first miracle, where the Son of Man is shown to have authority to forgive sins (2:10), to the two final scenes where the Son of Man declares he is lord of the Sabbath (2:28; 3:2).

The presentation of Jesus and the mounting opposition to him enables Mark the storyteller to introduce the shadow of the cross for the first time: "The days will come, when the bridegroom is taken away from them" (2:20), and that day is already being plotted as Pharisees and Herodians plan his destruction (3:6). It is not until Mark leads the reader to the second miracle story that a sense of repetition generates a need to look back across the passage, to appreciate the skill of the storyteller. Whether this impresses the reader, however, is not the point. The ongoing linear development of the story continues to announce Jesus' gospel of the kingdom, only to meet increasing opposition, which will lead to death (see 2:20; 3:6).

One event is linked to another, with each episode looking back and forward for its full meaning. Jesus' words and deeds demonstrate the power of the kingdom, yet raise opposition. Through this collection of episodes, however, the storyteller subtly interweaves an increasing interest and wonder in Jesus' person. Characters in the story who have not read the prologue encounter Jesus and raise questions: "What is this? A new teaching!" (1:27); "Everyone is searching for you" (v. 37); "We never saw anything like this!" (2:12). The storyteller informs the reader: "They were astonished at his teaching" (1:22); "His fame spread everywhere" (v. 28); "And the whole city was gathered together about the door" (v. 33); "People came to him from every quarter" (v. 45); "They were all amazed and glorified God" (2:12). Yet Jesus forbids the demons, who know who he is, to speak (1:34), and insists that his deeds not become the focus of attention (1:44). Mark 1:14–3:6 vigorously addresses the question of Jesus' identity.

Looking back across the narrative that flows from 1:14 to 3:6, we can trace the careful work of Mark the storyteller. Jesus has begun his proclamation of the gospel in Galilee (1:14–15), called others to follow (vv. 16–20), and together they have gone forth. Demons (vv. 21–28, 32–34), sickness and taboo (vv. 29–31, 32–34), and leprosy (vv. 40–45) cannot resist the power of the kingdom present in Jesus' response to God as he goes throughout all Galilee (vv. 35–39). Mark has established a truth essential to his story: Jesus brings in the reigning presence of God as king. He is entirely subject to the design of God, and overcomes the powers of evil. However, Mark writes a story that will end in a cross. Already in 1:14–45 he introduces words and events hinting that all is not well (see 1:22, 27, 45). Jesus conquers the powers of evil, but human beings remain puzzled, and he is unable to move freely in the towns. This initial puzzlement is more fully developed by Mark in 2:1–3:6. In this collection of passages, puzzlement becomes conflict. The storyteller places two crucial themes at the center of 2:1–3:6: the eschatological significance of the death of Jesus, and the radical newness that this event will introduce into salvation history (2:18–22). But the gradual progression and intensification of the opposition to Jesus, from the scribes (2:1–12, 13–17), the people (2:18–22), and the Pharisees (2:23–28; 3:1–6) leads inexorably to the collusion between the Pharisees and the Herodians that Jesus must be destroyed (3:6).

Despite the opposition, the kingdom is proclaimed by Jesus' words and deeds. People are "raised" (2:1–12; 3:1–6), disciples are called, and Jesus offers healing to sinners (2:13–17). The presence of the Son of Man (2:10, 28) and the bridegroom (2:18–20) shows that the coming of the kingdom *of God* is marked by a new authority over sin, fasting and Sabbath, an authority previously allowed only to God. Mark is convinced that a radically new era has come that cannot be contained by former traditions and ways of life (2:21–22), and he writes his story to convince his readers of that truth. He enhances this teaching by means of another simple but effective literary feature, the frame around 2:1–3:6 created by 1:45 and 3:7–8. In 1:45 the storyteller reports: "People came to him from every quarter." He repeats the same theme in 3:7–8: "A great multitude from Galilee followed; also from Judea and Jerusalem and Idumea and from beyond the Jordan and from Tyre and Sidon a great multitude, hearing all that he did, came to him." However much the opposition increases in 2:1–3:6, the immediate context, provided by Mark the storyteller in 1:45 and 3:7–8, indicates that the person and teaching of Jesus is becoming increasingly well known, and attracting more and more people.

Regardless of the mounting opposition to Jesus across 2:1–3:6, he continues to proclaim the kingdom, and people stream to him from every corner (3:7–8; see 1:45). The first major series of episodes in Mark's story announces that Jesus' presence to Israel has not been fruitless, despite the leaders' decision that he must be destroyed. It has been rightly suggested that among the many themes in 1:16–45 "the note of 'authority' rings out louder than the others."[23] In all five conflict stories Jesus has the last word. The gospel of the coming kingdom (1:14–15) continues as the ministry of Jesus proceeds in the midst of opposition and plans for his death.

## Jesus and His New Family (3:7–6:6a)

Mark reintroduces the cycle of summary, disciples, narrative, and decision with the introductory summary of 3:7–12. It is made up of narratives associated with the life of Jesus (vv. 3, 7, 9–10) and more obvious summary material in vv. 8 and 11–12. The storyteller combines elements from the tradition and important summary additions to cross into a new stage in the first half of the gospel. As Jesus' ministry continues, people from every quarter enthusiastically receive him (vv. 7–8). He effects cures and drives out evil spirits who know who he is (vv. 9–10). As happens so often throughout the gospel, these vanquished spirits, who have access to knowledge beyond the limitations of the human mind, are commanded to silence (vv. 11–12).

As in 1:14–3:6, Mark adds a discipleship story to the summary of 3:7–12. Jesus calls disciples (v. 13), and appoints the Twelve to be with him, to do the things that Jesus has done: He will send them out to preach and have authority to cast out demons (vv. 14–15). The Twelve are named (vv. 16–19), and having established this new group who will "be with him" (3:14), a series of episodes that are held together by the theme of belonging to Jesus follows, down to 6:1–6a. In 3:20–25 Jesus turns to face the misunderstanding, the hostility, and the rejection of those who might understandably be seen as "his own." Jesus goes home (v. 20a: ἔρχεται εἰς οἶκον; *erchetai eis oikon*). People flock to him, and his family express concern for his sanity (vv. 20b–21).

As well as his blood family, his religious and ethnic family has difficulties with who he is and what he is teaching. The scribes from Jerusalem deny the source of Jesus' authority: his authority cannot come from God, and thus it must be from the powers of evil. Jesus points out their error, and condemns them as guilty of an eternal sin. Anyone who cannot accept that the Son of God works in the power of the Spirit, denies the Spirit. This decision places them in a situation where forgiveness is impossible (vv. 22–30).

In vv. 31–35, the same group of people who were present in vv. 20–21 return. Jesus encounters his blood family, as his mother and his brothers and sisters come to him while he is teaching. He tells those listening to him that his family are "outside," while for those inside, those listening to him, he establishes a new criterion for belonging to his family: doing the will of God (vv. 31–35). Mark the storyteller has again carefully placed passages that deal with Jesus' blood family (vv. 20–21 and vv. 31–35) around other passages where he encounters his national and religious family (vv. 22–30). None of the universally accepted criteria for belonging can apply to the new community established by Jesus. He turns away from the established criteria for being a member of the family of Jesus. As vv. 20–35 conclude, he establishes a new criterion for such belonging: "Whoever does the will of God" (v. 35).

Jesus is now surrounded by this new family, the Twelve and those who are with him (see v. 10). The storyteller leads the reader into an encounter with the longest sequence of Jesus' teaching in the gospel.[24] Expressions from the verb "to teach" (διδάσκειν; *didaskein*) appear three times in the first two verses (4:1–2) as Jesus uses a boat as a pulpit, initially to tell the crowds the parable of the sown seed (vv. 3–9). But after the parable he withdraws with his disciples, indicates to them that they have been chosen and are privileged insiders (vv. 10–13), and proceeds to explain the meaning of the parable of the sown seed to them (vv. 14–20). The privileged insiders, who struggle to understand Jesus' teaching, are challenged by the parable of the light under a bushel (vv. 21–25). What they have received must be seen, and not hidden. Jesus turns back to address the larger assembly in two short parables of the growing seed (vv. 26–29) and the mustard seed (vv. 30–32). They build on the theme of growth that has been present through all the parables. However small and insignificant, however oppressed, the kingdom preached by Jesus will blossom and bear fruit. This section, dedicated to Jesus' teaching the crowds and his new family by means of parables, is solemnly closed in vv. 33–34: "With many such parables he spoke the word to them, as they were able to hear it; he did not speak to them without a parable, but privately to his own disciples he explained everything."

The primary focus of Jesus' attention throughout his teaching is his new family, those who are inside and to whom has been given the gift of the mystery of the reigning presence of God (see vv. 11–13). They remain as major, but fragile, witnesses to the series of miracles that follow in 4:35–5:43.[25] Across Mark's reporting of four miracles, in rapid succession, the focus of the storyteller is twofold. Mark has gathered a series of miracles from his tradition and placed them side by side to show, in the first place, the power of Jesus' presence, and second, the difficulty that the disciples experience in accepting and understanding the full significance of this presence. The miracles open with victory over the stormy seas (vv. 35–41). Jesus calms the seas, while the disciples tremble with fear, and ask: "Who then is this, that even the wind and the sea obey him?" (v. 41). He then moves into Gerasa, a Gentile land, and drives out the legion of unclean spirits. In doing so, he also purifies the land, sending the unclean pigs to destruction in the sea (5:1–20). When the villagers come to see who had done this deed, and wish to know what had happened, it is most likely the disciples who inform them: "Those who had seen it told what had happened to the demoniac and to the swine" (v. 16).[26] Although the cured man asks to be with Jesus (v. 18; see 3:14), Jesus has other plans for him. He is sent off to his village to proclaim what "the Lord" has done for him, and he does so, proclaiming what *Jesus* had done for him (vv. 19–20). Thus, he is the first person in the Gospel of Mark to preach Jesus in a Gentile land, no doubt the forerunner of many in the Gentile mission at the time Mark was telling his story.

Jesus' works of wonder deal with nature (4:35–41) and the demonic (5:1–20). In the combined account of the woman with the flow of blood and the raising of Jairus's daughter, he overcomes human ailment, and even death (5:21–43). The pairing of these two miracle stories is one of Mark's favorite literary techniques. Mark wants the reader to understand these two miracles in the light of each other: the Jairus story that provides the frame (5:21–24a, 35–43), and the story of the woman with the flow of blood that is found at the center (vv. 24b–34). He opens the narrative with the approach of Jairus and his humble prostration before Jesus, requesting a cure for his daughter (5:21–24a). On the way to the home of Jairus, the woman who has had a flow of blood *for twelve years* also approaches Jesus, believing that his touch would cure her. Feeling her touch, Jesus asks who touched him, and is ridiculed by his disciples for such a question as so many people are thronging about him (v. 31). The courageous woman comes forward, and Jesus assures her that her faith has made her whole, and that she can go in peace (vv. 24b–34). Proceeding to the home of Jairus, Jesus is again ridiculed by the mourners when he announces that the child is only asleep. He sends them away, *takes her by the hand* and summons her to rise. She rises from the dead, and Jesus insists that she be fed and that this story not be spread abroad.

Several themes affirming the authority of Jesus are broached by these two miracles. First, the power and authority of Jesus overcome sickness and death. Second, the faith of Jairus and the woman with the flow of blood restore health, life, and peace to the afflicted. Finally, these two miracles both have women at their center. Jesus allows himself to be *touched* by a woman who was perpetually ritually unclean. By his touch he restores her to wholeness and peace (v. 34). Similarly, he *touches* a dead girl *of twelve years of age*.[27] If she is dead, then he renders himself impure by touching a dead body; if she is only asleep, then he touches a young woman who is marriageable. Yet his touch restores her to life. Both women are restored to wholeness and peace because they have been "touched" by God's reigning presence in and through the person of Jesus.[28] But the disciples and others find Jesus' healing and life-giving presence hard to understand and accept (see vv. 31, 40).

The second section of Jesus' Galilean ministry (3:7–6:6a) inevitably leads to a decision (see also 3:6). Jesus returns to his hometown (v. 1: ἔρχεται εἰς τὴν πατρίδα; *erchetai eis tēn patrida*), followed by his disciples (6:1). The people from his hometown ask the right question. They want to know the source of his wisdom (see 4:1–34: his parables) and his mighty power (see 4:35–5:53: his miracles; 6:2). But they give the wrong answer. They limit his origins to his mother, and they know his brothers and sisters (vv. 3–5). The reader, who has read the prologue (1:1–13), is aware that Jesus' wisdom and power reflect the reigning presence *of God*, but Jesus' townsfolk cannot see beyond his blood family. Jesus is amazed at their lack of faith, and is rendered powerless among them (6:5–6a).

Jesus' Galilean ministry continues in 3:7–6:6a, but the storyteller's focus on the new family of Jesus is unmistakable. After the introductory summary (3:7–12) Jesus generates a new family (3:13–19), and provides a new criterion for belonging to that family (3:31–35). He continues his powerful proclamation of the reigning presence of God as king in both word (4:1–34) and deed (4:35–5:43). Nature, demons, sickness, and death succumb, but human beings remain ambiguous or hostile. Those most likely to accept him, his blood family and his fellow Jews, either consider him insane (3:20–21), driven by the prince of evil spirits (3:22–30), or of no consequence, as they know his mother, brothers, and sisters (6:1–6a). Faced by this opposition and rejection, Jesus teaches enigmatically, by means of parables, but explains their deeper meaning to his new family, the disciples (4:10–13; 14–20, 33–34), insiders, specially gifted with the mystery of the kingdom of God (4:11).

Despite their privileges as insiders, Mark has insinuated the first signs of the disciples' inability to accept Jesus as he tells the parables of the kingdom. He questions their ability to understand the parable of the seed sown (4:13), and across the collection of parables issues a warning, that those with ears must hear (see vv. 9, 23, 33). Their difficulties increase as Mark tells his series of miracle stories. After the miracle of the calming of the sea, where the disciples do not yet understand who Jesus is (4:41), they are present with him at Gerasa (5:1). They may be the ones who make an unfavorable report on his actions to the Gerasenes, who ask Jesus to leave their land (v. 16). They join those at the house of Jairus and the professional mourners who regard Jesus' presence as a waste of time (see v. 35) and laugh at him (see v. 40a). Similarly, the disciples mock Jesus when he asks who touched his garment in the milling crowd (v. 31). Israel has decided against Jesus (3:6), and so have his own townsfolk (6:1–6a), but the disciples cannot be regarded as belonging to any group that rejects him. These fragile disciples are still with him, following him, despite their shortcomings (6:1). They become the focus of the storyteller's attention in the following, and final, section of the first half of the gospel.

## Jesus and the Disciples (6:6b–8:30)

Jesus' rejection (6:1–6a) leads to one of the briefest summaries in the gospel, "And he went about among the villages teaching" (6:6b). However brief, Mark uses this summary to introduce the next section of the story (see 1:14–15; 3:7–12). Like the earlier summaries, 6:6b is followed by discipleship material (vv. 7–30). The storyteller has introduced the next stage of his presentation of Jesus' Galilean ministry. The presentation of the disciples in vv. 7–30 involves another sandwich construction. Fulfilling the promise Jesus made to those whom he chose to be with him in 3:14, the Twelve are sent out to continue the work of Jesus, teaching with authority, healing the sick, and driving out demons (vv. 7–13), but while they are on the mission, Mark tells of the death of John the Baptist (vv. 14–29). As a messenger of God (see 1:2–3) who announces Jesus (1:7–8), the Baptist has an unswerving commitment to his mission. It costs him his life (6:17–29). His life and death have close parallels with the life and death of Jesus, who is also put to death by a ruler who recognizes his goodness (see 15:9–10, 12, 14 [Jesus], and 6:20, 26 [John the Baptist]), but who succumbed to pressure (see 15:10, 14–15 [Jesus], and 6:22–26 [John the Baptist]). Jesus announces the present and future coming of God, cost what it may (15:48; 16:60–62), and the Baptist stands by his God-given task, continuing his call to repentance and forgiveness (see 1:14) even into the court of the king (6:17–19). For both of them, it leads to death. When the disciples return, they are full of the success of the teaching and wonders they have done. They tell Jesus, the authority from whom all their authority flows, of their great achievements (v. 30). They are moving away from unconditional dependence upon Jesus (3:14) into a world of their own (6:30).[29]

The storyteller shapes the remainder of this part of the story around two bread miracles (6:31–44; 8:1–10), and a series of repeated events that follow the miracles. There are two boat trips (6:45–56; 8:10),[30] two conflicts (7:1–23; 8:11–21), and two healing miracles (7:24–37; 8:22–26). The feeding miracles seem to set the tone for much of the story at this stage. For example, food and eating dominate the angry debate between Jesus and Israel in 7:1–23 and the subsequent encounter between Jesus and the Syrophoenician woman (7:24–30). But by introducing the question of allowing a Gentile to consume the bread that falls from the table, the storyteller has introduced another theme into the sequence: Jesus' movement from Israel into a Gentile land. This continues into the curing of a Gentile man in 7:31–37, and leads into further feeding, this time the feeding of Gentiles in 8:1–9. The Pharisees return to the story, arguing with Jesus (8:11–13). This enables Jesus to present the theme of the leaven of the Pharisees and the Herodians, leading to conflict between himself and his disciples as he crosses the sea (8:14–21). Mark uses these closing moments of the first half of his story to show that the disciples are becoming increasingly blind to what is happening around them. They are unable to understand the miracles of the multiplication of the bread, despite their being Jesus' agents in both events (see 6:41; 8:6–7). The theme of blindness is continued into the story of the curing of the blind man at Bethsaida, in stages (8:22–26), leading directly into the questions concerning Jesus' identity, Peter's reply, and Jesus' warning (8:27–30). As always, the section closes with a decision. In the name of the disciples, Peter confesses, "You are the Christ" (8:29).[31]

## The first bread miracle and its aftermath (6:31-7:37)

In 6:31–44 Mark reports *the first multiplication of the loaves and fish.* The story indicates that this miracle takes place in Israel, on the Jewish side of the lake. One also finds indications that the eucharistic celebrations of the community are recalled in the words and actions of Jesus, in the feeding of the multitude, and in the gathering of the fragments so that the meal can continue. While Jesus has compassion on the lost sheep, without a shepherd (v. 35), the disciples want Jesus to send them away. He commands them: "You give them something to eat" (v. 37). Out of the poverty of the disciples, Jesus generates a great meal and enables them to nourish the five thousand who are gathered there. The miracle is followed by *the first sea journey, and contrasting responses to Jesus* (6:45–56). The disciples do not recognize Jesus, who comes to them across the stormy seas, because their hearts are hardened and they have not understood about the loaves (vv. 45–52). On arrival at Gennesaret, the opposite reaction takes place. Unlike the disciples, people "recognized him" and he works many miracles (vv. 53–56).

But the life and practice of Jesus and his disciples generates *the first conflict* in the cycle, a conflict between Jesus and the traditions of Israel. In a bitter encounter, the Pharisees and the scribes attack Jesus on his lack of observance of purity traditions. He accuses them of rejecting the commandments of God and replacing them with human traditions (vv. 7:1–13). He instructs "the people" on the importance of what comes out of a person, rather than that which is outside and superficial (vv. 14–15). He further instructs his disciples on why this is so (vv. 17–23). Much of the discussion surrounds the issue of food and eating, and this continues into *the first miraculous healings* in the cycle, two healings that take place in Gentile territory (vv. 24–37). Following Jesus' harsh rejection of the human traditions of Israel, Mark's description of his movements in v. 24 place him in a Gentile location. There Jesus grants the request of the Syrophoenician woman in the region of Tyre and Sidon, all the while challenging her to recognize that she does not deserve to receive the gifts reserved for God's chosen people. She recognizes this, and is blessed by the miracle in the midst of her nothingness (vv. 24–30). Again the storyteller moves Jesus from one place to another, by way of the Decapolis, ten Greek cities to the northeast of the Lake of Galilee. Jesus remains in a Gentile land (v. 31), where he cures a deaf mute, and the Gentiles become the first to suggest that Jesus might be the Messiah (vv. 31–37). They praise him in terms of Isa 35:5–6, an accepted messianic text, suggesting that when the Messiah comes the deaf will hear and the dumb will speak (v. 37).

## The second bread miracle and its aftermath (8:1–26)

The storyteller prompts the reader by reporting *the second multiplication of the loaves and fish* in 8:1–9. There are similarities and even parallels between the two bread miracles, especially concerning the eucharistic nature of the meal, the responsibility of the disciples to feed the crowd of about four thousand people and the gathering of the fragments at the end of the meal. The table remains open. But Jesus is in a Gentile land, on the other side of the lake. Other details in the narrative indicate that this feeding is a symbol of Jesus' ongoing eucharistic presence to the Gentiles, for some of them have come a very long way (v. 3).[32] Following the miracle, Jesus dismisses the crowd, and sets out on *the second sea journey, to Dalmanutha* (8:10).[33]

Pharisees appear on the scene, and Jesus debates with them as *the second conflict* opens (8:11–13b). They ask for a sign from Jesus that will give authority to what he says and does, but he rejects their request, condemning them as "this generation." They are locked in a closed religious system that will allow no entry to the person and message of Jesus. Although the boat trip that follows may have originally belonged to the journey to Dalmanutha (vv. 13c–21), Mark has inserted the conflict with the Pharisees in vv. 11–13b to teach the disciples not to be of the "leaven" of the Pharisees and the Herodians (v. 15). But they show they are moving dangerously close to that leaven in their inability to recognize "the bread" they have with them, and in their misunderstanding of the two bread miracles. In the storyteller's reordering of this material, the disciples in the boat have become part of the *second conflict* in the cycle. As Jesus asks them: "*Having eyes do you not see,* and having ears do you not hear?*" he accuses them of blindness, a theme that becomes central in vv. 22–26, *the second miraculous healing.* At Bethsaida, a blind man is cured, in stages. He moves from total blindness through partial sight to full vision.

## Climax (8:27-30)

Mark first raises the theme of blindness in Jesus' accusation of the disciples in 8:18. It continues in the miracle of the man who gradually comes to full sight in vv. 22–26. Although not explicitly mentioned, *the confession at Caesarea Philippi* (vv. 27–30) needs to be read in the light of the story of the blind man. The people who suggest that Jesus might be one of the precursors to the messianic era are totally blind to Jesus' identity (vv. 27–28). This blindness matches the total blindness of the man at Bethsaida (see v. 22). Peter's confession of the faith of the disciples, "You are the Christ," must be understood as sight, but only partial sight (v. 29), matching the intermediate experience of the blind man (see v. 24). For this reason, they are to say nothing about their partial understanding of Jesus. It would be misleading to proclaim Jesus' messianic status as Peter and the disciples understand it at this stage of the story (v. 30). The rest of the story needs to be told for fullness of vision (matching the final experience of the blind man [v. 25]). Jesus' words in v. 31 will introduce that vision for the first time. He predicts that he is going to Jerusalem to suffer, to be slain, and to rise again.

The confession at Caesarea Philippi is surely a moment of climax, but we should be careful not to separate one part of the story from another.[34] For Mark, the gospel is one long story. Thus, as the first half of the story comes to a close, the second half is already under way.

The curing of the blind man at Bethsaida in 8:22–26 is taken up in the curing of blind Bartimeus in 10:46–52. Between these two stories of blind men (closely associated with the blindness of the disciples) Jesus will three times tell of the forthcoming passion, death, and resurrection of the Son of Man (8:31; 9:31; 10:32–34). This is a deliberate literary overlap in which 8:22–30 concludes 1:14–8:30 and introduces 8:31–15:47.[35]

# Conclusion

The same literary pattern is followed in 1:14–3:6, 3:7–6:6a, and 6:6b–8:30, but the storyteller's argument develops as Jesus and the disciples, the protagonists central to the Gospel of Mark, emerge more clearly. Each section has led into the next, and this is particularly obvious in 6:6b–8:30, where 8:22–26 forms a bridge out of the first half of the story, raising the question of blindness, into the second half, where the issue develops further (see especially 10:46–52). Yet, there is some sense of climax to the first half of the gospel, where puzzlement has been regularly expressed over Jesus' identity (1:14–8:30). It closes with Peter's confession and Jesus' warning at Caesarea Philippi (8:27–30). Peter's confession may not have fully understood the nature of Jesus' messiahship, but a major character in the story has at last spoken part of the truth: "You are the Christ" (v. 29). As in the earlier sections of the first half of the gospel, this final section closes with the decision of Peter, in the name of the disciples. Jesus is the Christ (8:27–30).

In the story to its midpoint, it is becoming clear that Mark has two major concerns: a presentation of the life and person of Jesus, and the increasing fragility of the disciples. The first signs of the disciples' lack of faith, encountered in 3:7–6:6a, become a major theme in 6:6b–8:30. It is understandable, and part of Mark's storytelling technique. Unlike the storyteller's readers, the disciples have not read the prologue (1:1–13). They do not know everything about Jesus' relationship to God, and his role as God's beloved Son. On the contrary, they have witnessed the ominous increase of tension between Jesus and the leaders of Israel (see 2:1–3:6; 7:1–23; 8:11–13, 15). The slaying of John the Baptist (6:14–29) adds to the atmosphere of impending violence and Jesus warns that the day will come when he will no longer be with them (2:20). From a merely human perspective, there is reason for the disciples' increasing lack of confidence in the man they chose to follow. The stage is set for the reading of 8:31–15:47.

## Notes

1. See also the perceptive narrative reading of Mark 1:1–8:30 in F. J. Matera, *New Testament Christology* (Louisville: Westminster John Knox, 1999), 6–17.

2. I mention "the midpoint" twice in this division because Mark 8:22–30 serves both as a conclusion to 1:1–8:30 and as a lead into 8:31–16:8. As such, it can be called a bridge passage.

3. See, among many studies of the Infancy Narratives, R. E. Brown, *The Birth of the Messiah: A Commentary on the Infancy Narratives of Matthew and Luke* (New York: Doubleday, 1977).

4. See, among many studies of the Johannine prologue, F. J. Moloney, *The Gospel of John* (SP 4; Collegeville: Liturgical Press, 1998), 33–48. For a study of all four prologues to the Gospels, see F. J. Moloney, *Beginning the Good News: A Narrative Approach* (Collegeville: Liturgical Press, 1993).

5. On this, see D. E. Smith, "Narrative Beginnings in Ancient Literature and Theory," *Sem* 52 (1991): 1–9.

6. See, for example, L. Keck, "The Introduction to Mark's Gospel," *NTS* 12 (1965–1966): 352–70; D. Lührmann, *Das Markusevangelium* (HNT 3; Tübingen: J. C. B. Mohr [Paul Siebeck], 1987), 32–33; M. E. Boring, "Mark 1:1–15 and the Beginning of the Gospel," *Sem* 52 (1991): 43–81; J. Marcus, *Mark 1–8* (AB 27; New York: Doubleday, 2000), 137–39.

7. On the Markan use of this literary technique, see R. M. Fowler, *Let the Reader Understand: Reader-Response Criticism and the Gospel of Mark* (Minneapolis: Fortress, 1991), 134–40. "Immediatel?y" (εὐθύς; *euthys*) is used more times in Mark's sixteen chapters than in all the rest of the New Testament put together.

8. For further information and discussion of this issue, see F. J. Moloney, *The Gospel of Mark: A Commentary* (Peabody: Hendrickson, 2002), 27–30, and F. J. Matera, "The Prologue as the Interpretative Key to Mark's Gospel," *JSNT* 34 (1988): 3–20.

9. Many ancient manuscripts do not contain the words "son of God" (υἱοῦ θεοῦ; *huiou theou*), but many others do. I am tentatively accepting it. For a full discussion, coming to the same conclusion, see C. R. Kazmierski, *Jesus, the Son of God: A Study in the Marcan Tradition and Its Redaction by the Evangelist* (FB 33; Würzburg: Echter Verlag, 1979), 1–9. John Painter, who suspects that it is an addition to the original, nevertheless claims: "The title is entirely appropriate" (*Mark's Gospel: Worlds in Conflict* [New Testament Readings; London: Routledge, 1997], 25). The use of the expression "my beloved son" in the description of Jesus by the voice from heaven at the end of the prologue (v. 11), leaves the reader in no doubt that Mark regarded Jesus as the Christ and the Son of God.

10. Although Mark says that "it is written in Isaiah the prophet" (v. 2), the passage is really a conflation of Mal 3:1 and Isa 40:3, with some help from Exod 23:20. On this, see Moloney, *Mark*, 32.

11. For extensive Jewish documentation in support of this link with creation themes, see W. D. Davies and D. C. Allison, *A Critical and Exegetical Commentary on the Gospel according to Saint Matthew* (3 vols.; ICC; Edinburgh: T&T Clark, 1988–1998), 1:356–57. (See *T. Naph.* 8:3–4; *b. Sanh.* 59b.)

12. This suggestion is perhaps made by means of an allusion to Abraham's preparedness to slay his beloved son, Isaac (see Gen 22:2, 12, 16) in response to the demand of God. See Moloney, *Mark*, 37; B. B. Thurston, *Preaching Mark* (Fortress Resources for Preaching; Minneapolis: Fortress, 2002), 16.

13. It is sometimes claimed that Mark 1:1–13 tells the reader everything that needs to be known. See, for example, M. D. Hooker, *Beginnings: Keys That Open the Gospels* (Valley Forge: Trinity Press International, 1998), 16–22. This is not the case, as the reader still has a great deal to learn and experience via the story of Jesus. On this, see Matera, "The Prologue," 9–15, and Matera, *New Testament Christology*, 6–10. On the role of telling and showing in narrative, see W. C. Booth, *The Rhetoric of Fiction* (2d ed.; Chicago: University of Chicago Press, 1983), 3–20.

14. This rare but important comment, "Let the reader understand" (Mark 13:14), is an indication that, despite the fact that the storyteller does not regularly address the reader in this way, he or she is always the focus of the storytelling.

15. J. Drury, "Mark," in *The Literary Guide to the Bible* (ed. A. Alter and F. Kermode; Cambridge, Mass.: Harvard University Press, 1987), 405, puts it well: "Between the understanding given us in its first verse and the radical insecurity and incomprehension of the subsequent tale, Mark's book gets its energy." See also Boring, "Mark 1:1–15," 63–67.

16. On these two groups within first-century Judaism, see J. P. Meier, *A Marginal Jew: Rethinking the Historical Jesus* (3 vols.; ABRL; New York: Doubleday, 1991–2001) 3:289–388 (the Pharisees), 560–65 (the Herodians).

17. See V. Taylor, *The Gospel according to St. Mark* (2d ed; New York: St. Martin's, 1966), 44–54. Taylor remarks: "Mark's Gospel is written in a relatively simple and popular form of Greek which has striking affinities with the spoken language of everyday life as it is revealed to us in the papyri and inscriptions" (p. 52). But simple language can be used skillfully. See especially M. A. Beavis, *Mark's Audience: The Literary and Social Setting of Mark 4:11–12* (JSNTSup 33; Sheffield: Sheffield Academic Press, 1989), 13–44. These pages show that "Mark is not an artless jumble of transcribed oral stories, but the result of conscious artifice" (p. 21).

18. L. E. Keck, *Who Is Jesus? History in the Perfect Tense* (Studies in Personalities of the New Testament; Columbia: University of South Carolina Press, 2001), 71. The Greek words ἡ βασιλεία τοῦ θεοῦ *(hē basileia tou theou)* form an extremely elusive concept. It certainly goes back to Jesus' own preaching, but should not be understood as a "kingdom" in the normal sense of that expression. It is present, yet to come, it is active among us, yet we wait for it. I will move between the traditional expression "Kingdom of God" and the more dynamic "the reigning presence of God" in the pages that follow. See the fine pages on this in Keck, *Jesus*, 65–112, and the definitive study of the meaning of the expression in the teaching of Jesus of Nazareth in Meier, *A Marginal Jew*, 2:237–506.

19. This understanding of Mark 2:1–3:6 depends on the work of J. Dewey, *Markan Public Debate: Literary Technique, Concentric Structure, and Theology in Mark 2:1–3:6* (SBLDS 48; Chico: Scholars Press, 1980). An earlier summary can be found in J. Dewey, "The Literary Structure of the Controversy Stories in Mark 2:1–3:6," *JBL* 92 (1973): 394–401. It is now available in W. R. Telford (ed.), *The Interpretation of Mark* (IRT 7; Philadelphia: Fortress, 1985), 109–18.

See also D. Rhoads, J. Dewey, and D. Michie, *Mark as Story: An Introduction to the Narrative of a Gospel* (2d ed.; Minneapolis: Fortress, 1999), 52–54.

20. In the scheme on p. 65, I have stressed key expressions to indicate the care of the storyteller's assembling of his material at this point of the story.

21. Some New Testament scholars trace many chiasms, and interpret passages in the light of the chiasm. See, most recently, J. Breck, *The Shape of Biblical Language: Chiasmus in the Scriptures and Beyond* (New York: St. Vladimir's Seminary Press, 1994). No doubt ancient authors wrote in this way, but readers do not read in chiasms. One needs a printed page and a scholar's desk to "lay out" a chiasm. Readers come to the end of a passage and are aware of a *reprise* of an earlier passage, its thought and its language. It may be better to call these literary patterns "ring compositions." The reader becomes aware of having come full circle. The temporal and linear development of the story must be allowed to proceed. See the remarks of Fowler, *Let the Reader Understand,* 151–52.

22. Scribes (lawyers) were people trained in the interpretation of the law. They were generally attached to either the Sadducees or the Pharisees. Thus, v. 16 has "a scribe of the Pharisees." See Meier, *A Marginal Jew,* 3:549–60.

23. R. A. Guelich, *Mark 1–8:26* (WBC 34A; Dallas: Word, 1989), 47.

24. For a detailed treatment of the wise teaching of Jesus in 4:2–34, see Moloney, *Mark,* 84–97. One of the most difficult passages in the Gospel of Mark is found in vv. 11–12. The passage may be best understood by uniting vv. 11–13. This highlights the lack of understanding of the insiders. The suggestion that the outsiders will never understand or perceive must be explained in terms of the definitive rejection of Christian preaching at the time Mark was writing. On this, see Moloney, *Mark,* 88–91.

25. For a detailed treatment of the mighty wonders wrought by Jesus in 4:35–5:43, see Moloney, *Mark,* 97–111.

26. Not all commentators would accept this understanding of v. 16. See the more detailed discussion in Moloney, *Mark,* 104–5.

27. One cannot be sure whether these stories were already connected before Mark wrote them into his Gospel, or whether he locked them together. One of the elements that may have led to their being paired is the presence of "twelve" in both accounts. For the woman, it indicates a long and relentless suffering; for the girl it means that she has been cut off from life just as she comes to full womanhood. Jesus reverses both of these situations.

28. See E. Schüssler Fiorenza, *In Memory of Her: A Feminist Theological Reconstruction of Christian Origins* (New York: Crossroad, 1983), 122–24.

29. See further, F. J. Moloney, "Mark 6:6b–30: Mission, the Baptist, and Failure," *CBQ* 63 (2001): 647–63.

30. In current literature, much is made of the sea, and the various crossings. See, for example, E. S. Malbon, "The Jesus of Mark and the Sea of Galilee," *JBL* 103 (1984): 363–77, and especially the figures on pp. 365 and 369. See also, E. S. Malbon, *Narrative Space and Mythic Meaning in Mark* (New Voices in Biblical Studies; San Francisco: Harper & Row, 1986), 76–79; B. van Iersel, *Reading Mark* (trans. W. H. Bisscheroux; Collegeville: Liturgical Press, 1988), 86–92. Many of these suggestions are enlightening (especially the links between 4:35–41, 6:45–52, and 8:14–21 [see Malbon, *Narrative Space,* 77–78; van Iersel, *Reading Mark,* 95–98]).

31. The following presentation of 6:31–8:26 as two cycles flowing from the bread miracles of 6:31–44 and 8:1–9 is strongly influenced by R. H. Lightfoot,

*History and Interpretation in the Gospels* (The Bampton Lectures 1934; London: Hodder and Stoughton, 1935), 114–17. Other scholars have traced similar patterns. See, for example, W. L. Lane, *Commentary on the Gospel of Mark* (NICNT; Grand Rapids: Eerdmans, 1974), 269. I have modified Lightfoot's suggestion somewhat, as his sequence is governed more by form than by content. I take the opposite position, allowing content to determine the flow of the reading process. Lightfoot was not the first to trace "cycles" between the two bread miracles. For a survey of suggestions, from 1864–1982, see G. van Oyen, *The Interpretation of the Feeding Miracles in the Gospel of Mark* (Collectanea Biblica et Religiosa Antiqua IV; Brussels: Wetenschappelkijk Comité voor Godsdienstwetenschappen Koninklijke Vlaamse Acadamie van België voor Wetenschappen en Kunsten, 1999), 1–19.

32. See, most recently, J. R. Donahue and D. J. Harrington, *The Gospel of Mark* (SP 3; Collegeville: Liturgical Press, 2002) 246; Thurston, *Preaching Mark*, 91–92. The understanding of 6:31–44 as a message of Jesus' eucharistic presence to Israel and vv. 8:1–9 as his presence to the Gentile world is widely accepted. However, some would question it. For a full discussion of the debate, and a detailed explanation for the position taken above, see Moloney, *Mark*, 129–33, 152–56. R. A. Horsley, *Hearing the Whole Story: The Politics of Plot in Mark's Gospel* (Louisville: Westminster John Knox, 2001), 104–7, offers no comparative study of the two miracles, but rejects the notion of a Jewish (6:31–44) and a Gentile (8:1–9) feeding. For Horsley, Jesus is a new Moses and a new Elijah, liberating and restoring the true Israel.

33. In the original form of the cycle, this sea journey may have gone to Dalmanutha and beyond (see 8:10, 13c–21), but, Mark has rearranged this for his own purposes. On this, see Moloney, *Mark*, 156–57.

34. This is true of all the so-called "divisions" of the gospel. On this feature across the gospel, see J. Dewey, "Mark as Interwoven Tapestry: Forecasts and Echoes for a Listening Audience," *CBQ* 53 (1991): 221–36; E. S. Malbon, "Echoes and Foreshadowings in Mark 4–8: Reading and Rereading," *JBL* 112 (1993): 211–30.

35. Despite the obvious importance of the confession at Caesarea Philippi, there is little agreement on its role in the unfolding narrative. For some it serves as a climax to the first half of the gospel, and for others it is already part of a second section, beginning in 8:22. Once one recognizes that 8:22–26 serves to conclude the first half and introduce the second, some of these difficulties are eased.

# CHAPTER 5

# Mark 8:31–16:8: Son of Man, Christ, and Son of God

We have already seen that the miracle of the cure of the blind man at Bethsaida (Mark 8:22–26) picked up the theme of the blindness of the disciples, first raised by Jesus in 8:18, and opened a bridge passage (8:22–30) that led out of the first half of the story (1:1–8:30) and into the second half (8:31–16:8). This becomes very clear once one sees the close link between 8:22–26 and the second cure of a blind man, Bartimaeus, in 10:46–52. Between the two miracles where Jesus heals blindness, he predicts his passion three times (8:31; 9:31; 10:32–34).[1] Already foreshadowed by 8:22–30, the first main section of the second half of the gospel thus begins with the textual marker of the first passion prediction of 8:31, and is concluded by the second account of the curing of a blind man in 10:46–52 (see 8:22–26). Further textual markers will make the other major moments in the second half of the narrative clear to the reader.

In 11:1–11, Jesus will enter Jerusalem for the first time in the gospel. He will not leave there until he leaves the temple in 13:1. From 11:27 to 12:44 Jesus will be in Jerusalem, overturning temple worship, and in continual conflict with Jewish leadership, reducing them to silence. On the Mount of Olives in 13:1–37 he will speak to his disciples about the end of Jerusalem and its temple, and the end of the world. Mark 11:1–13:34 is a story of endings. The third section of this second half of the gospel runs from 14:1 to 15:47. It opens with the plot to kill Jesus, and ends in his death and burial. But God will have the last word, and this is found in a section that appears to be an epilogue, the story of the empty tomb and the Easter message in 16:1–8.[2]

# Jesus and the Disciples on the Way to Jerusalem (8:31–10:52)

It is not precise to speak of three cycles in 8:31–10:45, matching the cycles following the two bread miracles. However, already foreshadowed by 8:22–30, which closed the first half of the gospel, the same literary and theological concern is repeated three times across this opening section of the second half. The three passion predictions will be followed by the unwillingness or inability of the disciples to accept what Jesus is telling them. However, he will not abandon them in their increasing fear and hardness of heart. He calls them, instructs them, and further challenges them to a deeper understanding of what it means to be his disciple.[3]

## The first passion prediction and its aftermath (8:31–9:29)

Jesus begins to teach his disciples he must suffer, be rejected by the leaders of Israel, be killed, and after three days rise (v. 31). This is Jesus' *first prediction of his passion*, and it marks a turning point in the narrative.[4] After Peter's confession that Jesus was the Christ, the disciples were warned not to say anything about this (vv. 29–30), but Jesus proclaims his destiny as the suffering Son of Man "plainly" (v. 32a: παρρησίᾳ; *parrēsiai*). Peter refuses to accept Jesus' words, takes hold of Jesus and rebukes him (v. 32). Jesus' sharp reply to Peter indicates he has *failed to understand and to accept the destiny of Jesus*. Disciples were called to follow Jesus (see 1:16–20), but Peter is blocking his way as he heads toward Jerusalem. He is accused of siding with Satan, and is commanded to take his place as a disciple—behind Jesus.[5] But Jesus does not allow this failure to deter him in his response to the design of God. *He calls the disciples and the crowd and instructs them* on the need to take up their cross, to lose their lives for the sake of the gospel. In this way they will gain their lives, and join Jesus in the glory he will attain by means of his death and resurrection (8:34–9:1). Disciples who follow Jesus are to hear his word concerning his death and resurrection in Jerusalem, and also be prepared to follow him to their resurrection, by means of self-loss and death for the sake of the gospel. The destiny of Jesus is to be the destiny of the disciple.

A pattern is emerging: the passion prediction is followed by failure on the part of the disciples, yet Jesus does not abandon them in their failure. He calls them and instructs them further on the nature of true discipleship. The episodes that follow are placed side by side to continue this instruction. The transfiguration (9:2–8) reveals to Peter, James, and John that Jesus, who has asked them to give up their lives and follow him down the way toward the cross, is the Son of God (v. 7). The three disciples are full of fear, and yet want to hold that moment on the mountain, to build three tents (vv. 5–6). But it fades, and only Jesus remains (v. 8). Leading them down the mountain, he teaches them further about the need for the Son of Man to suffer, just as John the Baptist suffered (vv. 9–13). They do not understand (v. 10). The disciples continue to fail in the next episode (vv. 14–29), unable to understand why—by their own authority—they cannot cure the epileptic boy (vv. 18, 28). In a context highlighted by the faith and trust of the boy's father (v. 24), Jesus has a moment of exasperation: "O faithless generation, how long am I to be with you? How long am I to bear you?" (v. 19).[6] Yet he takes them aside and instructs them that authority to work such marvels has its source in God: "This kind cannot be driven out by anything but prayer" (v. 29).

## The second passion prediction and its aftermath (9:30–10:31)

In 9:31, Mark informs the readers that Jesus is journeying with the disciples, and teaching them. His teaching is summed up in *the second prediction of the passion:* "The Son of Man will be delivered into the hands of men and they will kill him."[7] This marks the *second failure of the disciples to understand and to accept* the destiny of Jesus. Again the storyteller intervenes, informing the readers that they did not understand, and uncovering their false messianic agendas, as they were discussing along the way who was the greatest (vv. 33–34). Jesus *instructs his failing disciples* on their call to be the servants of all and last of all, and on the receptivity of a true disciple by means of the receptivity of a small child (vv. 35–37). But still the disciples fail. John reports that they forbade someone from casting out demons in the name of Jesus, because that person was *not following them!* Jesus affirms that the reigning presence of God is made manifest in those who do things in his name, not by those who are following the disciples (vv. 38–41). The criterion on following is to follow Jesus (see 1:16–20), not the disciples. The message on receptivity does not seem to have penetrated. A series of warnings by Jesus follows, further instructing the disciples on the seriousness of their responsibilities as receptive servants, and not lords. The kingdom is more precious than any part of one's body, and salt that has lost its saltiness has lost its worth. The disciples must put first things first. Among these is a final insistence that disciples of Jesus "be at peace with one another" (vv. 42–50).[8]

To this point, Jesus' instruction of the disciples has focused on three major themes: the call to take up the cross (8:34–9:1), the need for service, and the need for receptivity (9:32–37). In 10:1–30 these demands continue, but no longer at the level of theory. In 10:1–12, by means of a debate with the Pharisees who wish to test him (v. 2), Jesus asks that God's original design of creation be restored, that one man cleave to a lifelong bond with one woman (vv. 2–9). The disciples find this a difficult teaching, so he gathers them in the house and reaffirms the teaching (vv. 10–11). The focus on the disciples must be noticed. In a brief interlude, the theme of the receptivity of the disciple is restated, as Jesus again takes children in his arms and blesses them (vv. 13–16). This episode is followed by the story of the man who wishes to inherit eternal life. He is called by Jesus to reach beyond the observance of the social commandments of the law, to give up his riches so that he might become one of his followers. The man cannot take this step, and walks away, losing a vocation to discipleship (vv. 17–22). Again Jesus turns to the disciples and speaks about riches, insisting that "It is easier for a camel to go through the eye of the needle than for a rich man to enter the kingdom of God" (v. 25). But this is impossible! Looking back across Jesus' teaching on divorce, and now his teaching on possession, the disciples ask: "Then who can be saved?" (v. 26). Jesus appears to be asking the impossible, but to the disciple who is receptive to the action of God, everything is possible: "With men it is impossible, but not with God; for all things are possible with God" (v. 27).[9] Peter's awareness that the disciples have made such sacrifices enables Jesus to praise them, and promise them a hundredfold, both now and hereafter (vv. 29–31). Mark the storyteller has tolled the same bell throughout 9:31–10:31: serving and receptive disciples are called to follow Jesus' way, through death, to life and the kingdom that only God can give.

## The third passion prediction and its aftermath (10:32–45)

The journey of Jesus and his disciples to Jerusalem continues, as Jesus strides ahead and his followers are full of fear and amazement (10:32). In that situation, Jesus utters *the third passion prediction*, replete with the details of his suffering and passion (v. 33–34). There should be no misunderstanding the full implications of this final prediction, but

James and John do. They ask for positions on the right and on the left of Jesus when he comes to his glory in Jerusalem. They seek positions of power and authority in the messianic kingdom that Peter dreamed of in his confession of 8:29. *The third failure of the disciples to understand and accept* the destiny of Jesus is again met by a patient Jesus. The anger of 9:19 does not return, as he promises them a share in his sufferings, and tells them that a position on the right or the left is not his to give. When Jesus does come to Jerusalem, two criminals will hang on his right and his left (see 15:27). This third failure is compounded by the indignation of the other members of the Twelve. They are annoyed that James and John are jockeying for positions of power, and Jesus turns to them, and continues *to instruct his failing disciples*. Summarizing everything he has asked from his disciples from 8:31 to this point, Jesus insists that they are not to imitate accepted patterns of so-called greatness: "whoever would be great among you must be your servant, and whoever would be first among you must be the slave of all" (vv. 43–44).

Jesus' final words to the disciples bring to a close all he has said to them by pointing to his own self-understanding. The Jesus of the Markan story has spelled out the paradigm for discipleship. His disciples are to accept the cross, to be receptive and to be servants and slaves. However, he does not ask this of his followers like a distant lawmaker. His is an invitation to follow him down his way. In the end, Jesus is the model of all disciples: "For the Son of Man also came, not to be served, but to serve, and to lay down his life as a ransom for many" (v. 45). Jesus, ever open to the design of God, comes to serve and to lay down his life. Vincent Taylor has aptly remarked concerning this saying of Jesus, and its location at the end of this long section devoted to the never-failing presence of Jesus to his ever-failing disciples: "This saying is one of the most important in the Gospels."[10]

## Closure: The cure of a blind man (10:46–52)

The disciples, as they have been presented by Mark the storyteller across 8:31–10:45, have never reached beyond Peter's messianic expectations (see 8:29). They have never reached the third stage of total sight, promised by the gradual movement to sight in the cure of the blind man at Bethsaida (8:22–26). They are not prepared to abandon all and follow the suffering Son of Man to Jerusalem. Jesus' curing of a blind man, blind Bartimaeus (10:46–52), shows that such self-abandon is possible. Jesus is journeying along the road to Jerusalem, as he comes out from Jericho *with his disciples* and a large crowd of people

(v. 46a). Bartimaeus is stationary, sitting blindly at the side of the road (v. 46b). Jesus stops to associate himself with the blind man, who calls out to him in trust and faith (vv. 47–49). By "calling" Bartimaeus (see v. 49, where the verb "call" [καλέω; *kaleō*] appears three times), motion restarts. Bartimaeus leaps to his feet, leaves behind his only possession, and comes to Jesus with nothing but himself, ready to receive whatever Jesus will offer.[11] This faith makes him well, and Jesus tells him to go his way (vv. 50–51). The response of Bartimaeus is to join Jesus' journey, and to follow him down *his* way (v. 52). "The story of Bartimaeus stands in contrast to the preceding failure of the disciples and symbolizes the ability of those who have faith in Jesus to see the truth."[12] It also brings to closure the journey from one blind miracle (8:22–26) to another (10:46–52),[13] and opens the way for the arrival of Jesus and his disciples in Jerusalem.

# Endings in Jerusalem (11:1–13:37)

Jesus' words and deeds in 11:1–13:37 bring significant Jewish institutions to an end, and forecast the destruction of Jerusalem and the end of the world.[14] Jesus halts Israel's cultic practices in the temple (11:1–25). He then systematically challenges and reduces to silence the religious leaders of Israel: Sadducees, Pharisees, and scribes (11:27–12:24). Finally, sitting on the Mount of Olives, looking across the valley toward the splendor of Jerusalem and its temple (13:1–2), he foretells the destruction of the Holy City (13:3–23) and the end of the world (13:24–37).[15] Mark has told a story of Jesus' presence in Jerusalem during which Jesus brings about, or foretells, *endings in Jerusalem.*[16]

## The end of Israel's cult (11:1–25)

In 11:1–25, Mark describes three major events. Jesus enters Jerusalem in the first episode (vv. 1–11). He then brings to an end the commercial and cultic activities of the temple (vv. 12–21). Finally, alone with his disciples, he replaces Israel's cult with a new approach to God, elaborating the need for faith, prayer, and forgiveness (vv. 22–25)

### The Entry into Jerusalem (11:1–11)

Master of the situation, on arrival at villages that lie on the outskirts of the great city, Jesus prepares to enter Jerusalem (vv. 1–7a). He tells two of his disciples where they are to go, what they will find, and what they must say and do. It happens exactly as Jesus said, and the

stage is set for Jesus' entry, riding the colt brought by the disciples.
Jesus is lavishly welcomed as he approaches the city. The spreading of
garments and laying of leafy branches accompany a cry *from those who
followed and those who went before* that welcomes Jesus as the Messiah:
"Hosanna! Blessed is he who comes in the name of the Lord! Blessed is
the kingdom of our father David that is coming! Hosanna in the high-
est" (vv. 9–10). These words go no further than the confession of Peter
in 8:29, and the false expectation of the disciples from 8:31 to 10:45.
Indeed, it is "those who followed" who utter this cry, recalling the use
of this expression across the earlier parts of the gospel (see, for example, 1:16–20). It is the disciples of Jesus who continue to misread
Jesus' messianic program. He has not come to bring the kingdom of
David, but the kingdom of God. Only after this false acclamation does
Jesus enter Jerusalem, go to the temple, and look round at everything
(v. 11). There is something ominous about this survey of the temple,
and his anger will burst forth in the next scene. For the moment, he
leaves the city and goes to Bethany.[17]

### The End of the Temple Cult (11:12–21)

One of our storyteller's favorite techniques reappears. On the way
from Bethany to Jerusalem, Jesus sees the fig tree in leaf, seeks its fruit,
and curses it. The fig tree is cursed because it was not the "proper time"
(καιρός; *kairos*) for fruit (vv. 12–14). Why curse the fig tree on these
grounds? The answer will be provided during and after the next episode (vv. 15–19). Jesus brings to an end the money dealings that went
on at the entry to the temple. But these deals were essential to the cultic
activity of the temple. On the one hand, people who carried coins with
effigies had to exchange them for coins bearing no image in order to
respect the holiness of the place they were entering. On the other hand,
the pigeons were the sacrificial victims used by the very poor. The storyteller then adds: "And he would not allow anyone to carry any sacred
vessel (σκεῦος; *skeuos*) through the temple" (v. 16). This translation
catches the meaning of the episode.[18] All cultic activity within the
temple comes to a standstill, as Jesus takes over and insists that his
house is to be a house of prayer for all the nations. It has been reduced
to a den of robbers (σπήλαιον λῃστῶν; *spēlaion leistōn*).[19] This situation must change! The next day, as Jesus and the disciples again return
to Jerusalem, Peter notices that the fig tree has died and withered
(vv. 20–21). The fig tree is a symbol of an Israel that did not recognize
its "proper time" (καιρός; *kairos*), and thus has lost its life-giving authority, and has withered.

## Approaching God with Faith, in Prayer, and with Forgiveness (11:22–25)

In response to Peter's amazement that the fig tree is withered (see v. 21), Jesus solemnly (v. 23: "Amen, I say to you") teaches his disciples that his coming, his presence among them, his teaching (and implicitly his death and resurrection) create a new way to God. The cult of Israel may have been symbolically brought to a standstill in 11:12–21, but in its place, Jesus insists, "Have faith in God" (v. 22), and teaches his disciples the power of such faith (v. 23). He further instructs them: "Whatever you ask in prayer, believe that you have received and it will be yours" (v. 24), and finally, lest prayer become mere words, not reflected in action, he adds, "And whenever you stand praying, forgive." In place of the cultic practices of Israel, Jesus teaches the way of faith, prayer, and forgiveness. In this way, the disciple of Jesus turns to God, and God turns toward the believer (see v. 25).[20]

# The end of Israel's religious leadership (11:27–12:44)

Jesus' encounters with the leaders of Israel take place within the temporal context of a single day and the never-changing geographical location in the temple in Jerusalem.[21] In 11:27 Mark announces that Jesus came again to Jerusalem, and was walking in the temple (see 11:11, 15). He does not move from the temple until 13:1a: "And as he came out of the temple." The unity created by these temporal and geographical considerations is reinforced by steady focus on the leaders of Israel. Jesus debates with the chief priests, the scribes, and the elders (vv. 27–33), and tells a parable that these same interlocutors recognize as "against them" (12:1–12). Three public conflicts follow: with the Pharisees (vv. 13–17), the Sadducees (vv. 18–27), and a scribe (vv. 28–34). Jesus silences his opponents: "And after that no one dared to ask him any question" (v. 34c). The section closes with a reflection on the relationship between the Christ and the Son of David, arguing that the scribal interpretation is incorrect (vv. 35–37), a denouncing of the scribes (vv. 38–40), which leads directly into the contrasting example of a poor widow, who gives her whole livelihood or life (vv. 41–44). Not only are the leaders of Israel reduced to silence, but the disciples, leaders of a new people of God (see 3:34–35), are challenged to recognize the need to give one's all.

## Jesus Reduces the Chief Priests, Scribes, and Elders to Silence (11:27–12:12)

Having returned to Jerusalem, and walking in the temple, Jesus is challenged by a collection of people from the Jewish leadership: the chief priests, the scribes, and the elders (v. 27).[22] They demand an explanation of his authority (v. 28). He outwits them by responding with a question of his own. He asks whether the baptism of John was from heaven or from men (vv. 29). Given the popularity of John the Baptist (see vv. 30–32), they remain silent, and thus this first encounter results in a stalemate, neither party responding to the questions posed (v. 33). But this leads Jesus to speak to these leaders "in parables" (12:1). In fact, he speaks only one parable, but the plural indicates the literary genre as Jesus clarifies his role to the leaders of Israel.[23]

The parable of 12:1–12 is loosely based on the image of a vineyard to speak of Israel in Isa 5:1–2 (see also Ps 80:8–13; Jer 2:21). The central message of the parable concerns a lord and master who had given tenants the privilege of caring for his vineyard, and tenants who do not live out their role in loyalty to the master. They wish to inherit the vineyard itself, beat and insult all the servants who come from him, and in the end kill the master's beloved son, and cast him out of the vineyard (vv. 2–8). The response of the master is rapid: The tenants are destroyed and the vineyard given to others. The story of Jesus, who proclaims and lives the reigning presence of God, only to be rejected and slain by those whom God had entrusted with the care of Israel, is close at hand. However, Jesus also speaks of himself, using an image that will grow in importance as the story closes. He reminds them of the word of God, found in Ps 118:2–3: "The very stone which the builders rejected has become the cornerstone. This was the Lord's doing, and it is marvelous in our eyes" (vv. 10–11). During his story of Jesus' passion and death, Mark the storyteller will exploit the idea that the rejected Jesus will become the foundation stone of a new temple.[24] Again the leaders of Israel slink off in silence . . . "for they perceived that he had told the parable against them" (v. 12).[25]

## Jesus Reduces the Pharisees and the Herodians to Silence (12:13–17)

Mark the storyteller has introduced Jesus' conflicts with the leaders of Israel in general in 11:27–12:12. He now presents three encounters with individual groups from that leadership. The first groups to challenge him are the Pharisees and the Herodians, who had plotted in 3:6 to destroy him. Attempting to trap him by placing him in an impossible position, they ask whether taxes should be paid to Caesar (vv. 13–15a). If he says "yes," they can accuse him of disloyalty to Israel (and thus objectionable to the Pharisees). If he says "no," he can be regarded as a revolutionary (and thus objectionable to the Herodians). He says neither, but asks his questioners to provide a coin (v. 15). They do so, and give him a coin bearing the effigy of Caesar (v. 16). *But they are in the temple (see 11:27), and should not be carrying coins bearing effigies (see 11:15).* It is on this basis that Jesus can utter his famous words, which have the immediate purpose of showing the duplicity of his questioners, but which have rightly taken on a broader meaning over the centuries: "Render to Caesar the things that are Caesar's, and to God the things that are God's" (12:17a). They are reduced to silent amazement (v. 17b).

## Jesus Reduces the Sadducees to Silence (12:18–27)

The Sadducees, who accept only books of Moses (the Torah) as the revealed word of God and thus do not believe in the resurrection of the dead, enter the scene (12:18).[26] They also test Jesus' loyalty to the word of Moses, citing the case of a woman who has married all seven brothers of a family, as each husband dies (vv. 19–23).[27] Jesus responds to them by charging them with ignorance of the Scriptures and the power of God (v. 24). He first explains the power of God, indicating that life after the resurrection will be a complete transformation of human experience. Their question reflects a total misunderstanding of the transforming power of God, who raises people from their tombs (v. 25).[28] He then turns to a text from Moses, Exod 3:6, taken from the famous episode of Moses' encounter with God at the burning bush (Exod 3:1–22). When speaking to Moses, God continued to identify himself as the God of the Patriarchs, Abraham, Isaac, and Jacob. If such were the case, then the word of God, who must be a God of the living, affirms that the patriarchs, long since dead as God speaks to Moses, must be alive in the resurrection (vv. 26–27a). Not only do the Sadducees not understand the transforming power of God, but they do not understand the Scriptures that came to them from Moses (v. 24). Jesus closes his encounter with the Sadducees by bluntly declaring: "You are quite wrong" (v. 27b).

## Jesus Draws a Scribe toward the Kingdom and Silences His Opponents (12:28–34)

The next figure to enter the story is a scribe (12:28a). Mark's way of presenting Jesus' encounter with the scribes is more subtle.[29] Initially, Jesus will draw this scribe close to the kingdom of God (vv. 28–34). However, he will then attack the scribal interpretation of Scripture (vv. 35–37), and then refer to the scribes, over against the example of a poor widow, as models of false religion, which parades itself and seeks public recognition, all the while behaving unworthily (vv. 38–44).

As the scribes were the legal specialists, this scribe asks Jesus' opinion concerning the first of all the commandments (v. 28b). Jesus responds by citing Deut 6:5, on the need to love God above all things, with one's heart, soul, mind, and strength, and adding a further citation from Lev 19:18, indicating that one must also love one's neighbor as oneself (vv. 29–31). The scribe accepts this teaching, and agrees with Jesus that these commandments exceed all the burnt offerings and cultic sacrifices (vv. 32–33). Jesus applauds *this scribe*, and tells him he is close to the kingdom of God. However, even in this encounter, it is Jesus' word that utters the truth. The scribe simply accepts it. The series of encounters in the temple with the chief priests, the scribes, and the elders (11:27–12:12), the Pharisees and the Herodians (12:13–17), the Sadducees (vv. 17–27), and a scribe (vv. 28–34) comes to a close with a comment from the storyteller: "And after that no one dared to ask him any question" (v. 34). Jesus has reduced the leaders of Israel to silence.

### The Scribes, and the Question of the Christ as the Son of David (12:35-37)

But Jesus' encounters with the scribal traditions of Israel have not come to an end. As he teaches in the temple, he questions the scribes' teaching that the Christ is the Son of David (12:35). By means of a careful exegesis of Ps 110:1, Jesus points out that David, inspired by the Holy Spirit, speaks of God the Lord's addressing the Messiah, whom the psalmist David calls "my Lord," as God places him at his right hand and subjugates all his enemies (v. 36). The Spirit-filled David thus speaks of the Messiah as "my Lord." It is impossible, therefore that the Messiah, who is David's Lord, can be his son (v. 37a).[30] In contrast to the silence generated by the earlier encounters with the leadership of Israel, this teaching meets with great approval from the crowd (v. 37b).

### The False Religion of the Scribes (12:38-44)

The theme of widows locks together the storyteller's closing presentation of Jesus' encounter with the leaders of Israel. As Jesus teaches, he warns against the superficiality of the scribes who like to wear long robes, be saluted in the marketplace, and have the best seats at celebrations (12:38–39). These gestures cover evil men who publicly make long prayers, for a pretense, but privately exploit the poor and suffering, as they "devour widows' houses" (v. 40ab).[31] They are promised condemnation (v. 40c). The scene changes, as Jesus and his disciples watch the wealthy put large sums of money into the treasury (v. 41). A poor widow comes, and puts in the two copper coins that made up a penny (v. 42). Turning to his disciples, Jesus, who has brought the leaders of Israel to silence and condemned false religion (11:27–12:40), points to her as the model of a disciple. While many give out of their abundance, and thus lose nothing in their gift, the woman gives her all. The Greek words used (ὅλον τὸν βίόν αὐτῆς; *holon ton bion autēs*), placed emphatically at the very end of the sentence and the passage as a whole, speak of what the woman gives. They are open to two meanings, both of which the story-teller wants his readers to understand. The woman has put in "her whole livelihood," and thus given all her possessions. But she has also given her very life. This is precisely what Jesus asked of his disciples as he instructed them in 8:34–9:1.[32]

Symbolically, Jesus has brought to an end the leadership of Israel. Earlier in his encounter with the leaders of Israel, Jesus has promised a new temple that will arise on the cornerstone rejected by the builders (12:10–11). After the death and resurrection of Jesus, the disciples will be part of this new temple (see 14:28; 16:7). They are instructed in this closing scene that they are to give their all, their very lives (vv. 43–44).

## The end of Jerusalem (13:1–23)

Mark the storyteller brings Jesus' ministry to a close with this final solemn discourse. It is delivered on the Mount of Olives and looking across toward Jerusalem and its temple. The discourse receives its narrative setting in vv. 1–4. Coming out of the temple, the disciples admire its wonder, and Jesus tells them that soon all will be destroyed. He then sits down with them on the Mount of Olives, and Peter, James, John, and Andrew, the first disciples to be called (1:16–20), ask two questions: When will this be and what will be the sign of its final accomplishment? These questions set the agenda for the discourse. In vv. 1–23 Jesus will answer the first question, telling them of the end of Jerusalem and its temple. In vv. 24–37 he will speak of other signs leading to the accomplishment of human history. He will speak of the end of the world.[33]

Mark has carefully arranged Jesus' teaching on the end of Jerusalem, focusing on the experiences of the city and its people, and the need to recognize that the disaster of the destruction of Jerusalem by Titus and the Roman armies in 70 C.E. was not the end of the world. First, the gospel had to be preached to all the nations.[34] The argument proceeds as follows:

• *False prophets (13:5–6)*

Jesus warns the disciples against those who will arise among them, and claim that the return of the Messiah is taking place. They will claim, "I am he!" and they will lead many astray. This must be prevented.

• *Wars and rumors of wars (13:7–8)*

The readers of the gospel hear of wars and rumors of wars, as reports of the tragic events of Jerusalem come to their ears. But this must not be understood as the end of time. There will be many wars, earthquakes, and famines between now and the end of time. This is but the beginning.

• *Preach the Gospel to all nations (13:9–13)*

A long experience of trial and suffering, at the hands and in the courts of both Jews and Gentile, lies ahead of the readers of the gospel. They must not fear betrayal and death, as they will be guided by the Spirit, and those who endure to the end will be saved. All this is necessary because before the end of the world "the gospel must first be preached to all the nations" (v. 10).

• *Wars and rumors of wars (13:14–20)*

Jesus now describes for the disciples events that can be reconstructed from existing reports about the Jewish War: Titus and his standard bearers in the holy of holies (v. 14: the abomination of desolation that the reader must understand), the need to flee in haste, and the tribulations for mothers and those with child, as they flee into a beginning wintertime. They will survive only because of God's care for those he has called.[35]

• *False prophets (13:21–23)*

Jesus returns to warn the disciples against any acceptance of the many voices who may be crying out that this is the end of time. They have now been told that first the gospel must be preached to all nations (v. 10). False prophets will come and go, as will wars and rumors of wars. None of this should shake them in their mission as Jesus comforts them: "I have told you all this beforehand" (v. 23).

# Jesus foretells the end of the world (13:24-37)

The disciples must not be led astray by the disasters surrounding the fall of Jerusalem and the destruction of the temple. These events do not mark the end of time and the final coming of the Son of Man as judge. However, that time will come, and all readers of the gospel must watch and wait. Making a clear break from what he has said about the end of Jerusalem in vv. 5–23, in v. 24, Jesus changes his focus by means of a strong adversative "but" (ἀλλά; *alla*). He now instructs disciples about the end of the world. In response to the question of the disciples in v. 4, he tells them of the signs for the accomplishment of all things including the sign of the coming Son of Man, in vv. 24–27, and in vv. 28–31, the many signs of the inevitable and imminent end time. In vv. 32–37 he exhorts disciples to watch and wait for the unknown day and hour.

## The Sign of the Coming of the Son of Man (13:24-27)

Many images are used in the Old Testament to speak of the end time. Jesus gathers some of them, darkness over the earth, the falling of the stars and the shaking of the heavenly powers (see Isa 13:10; 34:4; Joel 2:10; 3:4, 15), to promise that at the end of all time the Son of Man will come in the clouds with power and glory. The Old Testament serves as background for this presentation of the Son of Man that depends on Dan 7:13–14. However, the Gospel of Mark also provides background. The suffering Son of Man, to whom authority has been given over the Sabbath and to forgive sins (see 2:10, 28), but whose authority is always questioned or rejected, will come as the final judge. He will send out angels, to gather the elect from the four corners of the earth. Jesus spoke about the end of Jerusalem in vv. 5–23, insisting that the disciples must not read those signs as the end of the world. First the gospel had to be preached to all the nations (v. 10). Only when that has been done will the Son of Man be able to gather the elect "from the four winds, from the ends of the earth to the ends of heaven" (v. 27). Universal mission necessarily precedes the final coming of the Son of Man.

## The Signs of the Inevitable and Imminent End of Time (13:28-31)

The signs given in vv. 13:24–27 had to be read and understood, just as anyone who sees the sprouting of the fig tree must know that the summer is coming (v. 28). There can be no doubt that everything will change, and the world as the disciples know it will come to an end, and that end will be very soon (v. 30).[36] However, one thing will remain, and the disciples who have been with Jesus, as well as disciples to whom this gospel is addressed, must take comfort: "Heaven and earth will pass away, but my words will not pass away" (v. 31).

### The Need to Watch for the Unknown Day and Hour (13:32–37)

The exact time of the end remains, as in the Old Testament, the day *of the Lord*.[37] No one knows when it will be: not the angels in heaven, not even the Son, and certainly not the disciples (vv. 32–33). Jesus' tone changes. He no longer tells them of the events that are coming, nor does he continue to insist they should take heed (βλέπετε; *blepete*). He has used this warning verb throughout the discourse (see vv. 5, 9, 23, 33). From now on, even though he insists that his disciples "watch," warning becomes exhortation. In order to do this, he uses another Greek verb that insists that they act in a way that shows a preparedness to accept one's responsibilities. They are "to be on the watch" as a good door-keeper must do as his master leaves (v. 35: γρηγορεῖτε; *grēgoreite*).[38] This final part of the discourse, therefore, suggests that Jesus is about to leave the disciples, and that they must perform their task in his absence with diligence and care. But the reader knows that Jesus' departure will be through the cross. The disciples should also know, as on three occasions Jesus has told them of his imminent death and resurrection in Jerusalem (8:31; 9:31; 10:33–34). Thus, Jesus' final warnings and recommendations to his disciples match the time periods that mark his passion and death. The disciples are told that they do not know whether the master of the house will come in the evening (see 14:17), at midnight (see 14:32–65), at cockcrow (see 14:72), or in the morning (see 15:1). He will come suddenly, and find them asleep (see 14:32–42).[39] The fragile first disciples hear Jesus' words as he enters into his passion: "What I say to you I say to all: watch" (v. 37).

## The Passion of Jesus (14:1–15:47)

The single most difficult fact that the members of the earliest Christian church had to face was that Jesus of Nazareth, who they believed was the Christ, had been ignominiously crucified.[40] Some twenty years after the event of Jesus' crucifixion, Paul confesses: "We preach Christ crucified, a stumbling block to Jews and folly to Gentiles" (1 Cor 1:23). Paul's was not the only voice in the early church that preached the crucified Jesus of Nazareth as the Christ, the Son of God (see Mark 1:1, 11). The Markan storyteller's narrative also tells of the events,[41] but like Paul and other early Christians, he was not primarily interested in recording the facts. He aimed to convince readers and listeners that Jesus was the Christ, the Son of God, in whom the Father was well pleased. Each of the four gospels describes Jesus' final evening with his disciples, Gethsemane, an arrest, an interrogation before Jewish authorities, one before the Roman authority of Pontius Pilate, a crucifixion, and a burial.[42]

Mark tells the traditional story of Jesus' passion and death, therefore, but he employs two simple techniques to insinuate his understanding of this climactic moment in the story. In the first place, he continues his oft-used practice of intercalation into 14:1–15:47. Second, he tells the story ironically. Irony is "virtually as old as speech itself."[43] Mark's use of irony is both simple and subtle, exploiting two ways of understanding words or events. Events and words are reported factually, and can be taken on their face value. But the reader or listener is made aware that the real meaning of these reported words and events are in some kind of opposition to what is said or done. For example, people may insult the crucified Jesus by mocking his claims to rebuild the temple in three days (15:29). But the reader knows that he will rise after three days, and become the foundation stone of a new temple of God, a believing Christian community (see 12:10–11). The abuse hurled at Jesus in 15:29, can thus be called an ironic proclamation of the truth. As Camery-Hoggatt has aptly commented:

> Ironic narratives disrupt the superficialities of ordinary experience, opening up new and richer possibilities of understanding. In a sense, this is true of all narratives, since they are all in one sense or another interpretations of the experiences they convey. Irony, however, can carry that inherent tendency to an extreme, setting one interpretation of an event against another. In that sense the deeper reading of the narrative unmasks dimensions of the event to which its participants would have been fundamentally blind. Here, then, is the suggestion that in human experience "more is going on than meets the eye."[44]

Literary critics have traced various forms of irony,[45] but Mark's use of it is either verbal or dramatic. In "verbal irony," characters *say things* about Jesus that are intended to have one meaning, but in reality convey a deeper truth that is the opposite to the meaning intended by the speakers. The above-mentioned example of the mocking request that Jesus rebuild the temple in three days is a good example (15:29). In verbal irony, "The speaker . . . stands protected behind the screen of ostensible meaning, while the silent intent of the word shoots beyond to do its piercing work."[46] "Dramatic irony" occurs when certain events, for example, Jesus' entry into Jerusalem (11:1–11), appear to have an obvious meaning, but in reality they point the reader elsewhere. The people and those following Jesus may appear to be welcoming the Messiah, but Jesus' entry into Jerusalem ominously introduces a number of endings, including the ending of his own death. He will be the Messiah, but not in a way that matches the acclamation of Jesus as the long-awaited Son of David. Mark will weave verbal and dramatic irony into his account of the passion and death of Jesus, making the tragic and cruel *words* and *events* that marked the end of the life of Jesus a *proclamation* of the fulfillment of God's design. Irony is a strategy used by Mark to guide the reader and the listener into and around the world of the story of the passion and death of Jesus, and thus into an awareness of its inner significances.[47]

## Jesus, the disciples, and the leaders of Israel (14:1–72)

In 14:1–72 Mark leads the reader through a series of eleven discrete scenes. The focus shifts from the disciples (these scenes are marked [A]), to a focus on Jesus (marked [B]). The [A] scenes indicate the steady progress of the plot against Jesus, and the disciples' unwitting (except in the case of Judas) association with it. The [B] scenes mark Jesus' acceptance of the darkness portrayed in the [A] scenes.[48] The storyteller, unfolding his account of Jesus' passion in this way, develops and concludes a central feature of his understanding of what God has done in and through Jesus. Behind Jesus' journey to the cross lies the will of God, and Jesus' unconditional acceptance of that will. The theme of the alternation between the darkness of evil, and the majesty of Jesus' acceptance of its consequences as a revelation of God's design, enables Mark to state and restate this theme. In 14:21 Jesus will announce: "The Son of Man goes as it is written of him, but woe to that man by whom the Son of Man is betrayed." The Scriptures indicate God's plan for Jesus ("as it is written of him"), but this does not take away the tragedy and evil that surround the fulfillment of that design. Mark returns to this theme in his report of Jesus' prayer at Gethsemane. Jesus prays: "Abba, Father, all things are possible to you; remove this cup from me; yet not what I will, but what you will" (14:36).[49] Although God is never actively present in the drama, everything is in accordance with God's purposes.

The following presentation of the eleven scenes used by Mark to construct 14:1–72 isolates each moment of darkness and light. The individual scenes stand out clearly from one another, but together they form a powerful story that flows dramatically from one event to the other. What follows is a summary presentation of the eleven scenes, highlighting their intercalation, and drawing attention to the use of irony.

[A] *The Jewish leaders plot to kill Jesus (14:1–2)*

Mark sets the story of Jesus' passion two days before the celebration of the Passover, the feast of the unleavened bread
(v. 14a).[50] Chief priests and scribes hatch a plan to slay Jesus,
but are hesitant, as they fear an uprising from the people, who
have so enthusiastically welcomed Jesus (see 11:1–11).[51] Their
hesitation to act will be resolved when Judas, one of the Twelve,
will join the plot (vv. 10–11), and this first moment of darkness
will be move from a plot to the possibility of immediate action
against Jesus.

[B] *Jesus is anointed at Bethany (14:3–9)*

The discourse in which Jesus warns his disciples to "watch"
(βλέπετε; *blepete*) and to be ready to respond to their call
(γρηγορεῖτε; *grēgoreite*) (13:1–37), is framed by the story of
two women who give without reservation: the widow of
12:41–44 and the nameless woman of 14:3–9. As the widow
instructed the disciples by means of her unconditional gift
of all she had, and her very self, the woman who anoints
Jesus also steps forward as a moment of light in the increasing darkness. Mark tells her story here, as her unconditional gift of self to Jesus, symbolized by the smashing of
the precious flask, and the pouring out of the oil, broaches
the theme of Jesus' royal status (v. 3). The disciples are unhappy with such generosity, reproach her, and miss the
meaning of the gesture (vv. 4–5). Jesus corrects them, saying that she has anointed his body for burial, and that
"wherever the gospel is preached in the whole world, what
she has done will be told in memory of her" (v. 9). "The
story is itself a proclamation of the good news."[52]

[A] *Judas, one of the Twelve, joins the plot of the Jewish leaders
(14:10–11)*

The darkness deepens, as "one of the Twelve" turns against
Jesus. In 3:14, Jesus appointed Judas to the Twelve. But in 3:19,
Mark informed the readers that he would "hand him over"
(αὐτὸν παραδοῖ; *auton paradoi*). The process begins here (v. 10)
as the promise of money (v. 11) links Judas with a plot to kill
Jesus that began in stealth (vv. 1–2), but now becomes possible.
Jesus' executors have enlisted one of his intimate followers.[53]

[B] *Jesus attends to the preparations for a Passover meal (14:12–16)*

Mark brings Jesus back to the center of the action, not only accepting God's will, but also arranging for the events that follow. As the Passover is at hand, the disciples ask Jesus about the preparation for the meal (v. 12).[54] He gives them a series of commands (vv. 13–15). What he says will happen, does happen, and preparations are on the way for the meal that soon follows (v. 16). Despite what lies ahead, Jesus is master of the situation as he responds to God's will (see also 11:1–6).[55] The light of Jesus' response to God, in the midst of the surrounding darkness, continues to shine.

[A] *Jesus predicts his betrayal by Judas, one of the Twelve (14:17–21)*

In the three central passages (vv. 17–21, 22–25, 26–31) Jesus is with the disciples, and is the major actor. However, in vv. 17–21 and vv. 26–31 he predicts the future betrayals, denials, and flight *of the disciples*. All three scenes have Jesus at the center of the action. But in two of them (vv. 17–21, 26–31), he shows his awareness of the oncoming darkness of the betrayal, the denials and the flight of those he had chosen and appointed to be with him in a special way (see 3:14). In the first of these three scenes, Jesus sits at the meal "with the Twelve" (vv. 17–18), and predicts the horrible possibility that someone who shares his table fellowship will betray him. Amid consternation, and the dramatic repetition of "Is it I?" as each person at the table asks that question (v. 19), the breach of table fellowship by "one of the Twelve" is given as the sign (v. 20). Yet, this terrible act is paradoxically part of God's design, in fulfillment of what was written of the Son of Man (v. 21a). But there can be no exonerating the betrayer (v. 21bc).[56]

[B] *Jesus shares the meal, giving bread and wine to the disciples (14:22–25)*

At the heart of 14:1–72 (the sixth of eleven scenes), dedicated to Jesus' never-failing presence to his disciples, Mark tells of his sharing the intimacy of a meal with them. Jesus takes bread, breaks and gives it *to the disciples* (v. 22). He takes a cup, gives thanks and shares the wine *with the disciples*. The broken bread and the shared wine point forward to the events of the following day. Jesus tells *his failing disciples* that his broken body and spilled blood will set up a new covenant, recalling the words of Moses, as he ratified the original covenant with God. "Behold the blood of the covenant which the Lord has made with you in accordance with all these words" (Exod 24:8). Mark's telling of his story of Jesus reaches one of its most poignant moments in a meal at which Jesus establishes a bond of loving self-giving with his disciples, who are about to betray, deny, and abandon him.

Jesus sets up a new covenant through the sign of this broken bread and shared wine, a sign of his gift of self *for others*, establishing a covenant of freedom and oneness with God: "and they all drank of it" (v. 23b). The events of the following day will not bring this pact to an end. The word *until* rings out: "I shall not drink again of the fruit of the vine *until that day* when I drink it new in the kingdom of God" (v. 25). The readers must look beyond the coming death of Jesus. Mark has told this story of Jesus' final meal with his disciples to inform readers about his relationship with his disciples as well as his self-sacrifice in death, "seen as a new act of redemption, establishing a covenant between God and his people which supersedes the old covenant between God and Israel."[57] Mark's use of the story of the meal as the centerpiece of 14:1–72 allows him to highlight Jesus' unconditional response to the will of God in his unconditional gift of self for others (see 15:20b–25). Ironically, those to whom he gives himself will betray, deny, and abandon him (vv. 17–21, 26–31)

[A] *Jesus predicts the denials of Peter and the flight of all the disciples (14:26–31)*

The meal itself concludes with a hymn, but the focus of the narrative remains with Jesus and the disciples as, together, they move to the Mount of Olives (v. 26). On arrival, oncoming darkness and failure return to Jesus' words with his disciples. He, the shepherd, will be struck, and they will all be scattered (v. 27). However, in the midst of these threatening words, he makes a further prediction: "But after I am raised up, I will go before you to Galilee" (v. 28). They may flee in fear, but Jesus will go before them. Peter will not hear of failure. He swears unconditional adhesion to Jesus, however weak everyone else might be. But he is warned that before the cock crows twice, he will deny Jesus three times (29–30). Peter swears allegiance unto death all the more vigorously (v. 31a), and so do all the others: "And they all said the same" (v. 31b). The readers of the story, who know more than the characters in the story, in this case the disciples, sense the irony of these words of commitment to Jesus unto death. The readers know that Jesus will die alone, and the disciples will have fled. They wait for Jesus' prophecy to come true.

[B] *Jesus prays in Gethsemane (14:32–42)*

The passion of Jesus begins with his experience in Gethsemane.[58] The storyteller assembles his description of this important moment with great care.[59] Jesus and the disciples gather in Gethsemane, as Jesus leaves them so that he might pray (v. 32). He takes Peter, James, and John with him, instructing them to watch with him, in his moment of anguish (vv. 33–34). The storyteller gradually thins out the presence of the disciples as Jesus leaves the whole group, bringing only three of them with him. He prostrates himself before God in prayer, a prayer summed up in the words: "Abba, Father, all things are possible to you; remove this cup from me; yet not what I will, but what you will" (vv. 35–36). Returning to Peter, James, and John, he finds that they are not able to watch one hour with him, as they have fallen asleep (vv. 27–38). Jesus is now totally alone. The irony of Jesus' command to his disciples to watch (βλέπετε, γρηγορεῖτε; *blepete, grēgoreite*) in 13:33, 34, 35, 37 cuts deep, especially in the light of their recent vowing of adhesion to Jesus, even if this means that they must die (14:29–31). Jesus returns to his prayer again, repeating what he has already said, and laying himself open to all that lies ahead (14:39). He revisits Peter, James, and John, struggling against sleep and confusion (v. 40). The time for the action of the passion is in motion: "The hour has come; the Son of Man is betrayed into the hands of sinners. Rise, let us be going. See, my betrayer is at hand" (vv. 41–42). The light of Jesus' unconditional gift of self to the will of the Father turns toward the darkness of betrayal.

[A] *Judas betrays Jesus, and all the disciples flee (14:43–52)*

Judas, *one of the Twelve,* comes with weapons of violence and a crowd representing the Jewish leaders. Jesus' final words in Gethsemane (vv. 41–42) lead directly into the following scene. He accepts the darkness that follows the light of Jesus' acceptance of the Father's will (vv. 33–42). The hour has come (v. 43). Now called "the betrayer," Judas marks out Jesus with the title "Master," and a kiss, another breach of the intimacy established in 3:14 and in the shared meal (14:22–25). Jesus is taken by force (vv. 44–46). Violence surrounds the moment, as someone standing by takes a sword and cuts off the ear of the high priest's servant. But Jesus reminds them of his presence among them, of his teaching in the temple (see 11:11–13:37). Ironically, the suffering of the righteous one, long predicted in the Scriptures of Israel, must be fulfilled.[60] The scene rushes to an end as Jesus' prophecy in 14:27 is fulfilled. The shepherd is struck, "and they all forsook him and fled" (v. 50). The storyteller provides a commentary on what has just happened by adding a tiny parabolic action. Another young man "followed" Jesus, and his action comments on the present situation of the disciples. Just as they fled in fear, so does this young man, but he leaves behind the linen cloth, his only article of clothing (vv. 51–52). He, like the disciples who have fled, is naked in the nothingness generated by separation from Jesus.[61]

[B] *Jesus reveals himself at the Jewish hearing (14:53–65)*

This passage is a moment of climax in the gospel. As usual, Mark the storyteller constructs it with great care, and his use of irony turns this moment of accusation and condemnation into a moment when the truth about Jesus is revealed for the first time in the Gospel. Jesus, the leaders of Israel, Peter, and the guards assemble. Peter, who had followed Jesus "from a distance" (ἀπὸ μακρόθεν; *apo makrothen*), now draws ominously close to the guards. He is sitting with them, and the readers recall that Jesus has foretold that Peter will deny him (vv. 53–54; see v. 30). The process begins with a series of false charges, but there is no agreement in the testimony brought against Jesus. At the center of the passage, the high priest rises and asks directly: "Are you the Christ, the Son of the Blessed" (v. 61). The reader recognizes the titles given to Jesus in 1:1: the Christ

and the Son of God. For the first time in the narrative Jesus
affirms his role in God's design. He accepts the charge as
stated: "I am" (v. 62a), but adds another function that has
been growing in importance across the narrative. The Son
of Man who must suffer at the hands of his accusers will be
the same one who will be seated at the right hand of God,
and will come with the clouds of heaven (v. 62b). The accused will become the final judge.

Jesus proclaims the truth. The storyteller's presentation of
the person of Jesus is summed up in v. 62: Jesus is the
Christ, the Son of God and the Son of Man.[62] On these
grounds, Jesus is condemned, but he is condemned falsely.
The high priest asks: "What need have we of witnesses" (v.
63). Jesus is condemned for blasphemy, but on the basis of
his own witness. Such a process is false,[63] but Jesus' physical suffering begins as some spit at him and strike him, crying out "Prophesy!" (v. 65). Ironically, the reader has seen
the prophecies of Jesus concerning both Judas' betrayal
(see 14:17–21) and the disciples' flight (see 14:27) come
true. He has just prophesied about the final coming of the
Son of Man (v. 62). In the light of the very next episode,
there is deep irony in the insults of his opponents.[64] What
Jesus says will happen . . . does happen! This must be the
case, as the storyteller is shaping his tale to inform the
reader that this is a story of the fulfillment of God's will.
God will have the last word in and through the vindicated
Son of Man who will return as judge.

[A] *Peter denies Jesus three times (14:66–72)*

Enigmatically, part of God's design is the failure of the disciples. Thus, the last of Jesus' prophecies uttered at the meal
(14:17–31; see vv. 30–31) comes true. With increasing determi-
nation and vigor, Peter, now "with the guards" (v. 55), denies
any knowledge of the maid's suggestion that he was "with the
Nazarene, Jesus" (vv. 66–68a). The truth concerning the person
of Jesus has been ironically proclaimed in vv. 61–62, but, in
a further use of irony, Peter claims no knowledge of the
Nazarene.[65] He moves closer to the gateway, but is trapped
again as the maid makes more public that Peter was "one of
them," and again he denies (v. 68b–70a). Now a matter of public discussion, one of the bystanders identifies Peter as a Gali-

lean, and insists that he belonged to Jesus' followers. In his final denial, Peter rejects Jesus: "I do not know this man of whom you speak" (vv. 70b–71). As the cock crows, Peter has denied Jesus three times (see 14:30), and he broke down and wept (v. 72). Skilfully, the storyteller has thus told of the final appearance of a disciple in the gospel. Although the disciples have dominated 14:1–72, playing an active role in all the scenes marked [A], they will not appear again. They have disappeared into the darker side of the fulfillment of God's design.[66]

## Mark 15:1–47: The Roman trial, crucifixion, death, and burial of Jesus

A change of location marks another moment in the story of the passion of Jesus. In 15:1 he is led to Pilate. From here he will proceed to Golgotha (15:22), and to a grave (15:46). The steady movement from a focus on Jesus ([B]) to a focus on other agents continues over nine brief scenes ([A]).[67] As 14:1–72 closed with the Peter scene ([A]), 15:1–47 opens with a scene with Jesus at its center ([B]).

[B] *Jesus reveals himself at the Roman hearing (15:1–5)*

The crowing cock indicates that it is morning. The action described with care by the storyteller links the Jewish and Roman trials. Jesus is led from the leaders of the Jews and the Sanhedrin, his chief antagonists in 14:1–72, who "handed him over" (παρέδωκαν; *paredōkan*) to Pilate (15:1). It is the Romans who direct the action against Jesus from this point on. The Roman procurator asks a Roman question: "Are you the King of the Jews" (v. 2a), and as in 14:62, Jesus accepts this ironic proclamation of the truth (v. 2b).[68] The chief priests continue to accuse Jesus (v. 3), but Jesus remains silent. Pilate is amazed (v. 5).

[A] *The question of Barabbas (15:6–11)*

The storyteller takes great care to allow neither Jesus nor Barabbas into the action as he informs the readers of Barabbas. He was a revolutionary and murderer (vv. 6–7). There is no need to inform the reader about Jesus. Although they are both discussed in vv. 6–11, neither Jesus not Barabbas appears in person. Thus vv. 6–11 is to be seen as an independent literary united within the nine intercalated passages that form 15:1–47.

When the crowd asks that Pilate release a prisoner, as was his custom,[69] Pilate ironically proclaims the truth. In an attempt to divide the crowd, he presents Jesus as "the king of the Jews" (v. 9). The dramatic irony cuts deeper as the leadership sways the people, and they ask for Barabbas (v. 11). The storyteller has presented two absent characters to the reader, Barabbas the murderer and Jesus the king. The crowd chooses the murderer.

[B] *Pilate proclaims Jesus innocent and also proclaims him king (15:12–15)*

Mark will not allow his understanding of Jesus as a suffering king to slip away in the midst of this ironic tragedy. Pilate again presents Jesus to the crowd as "the king of the Jews," asking what they want done to him (v. 14). Unlike vv. 6–11, in vv. 12–15 both Jesus and Barabbas appear in person. The crowd demands that Jesus be crucified (vv. 13, 14), despite Pilate's insistence that he is innocent (v. 14). Mark reports Jesus' being handed over to death, despite the clear evidence that he is an innocent king. Ironically, these truths are met with rejection, as the crowd twice demands that Jesus be crucified. Both Jesus and Barabbas enter the scene as Pilate gives in: "So Pilate, wishing to satisfy the crowd, released for them Barabbas; and having scourged Jesus, he delivered him to be crucified" (v. 15). Jesus' opponents choose a violent revolutionary instead of the king of the Jews.[70] The simplicity, yet the depth, of the storyteller's use of irony is striking. The reader is aware that Jesus goes to the cross as an innocent king.

[A] *Roman soldiers ironically proclaim the truth (15:16–20a)*

Jesus is present, but entirely passive as the whole cohort of soldiers mockingly dress him as a king (vv. 16–17). The storyteller has the soldiers ironically proclaim the truth: "Hail, king of the Jews" (v. 18). They prostrate themselves fittingly, but they strike him and spit on him. These actions indicate that, while they proclaim the truth, they reject what they are proclaiming (v. 19). To make this clear, he is stripped of the purple cloak (v. 20a). Mark the storyteller makes it clear, even by means of the mockery and the insults, that Jesus goes to the cross as a king. This is dramatic irony at its best.

[B] *The crucifixion of Jesus (15:20b–25)*

A number of features single out vv. 20b–25 as a self-standing unit. In terms of the overall literary structure, there are nine brief scenes across 15:1–47, and this climactic moment in the story, the crucifixion of Jesus, forms the fifth (and thus central) passage. However, a close reading of the passage itself, set within this context, indicates that it bears all the marks of a deliberately contrived self-standing unit. The Romans continue to direct the action. As the passage opens we read: "And they led him out to crucify him" (v. 20b). It closes with the words: "they crucified him" (v. 25b). The surrounding scenes are full of violence and the screaming of abuse (vv. 16–20a and vv. 26–32). None of that is found in the storyteller's report of the crucifixion. Everything takes place in silence. There is no report of spoken words. Furthermore, every verb in the passage has "they" as the subject (meaning the soldiers), and tells of what the Romans do to Jesus: v. 20b: "they led," v. 21: "they compelled," v. 22: "they brought," v. 23: "they offered," v. 24: "they crucified," "they divided," v. 25: "they crucified." Almost all of these verbs report this past event by means of the what is called the historic present tense.[71] Mark has presented a unified and stark account of Jesus' crucifixion. As Jesus is led out (v. 20a), Simon of Cyrene, someone well known to the Markan community,[72] takes up the cross and follows Jesus (v. 21).

Usual Roman procedure is followed as Jesus is crucified at Golgotha, but the storyteller is interested in deeper themes. Jesus refuses anything that might lessen his unconditional response to the Father (v. 23). The division of his garments recalls Ps 22:19, and the reference to "the third hour" begins to mark the time frame for Jesus' agony. The storyteller's use of this time frame (see v. 33: "at the sixth hour;" v. 34: "at the ninth hour") shows "how carefully God took care of the events surrounding the death of his Son."[73] In a mysterious way, God's design is being worked out in this brutal murder (see 10:45; 14:36). The centerpiece of chapter 15, vv. 20b–25, finally describes Jesus' unconditional response to the will of God in his unconditional gift of self for others. This repeats the message of

14:20b–25, the centerpiece of 14:1–72.[74] The skills of an uncomplicated but profound storyteller are evident.

[A] *Passersby and the Jewish leaders ironically proclaim the truth (15:26–32)*

Mark continues his carefully constructed account in vv. 26–32. This passage is dedicated to the ironic presentation of the crucified Jesus as king, savior, and Christ. The passage opens with the kingship of Jesus proclaimed in the title on the cross—"The King of the Jews" (v. 26)—and the information that two robbers were crucified on either side of Jesus (v. 27). Two thieves have taken the positions of honor requested by the sons of Zebedee in 10:37, one on the left and one of the right of the crucified Christ. It closes with a development of v. 26 in another proclamation: "the Christ, the king of Israel" (v. 32a), and a remark from the storyteller that the two robbers joined in the abuse of Jesus (v. 32b).

Between the frame of vv. 26–27 and v. 32 (the proclamation of Jesus' dignity and the presence of the two thieves), passersby recall the tradition on the construction of a new temple of God (v. 29). They demand that Jesus show his authority by *coming down from the cross* (v. 30). The storyteller has already informed the readers that Jesus is the foundation stone of the new temple of God (see 12:10–11, 22–25), and that only by *remaining on the cross* will he found the new community of God. The Jewish leaders acknowledge Jesus' saving presence among others, but answer the request of the passers-by in telling them that he cannot save himself (v. 31). They will see and believe in Jesus' claim to be the Christ and the king of Israel (see 14:61–62a; 15:2) only if he *comes down from the cross* (v. 31a). But the storyteller makes his point of view clear in this irony: It is only *on the cross,* abused and insulted, that Jesus is savior, Christ, and king of Israel. The crucifixion of the Messiah and Son of God, accompanied by the abuse of bystanders and Jewish leaders, is perhaps the most powerful combination of verbal and dramatic irony in the Gospel of Mark.[75]

[B] *The death of Jesus, Son of God (15:33–39)*

Mark makes another reference to time: "and when the sixth hour had come" (15:33). These words introduce his dramatic report of the three hours that led to the death of

Jesus "at the ninth hour" (15:34). Jesus is the focus of attention at all times, as he sinks into desolation, crying out
in Aramaic, "My God, my God, why have you forsaken
me" (v. 34). The use of Ps 22, the lament par excellence of
the righteous sufferer that has dominated the Markan passion story (see 14:17; 15:24, 29, 30–31), reaches its climax
in these final words of Jesus in this cry from Ps 22:1. The
sense of abandonment, and the intensity of the question
that Jesus asks in death, must be maintained to capture
fully the storyteller's presentation of the crucified Christ.[76]
The use of Ps 22, and other OT texts related to the righteous sufferer, are the storyteller's way of indicating that
God's design is being fulfilled. The cry of "My God" (ἐλωί;
*elōi*) is misunderstood as a cry to Elijah, the helper of the
helpless. The bystanders are still hoping that, at this last
moment, Jesus will come down from this cross. His response is a further agonized scream, and he breathes his
last (v. 37).

Only *after* his death do things begin to happen. The holy of
holies, once hidden from the world by a curtain, is torn
from top to bottom. The temple is now available for the
world to see. The centurion, who, facing Jesus, has witnessed Jesus' death, confesses: "Truly this man was the Son
of God" (v. 39).[77] "The death scene is the summit of Mark's
narrative, the final resolution of the christological issues
apparent throughout the Gospel."[78]

[A] *The women at the cross (15:40–41)*

The narrator introduces a new set of characters in 15:40–41.[79]
He names three women: Mary Magdalene, Mary the mother of
James the younger and of Joses, and Salome (v. 40b).[80] He also
introduces other, unnamed, women (v. 41b). Mark provides
information about both the past and the present relationship
between these women and Jesus. The three named women,
and the larger group, have been associated with Jesus from
his time in Galilee. This information links the women with the
earlier teaching and ministry of Jesus. They followed him
(ἠκολούθουν αὐτῷ; *ēkolouthoun autō*) and they ministered
to him (διηκόνουν αὐτῷ; *diēkonoun autō*) during that time
(v. 41b).[81] The following, and the serving, must be given
their full Markan meaning. The storyteller wants the reader to

associate the women's past activities with Jesus' teaching on discipleship.[82] But now, at the cross, they are described as "looking on from afar" (v. 40: ἀπὸ μακρόθεν; *apo makrothen*). The language used for both the past and present activities of the women sets them in marked contrast with the other disciples, and especially the Twelve, who have abandoned, betrayed, and denied Jesus. They are still "with Jesus" (see 3:14). But Mark's careful indication of their looking on from afar associates them with the vacillating Peter as Jesus began his passion. Peter also remained with Jesus after the arrest, but looked on from afar (see 14:54: ἀπὸ μακρόθεν; *apo makrothen*). By means of this glance back to Peter's earlier relationship to Jesus in 14:54, Mark has dropped a first hint that the women may not overcome the scandal of the culminating irony of Jesus' death.

[B] *The burial of Jesus (15:42–47)*

> Mark focuses strongly on what happens to the body of Jesus in this episode. The arrival of the evening of preparation for the Sabbath generates the need for Jesus' body to be hastily buried. He must not be left hanging on the cross until after the Sabbath (v. 42). Joseph of Arimathea appears for the first time, a man of some influence. He has the courage to ask for the body, and after checking with the centurion on whether Jesus was already dead, Pilate grants the body to Joseph (vv. 43–45). The body is hastily buried, without washing and anointing. Yet Joseph wraps the body in a freshly purchased linen shroud mentioned twice in v. 46a, lays it in a tomb hewn out of the rock. A stone is rolled across the entrance to seal the tomb (v. 46b). These details highlight Joseph's influence and care for the body of Jesus, but also prepare for the events that will take place "after three days" (see 8:31; 9:31; 10:32–34).
>
> Two of the women who stood at the cross, Mary Magdalene and Mary the mother of Joses (see v. 40), see where Jesus was laid (v. 47). This is not the end of the story. The timing of the episode points the reader to the day after the Sabbath (v. 42; see 16:1). The body is not properly prepared for burial, and women who saw him die (vv. 40–41) have also watched to see where he was hurriedly buried

(v. 47; see 16:1). Jesus is wrapped in a σινδών *(sindōn)*, the covering used in the description of the young man who fled from Gethsemane, a parabolic comment on the flight of the disciples. The storyteller has led the readers through the tale of the death of the Son of God and the burial of his dead body. They now wait for God's response to Jesus' question in 15:34: "My God, my God, why have you forsaken me?" Ironically this story of a cruel and ignominious death is told for a reader aware that God did not abandon the Christ, the Son of God (see 1:1, 11; 9:7; 14:61–62; 15:39).

# The Epilogue (16:1–8)

Mark the storyteller closes his tale in a remarkable fashion in 16:1–8.[83] The setting of the first Easter morning is provided in vv. 1–4. Links are made with the passion story: the Sabbath has now passed, and the women who were at the cross, and at the tomb, bring spices to anoint Jesus' body. Light is dawning on this "first day of the week" as they approach the tomb, asking who will roll away the stone (vv. 2–3).[84] There are some strange things happening here. Why anoint a dead body after three days? Why did they not think of the stone before they left home? Indeed, the stone was very large, but it had already been rolled back (v. 4). The passive use of the verb in the sentence "the stone was rolled back" indicates that someone else has entered the story. Who might that be? There are more questions than answers in these opening verses.[85]

The answers come at the empty tomb (vv. 5–7). As the women enter it, they see a young man sitting on the right side, dressed in a white robe (v. 5). His description recalls the symbolic sign of the failing disciples, the young man who was dressed in a linen cloth and fled naked in his nothingness (see 14:51–52). Discipleship will be restored, despite fear and flight (see 14:50).[86] The words of the young man in v. 6 tell them that they are looking in the wrong place. They are seeking Jesus, the Nazarene, the crucified. They are told to look at the place where the dead body had been laid. He is not there, because *he has been raised!* The answer to the question concerning the rolling back of the stone is answered: God has entered the story, and has raised Jesus (v. 6). Jesus' question from the cross, "My God, my God, why have you forsaken me?" (15:34) has been answered. God has not forsaken Jesus. The Father has not abandoned the Son, in whom he is well pleased (see 1:11). The final words of the young man recall Jesus' promise of 14:28. The women are told to announce the Easter message: "But go, tell his disciples and Peter that he is going before you to Galilee; there you will see him, as he told you" (v. 7). In 14:28 Jesus promised that, despite the failure of the disciples, he *would go* before them to Galilee; in 16:7 the young man announces he *is going* before them into Galilee.

But the women run away from the tomb, associating themselves with the fear, trembling, astonishment, and flight of the disciples (see 14:50–52). They say nothing to anyone, for they were afraid (v. 8), and thus the Gospel of Mark comes to a close. Even the first readers of Mark knew of the tradition found in the other canonical gospels: women were the recipients of the Easter message, and they delivered it to the disciples (see Matt 28:7–10; Luke 24:8–9; John 20:1–2). Mark the storyteller has *deliberately changed a well-known tradition.* He does this because he wishes to lead his readers back to the point where they began. In 1:1–13 the storyteller challenged readers by means of his christological prologue. His main focus in 16:1–8 is again his readers, called to discipleship.

Mark's epilogue makes clear that God's action is *not* the result of human initiative, but rests entirely with God.[87] As with the promises of Jesus' forthcoming death and resurrection (8:31; 9:31; 10:33–34), the promises of 14:28 and 16:7 will be fulfilled. *What Jesus said would happen, will happen.* After Jesus had been challenged by his enemies to prophesy (14:65), the failure of the disciples (14:50; see v. 27), the betrayal of Judas (14:43–46; see 17–21), and the denials of Peter (14:66–72; see vv. 30–31), his arrest, his trials, and his crucifixion have all shown that Jesus' predictions come true. The *reader* has every reason to believe that the promises of 14:28 and 16:7 *have already come true.* But Jesus' meeting with the disciples and Peter in Galilee does not take place within the limitations of the story. It cannot, because the women do not obey the word of the young man. They, like the disciples, fail. As with the disciples, they flee in fear (16:8).

## Conclusion

When and how does Jesus' meeting with the failed disciples, women and men, take place? The answer to that question cannot be found *in the story,* but the very existence *of the story* tells the reader that *what Jesus said would happen, did happen.* The Gospel of Mark, with its faith-filled prologue telling of God's design for the human situation in the gift of his Son (1:1–13), addresses a believing community in its epilogue (16:1–8). This indicates that the disciples and Peter did see Jesus in Galilee, as he had promised (14:28; 16:7). As Jesus' prophecies came true (see 8:31; 9:31; 10:32–34; 12:11–12; 14:17–21, 27–31), the believing reader accepts that the promises of 14:28 and 16:7 also came true. For Mark, the consummate storyteller, there can be no record of any such encounter *within the narrative*. It is not required, as the believing community has the word itself: "Jesus has been raised" (16:6). Jesus' words to his disciples on the Mount of Olives ring out: "Heaven and earth will pass away, but my words will not pass away" (13:31). For this reason, the voice from heaven tells all disciples, readers and the listeners to the story of the Gospel of Mark: "Listen to him" (9:7). If the promise of 14:28 and 16:7 had been thwarted, there would be no Christian community, and thus no Gospel of Mark, read and heard within the community. "This is the end of Mark's story, because it is the beginning of discipleship."[88]

## Notes

1. The setting of the passion predictions and the instruction of the disciples between the two blind miracles are widely accepted. See, for example, N. Perrin, *What Is Redaction Criticism?* (Philadelphia: Fortress, 1969) 40–63; N. Perrin, "Towards an Interpretation of the Gospel of Mark," in *Christology and a Modern Pilgrimage: A Discussion with Norman Perrin* (ed. H. D. Betz; Missoula: Scholars Press, 1974), 6–21; E. Best, *Following Jesus: Discipleship in the Gospel of Mark* (JSNTS 4; Sheffield: JSOT Press, 1981) 1–16; D. Senior, *The Passion of Jesus in the Gospel of Mark* (The Passion Series 2; Wilmington: Michael Glazier, 1984) 28–36; and J. P. Meier, *A Marginal Jew: Rethinking the Historical Jesus* (3 vols.; ABRL; New York: Doubleday, 1991–2001), 2:686–87.

2. See also the perceptive narrative approach to 8:31–16:8 in F. J. Matera, *New Testament Christology* (Louisville: Westminster John Knox, 1999), 18–24.

3. This structure, and subsequent reading, of Mark 8:31–10:52 owes much to N. Perrin, "The Christology of Mark: A Study in Methodology," *JR* 51 (1971): 173–87. A slightly revised version of this article is also available in W. Telford, ed., *The Interpretation of Mark* (IRT 7; Philadelphia: Fortress, 1985), 95–108. For earlier suggestions along the lines eventually developed by Perrin, see R. H. Lightfoot, *History and Interpretation in the Gospels* (The Bampton Lectures 1934; London: Hodder and Stoughton, 1935), 117–20.

4. See W. L. Lane, *Commentary on the Gospel of Mark* (NICNT; Grand Rapids: Eerdmans, 1974), 292: "With verse 31 an entirely new orientation is given to the gospel."

5. There is no doubt a link being made between Peter and the mention of "Satan" in 1:12–13. However, the Aramaic word behind "Satan" means "stumbling block." Peter, standing in front of Jesus as he sets out for Jerusalem, is a potential stumbling block. In Matt 16:18, 23, Peter is called both "the rock" (Πέτρος; *Petros*) and "stumbling block" (Σατανᾶ . . . σκάνδαλον; *Satana . . . skandalon*). He must get behind Jesus. See B. A. E. Osborne, "Peter: Stumbling Block and Satan," *NovT* 15 (1973): 187–90; F. J. Moloney, *The Gospel of Mark: A Commentary* (Peabody: Hendrickson, 2002), 174–75.

6. For the interpretation of v. 19 as a rebuke directed at the disciples, see Lane, *Mark*, 332; J. Ernst, *Das Evangelium nach Markus* (RNT; Regensburg: Pustet Verlag, 1981), 267; Moloney, *Mark*, 183–84.

7. This is not a study of the Jesus of history, but Jesus of Nazareth perhaps spoke of his oncoming death, possibly in Aramaic reflected in the Greek of Mark 9:31 and Luke 9:44, and probably using the expression "the Son of Man" to speak of himself. For further discussion of this question, and references to further reading, see Moloney, *Mark*, 171, note 2, and pp. 212–13: "Excursus 1: The Son of Man Discussion." The other passion predictions (8:31 and 10:32–34) were enriched with greater detail (especially 10:32–34) as the storytelling of the early church developed.

8. The internal logic of vv. 42–50 is difficult to follow. Mark, or the tradition before him, has strung together a series of sayings that are joined by the link words of "causing to sin," "fire," and "salt." However, as D. E. Nineham, *The Gospel of St. Mark* (Westminster Pelican Commentaries; Philadelphia: Westminster, 1978), aptly remarks, "Readers may well feel slightly bewildered after a first glance at these verses" (p. 250). The final request, that disciples be at peace with one another, comes abruptly and reflects Mark's concern for the Christian community. For a more detailed explanation of the passage, see Moloney, *Mark*, 190–92.

9. The focus on the instruction of the disciples is highlighted by 10:10–12 and 10:23–31. Form and redaction critical studies often identify the passages on divorce and possessions as catechesis for the community in the post-Easter situation. See, for example, Ernst, *Markus*, 285–86, 294–95. This location of the passages in the tradition is no doubt true, but Mark has used them within the context of 8:22–10:52 *primarily* as instruction for the disciples in the story.

10. V. Taylor, *The Gospel according to St. Mark* (2d ed; New York: St. Martin's, 1966), 444.

11. See R. A. Culpepper, "Mark 10:50: Why Mention the Garment?" *JBL* 101 (1982): 131–32.

12. M. D. Hooker, *The Gospel according to St. Mark* (BNTC; Peabody: Hendrickson, 1991), 252. For further reflections along these lines, see C. D. Marshall, *Faith as a Theme in Mark's Narrative* (SNTSMS 64; Cambridge: Cambridge University Press, 1989), 142–44; J. Camery-Hoggatt, *Irony in Mark: Text and Subtext* (SNTSMS 72; Cambridge: Cambridge University Press, 1992), 48. See the remarks of H. C. Kee, *Community of the New Age: Studies in Mark's Gospel* (London: SCM Press, 1977), 58: "Both stories of the blind who see throw in sharp relief the portraits of the disciples who cannot understand even when an explanation is offered them."

13. See above, note 1.

14. See W. R. Telford, *The Barren Temple and the Withered Tree: A Redaction-Critical Analysis of the Cursing of the Fig-Tree Pericope in Mark's Gospel and Its Relation to the Cleansing of the Temple Tradition* (JSNTSup 1; Sheffield: JSOT Press, 1980), 39. In a perceptive essay, E. S. Malbon, "The Jewish Leaders in the Gospel of Mark: A Literary Study of Markan Characterization," in *In the Company of Jesus: Characters in Mark's Gospel* (Louisville: Westminster John Knox, 2000), 131–65, warns against the stereotyping of the Jewish leaders. Scribes and Pharisees on the one hand, and elders, chief priests, and scribes on the other, play a negative role (see pp. 138–52). However, some emerge positively (the scribe of

12:34, Jairus and Joseph of Arimathea; see pp. 157–65). Response to Jesus does not depend on one's social or religious role.

15. Many commentators separate 13:1–37 from 11:1–12:44, and thus miss the unifying theme of endings that Mark develops across these days of Jesus' presence in Jerusalem.

16. On this, see W. H. Kelber, *The Kingdom in Mark: A New Place and a New Time* (Philadelphia: Fortress, 1974), 67–147; W. H. Kelber, *Mark's Story of Jesus* (Philadelphia: Fortress, 1979), 57–70. E. Lohmeyer, *Das Evangelium des Markus* (17th ed.; Meyers Kommentar; Göttingen: Vandenhoeck & Ruprecht, 1967), 227, rightly comments on 11:1–13:37: "In the end, this passage has a single great theme, during which on only one occasion the shadow of Jesus' forthcoming suffering is cast (12:1–12): it is the message of Jesus for or against the holy city."

17. Mark shapes Jesus' presence in Jerusalem by having him come to the city and leave it. He arrives in vv. 1–11, but leaves in v. 11. He returns to the city in v. 15, by means of a short journey reported in vv. 12–14 (the fig tree), and leaves it again in v. 19. He returns again in v. 27, again via a short journey reported in vv. 20–21 (the fig tree). He is in the city and the temple from 12:27–44, but leaves the temple for the Mount of Olives in 13:1.

18. Most translations render this as he would not allow anyone "to carry anything" through the temple. The word σκεῦος *(skeuos)* has a wide range of meanings, but it is regularly attested, especially in the LXX, as meaning a vessel to be used in a cult. For more detail, see Moloney, *Mark,* 223–24.

19. The accusation that the Temple had become a den of robbers, using the word λῃστής *(lēistēs)* for "robber," would be very eloquent for Mark's readers. Toward the end of the siege of Jerusalem, the fanatical fringe of the Zealot party, always called λῃσταί *(lēistai)* by the historian Josephus, made the temple into a fortress, and committed atrocities there, including the spilling of human blood. The temple had indeed become a den of robbers.

20. For an outstanding study of this passage, see S. E. Dowd, *Prayer, Power and the Problem of Suffering: Mark 11:22–25 in the Context of Markan Theology* (SBLDS 105; Atlanta: Scholars Press, 1988). Most early textual witnesses do not contain v. 26: "But if you do not forgive, neither will your father who is in heaven forgive your trespasses." Early copyists inserted these words from Matt 6:15. For more detail, see Moloney, *Mark,* 216 n. 3.

21. This paragraph is lightly adapted from Moloney, *Mark,* 229.

22. The chief priests, the scribes, and the elders are the only characters who appear as leaders of Israel in the passion narrative. The Pharisees, the Herodians, and the Sadducees do not reappear in chaps. 14–15.

23. See C. E. B. Cranfield, *The Gospel according to St. Mark* (CGTC; Cambridge: Cambridge University Press, 1959), 364.

24. On this, see the important study of D. H. Juel, *Messiah and Temple: The Trial of Jesus in the Gospel of Mark* (SBLDS 31; Missoula: Scholars Press, 1977).

25. E. Schweizer, *The Good News according to Mark* (trans. D. H. Madvig; Richmond: John Knox Press, 1970), 240, aptly comments about Mark's use of parables in general, and this parable in particular: "For Mark, a parable is a way of speaking about God, to which a mere intellectual response is not possible. The only person who can understand a parable is one who is willing to accept or reject its message."

26. On the Sadducees, see J. P. Meier, *A Marginal Jew: Rethinking the Historical Jesus* (3 vols.; ABRL; New York: Doubleday, 1991–2001), 3:389–448.

27. This caricature is based on what is called levirate law, which had its origins in the early history of Israel as a nation. As the mother transmits the bloodline, and the tribal nature of the people had to be preserved, if a woman was left childless, it was the responsibility of the next of kin to raise up children by her, "that his name may not be blotted out of Israel" (Deut 25:6).

28. Jesus' description of the life of the risen one as not being given in marriage, but being like the angels, has long been misunderstood. See, for example, Hooker, *St. Mark*, 284: "a bloodless existence where the warmth of human relationships has ceased to matter." The issue is that God becomes the unique focus, and the angels are used to convey that message. As M.-J. Lagrange, *Évangile selon Saint Marc* (EB; Paris: Gabalda, 1920), 297, points out: "The comparison is aimed less at the nature of the angels than at their occupation."

29. On the scribes, see Meier, *A Marginal Jew*, 3:549–60.

30. This passage is important for an understanding of Markan Christology, which we will treat in more detail in Part 3 (Mark the Interpreter). In both 11:9–11 and 12:35–37 Jesus rejects any identification between the Messiah and the Son of David, even though this identification is made in other christologies of the New Testament (see, for example, Matt 1:1; Rom 1:3–4). Only in his encounter between Bartimaeus does Jesus appear to listen approvingly to the salutation, "Son of David" (see 10:47–48). The appeal of Bartimaeus, however, is not to Jesus as Messiah, but as someone who (like Solomon, the son of David) might heal him. On the link between "Son of David" and healing, see Moloney, *Mark*, 208–10, and especially J. H. Charlesworth, "The Son of David, Solomon and Jesus," in *The New Testament and Hellenistic Judaism* (eds. P. Borgen and S. Giversen; Peabody: Hendrickson, 1997), 72–87.

31. This is a serious accusation. Long-standing legal, prophetic, and wisdom traditions in Israel called for the respect and protection of widows (see, for example, Exod 22:21–24; Deut 24:17, 19–22, 27:19; Isa 1:17; Jer 7:6; 22:3; Zech 7:10; Mal 3:5; Ps 146:9; Prov 15:25). The woman without a husband was particularly fragile and open to physical, social, and financial abuse.

32. On this brief but important passage, and the need to link vv. 38–40 with 41–44, see A. G. Wright, "The Widow's Mite—Praise or Lament?—A Matter of Context," *CBQ* 44 (1982): 256–65, and especially E. S. Malbon, "The Poor Widow in Mark and Her Poor Rich Readers," in *In the Company of Jesus* (Louisville: Westminster John Knox, 2000), 166–88. See also H. Fledderman, "A Warning about the Scribes (Mark 12:37b–40)," *CBQ* 44 (1982): 52–67.

33. The discourse bristles with exegetical, historical, and theological challenges. For three recent full-scale studies of the discourse, see G. R. Beasley-Murray, *Jesus and the Last Days: The Interpretation of the Olivet Discourse* (Peabody: Hendrickson, 1993); K. D. Dyer, *The Prophecy on the Mount: Mark 13 and the Gathering of the New Community* (International Theological Studies 2; Bern: Peter Lang, 1998), and the succinct, but provocative study of V. Balabanski, *Eschatology in the Making: Mark, Matthew and the Didache* (SNTSMS 97; Cambridge: Cambridge University Press, 1998), 55–134.

34. For a strong case supporting the above, that 13:5–23 described the destruction of Jerusalem, see J. Marcus, "The Jewish War and the *Sitz im Leben* of Mark," *JBL* 111 (1992): 441–62, and especially W. A. Such, *The Abomination of Desolation in the Gospel of Mark: Its Historical Reference in Mark 13:14 and Its*

*Impact in the Gospel* (Lanham: University of America Press, 1999). For a case against any such identification, see M. Hengel, *Studies in the Gospel of Mark* (trans. J. Bowden; Philadelphia: Fortress, 1985), 14–28.

35. It is this section of the discourse that attracts most attention (and disagreement). It probably also provides traces of the "little apocalypse," a source that Mark used for his reports of the events surrounding the fall of Israel. For a discussion of these questions, see Moloney, *Mark*, 258–63. As D. Lührmann, *Das Markusevangelium* (HNT 3; Tübingen: J. C. B. Mohr [Paul Siebeck], 1987), 222, comments, all this reflects "something that actually took place during the Roman siege of Jerusalem in the Jewish War." On the "little apocalypse," see Balabanski, *Eschatology*, 86–97. She summarizes other positions, and gives her own. See also her excellent work on the idea of a "flight" from Jerusalem on pp. 105–34.

36. These texts lead scholars to ask whether Jesus himself thought the end time would come soon. Most likely he did, and so did many in the early church (see, for example, 1 Thess 4:13–18). Mark probably also suspected this, but he is prepared to leave the "when" to God, as we will see in vv. 32–33.

37. As Lane, *Mark*, 482, remarks: "The parousia is not conditioned by any other consideration than the sovereign decision of the Father, which remains enveloped with impenetrable mystery."

38. This verb appears in vv. 34, 35, and v. 37. While βλέπετε *(blepete)* warns, γρηγορεῖτε *(grēgoreite)* exhorts. For a full discussion of the importance of this shift in verbs, see T. J. Geddert, *Watchwords: Mark 13 in Markan Eschatology* (JSNTSup 26; Sheffield: Sheffield Academic Press, 1989), 81–87.

39. The evening, the cockcrow, and the morning, as well as the sleeping disciples, are explicitly mentioned in Mark 14–15. However, 14:32–65 is set across the middle of the night, even though this time frame is never explicitly mentioned. See R. H. Lightfoot, *The Gospel Message of St. Mark* (Oxford: Clarendon Press, 1950), 53.

40. This paragraph is adapted from Moloney, *Mark*, 275.

41. See G. S. Sloyan, *Jesus on Trial: The Development of the Passion Narratives and Their Historical and Ecumenical Implications* (ed. J. Reumann; Philadelphia: Fortress, 1973), 1–3. As Taylor, *St. Mark* (1966), 525 (paraphrasing K. L. Schmidt) remarks: "The Passion Narrative . . . is the oldest and most notable document in the garland of the acts of martyrs."

42. Of course, each evangelist has told the story in an original fashion, even in the passion narrative. See the useful study of F. J. Matera, *Passion Narratives and Gospel Theologies: Interpreting the Synoptics Through their Passion Stories* (New York: Paulist, 1986).

43. P. D. Duke, *Irony in the Fourth Gospel* (Atlanta: John Knox Press, 1985), 8. See the excellent summary of the use of irony in the history of language and literature on pp. 8–13. For a more ambitious attempt to situate the rhetoric of irony within the broader context of the social and literary function of narrative, see Camery-Hoggatt, *Irony in Mark's Gospel*, 15–56.

44. Camery-Hoggatt, *Irony in Mark's Gospel*, 32.

45. For a fuller description of these forms of irony, see Duke, *Irony*, 18–27. On verbal irony, see also Camery-Hoggatt, *Irony in Mark's Gospel*, 85.

46. Duke, *Irony*, 23.

47. See Camery-Hoggatt, *Irony in Mark's Gospel*, 40. Camery-Hoggatt's study uncovers a number of interesting ironic strategies across the Gospel of

Mark. However, he devotes only a few pages (pp. 171–77) to the climax of the Markan use of irony in 14:1–16:8.

48. J. R. Donahue, *"Are You the Christ?" The Trial Narrative in the Gospel of Mark* (SBLDS 10; Missoula: Scholars Press, 1973), 58–63, identified the importance of intercalation for the interpretation of 14:53–65. I have extended his suggestion across the whole of Mark 14–15.

49. I am grateful to Dr. Timothy Carmody, who pointed this out to me during the course of the work of the Catholic Biblical Association Task Force on "The Gospel of Mark in the 21st Century," at John Carroll University, Cleveland, Ohio, on Monday, August 5, 2002. This suggestion is an important addition to my thoughts in Moloney, *Mark*, 276–79, and would add to my more detailed exegesis of these passages in that work, 279–336.

50. Mark's chronology is difficult to follow. Most likely the "two days" of v. 1 would mean twenty-four hours, as a day was counted on each appearance of daylight. The evening of one day and the morning of the next would be "two days." The following *tentative* scheme is suggested by the narrative: plot and anointing (Wednesday), preparations and the Passover meal (Thursday), Gethsemane, arrest, and Jewish hearing (during the night between Thursday and Friday), Roman hearing, crucifixion, and burial (Friday). An empty tomb is thus discovered "after three days" (8:31; 9:31; 10:32–34) = end of daylight on Friday, daylight on Saturday, morning light on Sunday. See Hooker, *St. Mark*, 325–26.

51. The Jewish historian Josephus records that the celebration of major feasts brought great tension during the time of Roman occupation. See Josephus, *Ant.* 17.213–218; 20.105–112; *J.W.* 2.255; 2.280–281; 5.244.

52. Hooker, *St. Mark*, 330. This episode announces, at the beginning of the passion narrative, that Jesus is king, and his crucifixion, death, and burial will point to that truth.

53. Paradoxically, there is a connection between Judas' action and God's design. In the passion predictions, Jesus has already said that he *must* (8:31: δεῖ; *dei*) be "handed over" (9:31: παραδίδοται; *paradidotai*; 10:33: παραδοθήσεται; *paradothēsetai*). See Senior, *The Passion of Jesus*, 48–49.

54. There are problems with the chronology here, as the days outlined above in note 45 are hard to fit in with the information provided in v. 12. For more detail, which may not have bothered Mark as much as it does the modern interpreter, see Moloney, *Mark*, 283, note 33.

55. As Lohmeyer, *Markus*, 300, comments on vv. 12–16: "It creates but an example for the thought that stands over the whole passion account."

56. Judas's deliberate separation from Jesus (see 3:14, 19) is read by Mark, and by the early church as a whole, as worthy only of the worst condemnation: It would be better if he had never been born (v. 21bc). Yet, this tragic failure is part of God's design, fulfilling the Scriptures. The fundamental background of the unfolding of God's purposes across these intercalated passages must not be lost from sight.

57. Hooker, *St. Mark*, 340. For a further development of the Markan understanding of the Lord's Table, see Part 3 (Mark the Interpreter).

58. On the passage as a whole, see R. E. Brown, *The Death of the Messiah: From Gethsemane to the Grave. A Commentary on the Passion Narratives in the Four Gospels* (2 vols.; ABRL; New York: Doubleday, 1994), 1:216–27. See also the excellent studies of D. M. Stanley, *Jesus in Gethsemane: The Early Church Reflects on the Suffering of Jesus* (New York: Paulist, 1980), 119–54, and

R. Feldmeier, *Die Krisis der Gottessohnes: Die Gethsemaneerzählung als Schlüssel der Markuspassion* (WUNT 2. Reihe 21: Tübingen: J. C. B. Mohr [Paul Siebeck], 1987).

59. Scholars have found tensions and contradictions in vv. 32–42. It is a finely crafted narrative, unfolding as follows: (a) Introduction (v. 32), (b) Jesus, Peter, James, and John (vv. 33–34), (c) The prayer of Jesus (vv. 35–36), (d) Jesus, Peter, James, and John (vv. 37–38), (c′) The prayer of Jesus (v. 39), (b′) Jesus, Peter, James, and John, (a′) Conclusion (vv. 41–42). For a full interpretation of the passage along these lines, see Moloney, *Mark*, 290–97.

60. There is no specific "Scripture" referred to in v. 49c. On the background of the righteous sufferer for this passage, see Senior, *Passion*, 83–84.

61. On this enigmatic passage, see Brown, *Death*, 1:294–95; H. Fledderman, "The Flight of the Naked Young Man (Mark 14:51–52)," *CBQ* 41 (1979): 412–17.

62. For a further development of the Markan Christology, see Part 3 (Mark the Interpreter).

63. On the falseness of the procedure here, see Moloney, *Mark*, 305–6, especially p. 306, note 150.

64. Mark's skillful writing is again evident. This scene is made up of (a) introduction (vv. 53–54), (b) false charges (vv. 55–61a), (c) Jesus' self-revelation (vv. 61b–62), (b′) false condemnation (vv. 63–64), (a′) conclusion (v. 66). This series of events is a blend of both verbal and dramatic irony.

65. For a more detailed examination of the irony in Peter's performance, in the light of Jesus' prophecy and witness to the truth across 14:53–72, see Camery-Hoggatt, *Irony in Mark's Gospel*, 171–74.

66. For a further development of the Markan presentation of the disciples, see Part 3 (Mark the Interpreter).

67. The divisions into scenes in 15:1–47 are not as obvious as in 14:1–72, and at times subtle textual markers must be taken as indicating a move from one scene to another. For a detailed presentation of these scenes, see Moloney, *Mark*, 309–35.

68. The parallel between the Jewish interrogation, leading to the ironic proclamation of Jesus as the Christ, the Son of God, and the Son of Man (14:61–62) and the Roman interrogation, leading to the ironic proclamation of Jesus as king (15:2), should be noticed. These are all uses of verbal irony. Schweizer remarks of Pilate's question: "It is a Greco-Roman formulation of the question which the high priest asked of Jesus in a Jewish version in 14:61" (*Mark*, 336).

69. It is difficult to find any support for this practice. For a full discussion, see Brown, *Death*, 1:793–95.

70. This choice would have made a poignant impression on readers of the gospel as Jerusalem fell, thanks to the implacable rage and violence of the Zealots.

71. In Greek, the "historic present" tense of a verb is found when the verb is in the present tense, but it has a past meaning. This is used in narrative to create a dramatic effect. It certainly does so here.

72. This is indicated by the mention of his sons Alexander and Rufus, who need no introduction to the readers.

73. Brown, *Death*, 2:960.

120 Mark: Storyteller, Interpreter, Evangelist

74. For the parallel between 14:22–25 and 15:20b–25, I am grateful to Dr. Noël Keller, R.S.M., who pointed this out to me during the course of the work of the Catholic Biblical Association Task force on "The Gospel of Mark in the 21st Century," at John Carroll University, Cleveland, Ohio, on August 5, 2002.

75. The background of Ps 22 continues in this passage: "All who see me mock at me, they make mouths at me, they wag their heads" (Ps 22:7); "He hoped in the Lord, let him deliver him; let him save him because he wants him" (Ps 22:9). On the chain of allusions to Ps 22 across vv. 29–31, see D. J. Moo, *The Old Testament in the Gospel Passion Narratives* (Sheffield: Almond, 1983), 257–60.

76. Several attempts have been made to interpret Jesus' cry as an act of faith. See, for example, F. J. Matera, *The Kingship of Jesus: Composition and Theology in Mark 15* (SBLDS 66; Chico: Scholars Press, 1982), 132–35; Senior, *Passion*, 123–24. In support of the above, see Brown, *Death*, 2:1045–47. After reviewing attempts to soften the sense of abandon, Brown comments: "I find no persuasive argument against attributing to the Jesus of Mark/Matt the literal sentiment of feeling forsaken expressed in the psalm quote" (*Death*, 2:1051).

77. Again, both verbal and dramatic irony are present. Both these events are the subject of much debate. There is some doubt about which curtain is torn, and because the Greek for "was (the) Son of God" does not have the definite article (υἱὸς θεοῦ ἦν; huios theou ēn), some suggest that it does not have the full Markan sense of Jesus' being the Son of God. For a full discussion, and a detailed defense of the positions taken above, see Moloney, *Mark*, 325–31, especially notes 278, 279, 282.

78. Senior, *Passion*, 121.

79. See Moloney, *Mark*, 331.

80. The introduction of these names, and especially the reference to James and Joses, without explanation, could indicate that the Markan community knew the women and the two sons.

81. The use of the imperfect tense in the Greek verbs indicates the *durative* aspect of their following and serving.

82. See W. Munro, "Women Disciples in Mark?" *CBQ* 44 (1982): 225–41; E. S. Malbon, "Fallible Followers: Women and Men in the Gospel of Mark," in *In the Company of Jesus* (Louisville: Westminster John Knox, 2000), 57–67.

83. Because of the fear, flight, and failure of the women in v. 8, early scribes added further endings to 16:1–8, and most Bibles carry at least vv. 9–20. For a discussion of the problem of the ending, affirming (with most contemporary scholars) that v. 8 marks the authentic ending of the Gospel of Mark, see Moloney, *Mark*, 339–41. On the several longer endings that have been added to the Gospel, and a commentary on vv. 9–20, see Moloney, *Mark*, 355–62.

84. I have decided to separate 16:1–8 from 14:1–15:47. However, a good case can be made for it being a continuation of the long intercalation. In literary terms, it closes the series with a final [A] scene (see the opening [A] scene in 14:1–2). Theologically, in this final [A] scene all the evil is overcome by the hidden, but ever-present, major player in the drama: God. I am grateful to Dr. Paul Danove, who pointed this out to me during the course of the work of the Catholic Biblical Association Task Force, "The Gospel of Mark in the 21st Century," at John Carroll University, Cleveland, Ohio, on Monday, August 5, 2002. I am strongly attracted to this on both literary and theological grounds. In the end, however, because of the link I see between 1:1–13 and 16:1–8, and because

of the central roles of 14:22–25 (sixth of eleven scenes) and 15:20b–25 (fifth of nine scenes), I have retained the structure, irony, and theology outlined in Moloney, *Mark,* 276–79. Maybe 16:1–8 is the culmination of all the foreshadowing that has been a feature of the Gospel of Mark. If this is the case, it is both the final [A] scene *and* the epilogue.

85. The Gospel of Mark is our earliest extended narrative of the Easter event. It bristles with exegetical, historical, and theological issues. For a full treatment, see Moloney, *Mark,* 339–54.

86. This link is not universally accepted. For further detail, and documentation of the discussion, see Moloney, *Mark,* 344–46. It is almost universally accepted that the young man in a white robe is an angelic figure, a messenger from God (see 2 Macc 3:26, 33; Tob 5:9; Mark 9:3; Acts 1:10; 10:30; Rev 6:11; 7:9, 13; Josephus, *Ant.* 5.277). This is no doubt true, but that does not exclude the interpretation proposed above.

87. Markan theology and Pauline theology agree. Fundamental to Pauline thought is the belief that God has saved sinful humankind by his free gift of grace, made available in and through the death and resurrection of Jesus Christ (see Rom 3:21–26). It is not so much a question of how good believers might be, or how good their performance (although a life modeled on that of Jesus is demanded [see the "ethical excursus" of Rom 5:1–8:39]). What ultimately changes the relationship between God and the human story, lost since the fall of Adam, is the boundless goodness of God (Rom 5:12–21), made visible in Jesus Christ (see Rom 8:31–39). See also Marcus, *Mark,* 73–75; J. Marcus, "Mark—Interpreter of Paul," *NTS* 46 (2000): 473–87.

88. Hooker, *St. Mark,* 394. See also A. Lindemann, "Die Osterbotschaft des Markus: Zur theologischen Interpretation von Mark 16.1–8," *NTS* 26 (1979–1980): 298–17; H. Paulsen, "Mk XVI 1–8," *NovT* 22 (1980): 138–75; J. L. Magness, *Sense and Absence: Structure and Suspension in the Ending of Mark's Gospel* (Society of Biblical Literature Semeia Series; Atlanta: Scholars Press, 1986); E. S. Malbon, "Texts and Contexts: Interpreting the Disciples in Mark," in *In the Company of Jesus* (Louisville: Westminster John Knox, 2000), 100–30.

# PART THREE

# MARK THE
# INTERPRETER

# CHAPTER 6

# Mark the Interpreter of Jesus of Nazareth

Our reading of Mark 1:1–16:8 has shown that the story of the gospel as we now have it is the result of careful, skillful, and at times remarkable storytelling techniques. The Greek may be rudimentary but the storytelling is refined. *Mark the storyteller* was not primarily interested in reporting, in a dispassionate fashion, the brute facts of the life of Jesus. On numerous occasions during our reading of the gospel through Chapters 4 and 5, we commented that Mark received traditions from his own community, and perhaps from other sources. In fashioning his story, he has shaped those sources to provide the tale of the Gospel of Mark. This process of respectfully receiving traditions that came to him, and shaping them in order to tell a story with its own point of view, means that Mark was an *interpreter* of the traditions. Many of the traditions may have come to Mark because of a desire in the early church, especially among second-generation Christians, to preserve the brute facts of the story of Jesus. But *Mark the interpreter* wished to go beyond that concern, all the while not abandoning his responsibility to tell the story of Jesus to a newer generation. Mark's Gospel indicates his desire to communicate a particular understanding of Jesus of Nazareth. He makes his intentions clear in the first line of his gospel: "The beginning of the good news of Jesus *Christ, the Son of God*" (Mark 1:1).

Part 3 of our study of the Gospel of Mark will be devoted to an analysis of Mark's two major interpretative activities. This chapter will be devoted to Mark's interpretation of the imminence of the reigning presence of God in the person, teaching, death, and resurrection of Jesus and to his being the Christ, the Son of God, and the Son of Man.

Chapter 7 will trace his understanding of the Christian community, reflected in the relationship between Jesus and the disciples and in his interpretation of the community's celebration of the Lord's Supper.

The structure of the Gospel of Mark indicates an interpreter's interest in Jesus as "the Christ, the Son of God" (see 1:1, 11; 9:7; 15:39 [the Son of God]; 1:1; 8:29; 14:61–62; 15:31–32 [the Christ]). The expression "the Son of Man" is used by Jesus to speak of himself on fourteen occasions (see 2:10, 28; 8:31, 38; 9:9, 12, 31; 10:33, 45; 13:26; 14:21 [twice], 41, 62). Until relatively recent times, it was thought that the best way to come to grips with the Christology of the New Testament was through the study of the use of these so-called christological "titles" for Jesus across the gospels and the letters of Paul.[1] Much of the subtlety of the christological perspective of the NT authors, however, can be lost in this approach. There is more to the identity of a character in a story than the names attributed to that character. This is particularly important for a proper understanding of the Markan interpretation of Jesus. Therefore, before a study of the more traditional approach to the Markan Jesus by analyzing the titles used in the gospel, some consideration must be given to Mark's more subtle insistence that Jesus is the person whose coming introduces the reigning presence of God as king.

## Jesus and the Kingdom of God

Mark's use of the expression "the kingdom of God" (ἡ βασιλεία τοῦ θεοῦ; *hē basileia tou theou*) came to him from one of the earliest church's most precious memories of Jesus. Scholars are in universal agreement that Jesus saw his mission as the establishment of the kingdom of God among men and women. They do *not* agree, however, on what is meant by the expression "the kingdom of God."[2] Jesus, Mark, and the other evangelists who carried on the Jesus tradition, never bothered to explain what the expression might mean. It was taken for granted that listeners and readers would know what it meant, but it is not a simple concept. Passing from Jesus' original Aramaic into the Greek of the Gospels, and then into our English translation, "the kingdom of God" has lost its dynamism and urgency. Our word "kingdom" is static. It carries with it the idea of a territory with borders within which a king has authority. For Jesus, and the Christian tradition that followed, it had no such limitations.

Many scholars helpfully suggest that we would better catch the original meaning of Jesus' expression by means of the paraphrase "the reigning presence of God as king," or simply "God's reigning presence."

Jesus understood his presence, his works, and his words as bringing into the human story the possibility that God would reign in the lives, hearts, and minds of men and women. This sounds simple, but it has profound ethical and eschatological consequences. Such preaching demanded un-conditional conversion (see Mark 1:14–15), and insisted that, while God's reign impinged on the human story in the person of Jesus, it was not yet fully realized. The final realization of the reigning presence of God as king would mark the end of all time, the end of all human at-tempts to thwart God's design. Leander Keck succinctly and accurately described Jesus' preaching of the reigning presence of God as "the recti-fying power of the impinging future."[3] This expression catches both the demand for conversion for entry into the kingdom (the rectifying power), and the tension that exists in Jesus' teaching of a kingdom that is both present, and yet to come (the impinging future). Nevertheless, every attempt to explain what is meant by the reigning presence of God fails to explain fully all its implications, because the major player is God. Jesus, therefore, and those of us who attempt to understand these concepts, must have recourse to parable and symbol. As God and God's design lie beyond our knowledge, we are forced to speak of them as best we can.[4]

Mark takes much of this urgency, tension, and mystery from the tradition, and uses the expression "the kingdom of God" fourteen times. As always, however, Mark does not simply repeat the tradition; he inter-prets it by associating the life, death, and resurrection *of Jesus* with the advent of the reigning presence *of God* as king. As Jesus bursts onto the scene, he announces that the reigning presence of God is at hand, and that entry into the kingdom calls for radical conversion (1:14–15). This idea of the nearness of the reigning presence of God, to be experienced in the presence of Jesus, is sustained across the episodes that follow these first words of Jesus. As the reign of God breaks into the human story, the first followers of Jesus respond wordlessly to the call of Jesus to join him on his journey (1:16–20). The powers of evil are overcome: de-mons (1:21–28), sickness and taboo (vv. 29–31), sickness and demons (vv. 32–34), leprosy and taboo (vv. 40–45). As the narrative unfolds, Jesus' presence continues to overcome evil powers (2:1–12; 3:1–6), but opposition to Jesus mounts. One does not have to accept that God's reigning presence is impinging on one's world. Human beings are free to choose (2:1–3:6). The first disciples accept it (1:16–20), but the leaders of Israel do not. They decide that Jesus must be destroyed (2:1–3:6; see 3:6). Although the expression "the kingdom of God" is not found across these passages, what happens here flows from Jesus' proclamation of the approach of the reigning presence of God (1:14–15). These first pages of the Gospel of Mark insist that in the presence *of Jesus* one encounters the reigning presence *of God* as king.

The same notion lies behind Jesus' words to his disciples in 9:1. Having called his followers to take up the cross and follow him, he encourages them by telling them that it will not be long before they experience the coming of the reigning presence of God, "with power." Many who are standing there, called to follow Jesus into suffering, will experience the ultimate vindication of the suffering Son of Man by means of the action of God in the resurrection (8:34–9:1). The kingdom of God will come with power.[5] A similar time line is established for the coming of the kingdom at Jesus' final meal. As he looks beyond the broken body and the spilled blood of his crucifixion, he assures his puzzled disciples, that he will drink of the fruit of the vine anew "in the kingdom of God" (14:25). This passage points to the period after the resurrection, where the vindicating action of God assured the ongoing presence of the kingdom within the believing and praying Christian community, a new temple of God built upon the rejected cornerstone (12:10–11; see 11:22–25; 13:24–37; 14:57–58; 15:29, 38–39). The definitive establishment of the reigning presence of God is also promised to those who, like children, are open to all that God offers, and not determined by their own designs and agendas (10:14–15; see also 9:35–37). There are others who are close to the kingdom (12:34: the scribe) or looking for the kingdom (15:43: Joseph of Arimathea) in their openness to the person and the word of Jesus.

After Jesus' failed attempt to draw the rich man into discipleship, he insists how difficult it will be for the rich (10:23, 26), indeed for anyone (v. 24), to enter the kingdom of God. When the disciples ask the obvious question—Who then can be saved? (v. 26)—Jesus provides the key to its mystery. Human beings do not have the power or authority to break into God's reigning presence. No one can enter the kingdom by his or her own authority—but everything is possible with God (v. 27). All that Jesus is, says, and does, depends on God. The centrality of his preaching the kingdom of God points away from the person of Jesus. At the heart of Mark's *story of Jesus* is the proclamation of *the coming of God as king*. Jesus is unexplainably the one whose life, death, and resurrection brought in the kingdom. Nevertheless, it is the kingdom *of God*, not the kingdom of *Jesus*. For this reason, when Jesus wishes to teach about the kingdom, he is unable to describe it in ordinary terms; he must tell the parables of the kingdom (see 4:26, 30). One can only offer parables or similitudes, *comparisons* based on human experiences that illuminate the mystery of the kingdom of God. But they can never exhaust this mystery, because it is a gift of God. Thus, despite their failure and inability to understand the parables, Jesus tells his disciples and those who surround him that they are indeed blessed: to them "has been given the secret of the kingdom of God" (4:11).[6]

The Gospel of Mark was the first of the four gospels to appear. Continuing the Jesus tradition, Mark uses "the kingdom of God" to begin an interpretation of the life, teaching, death, and resurrection of Jesus that will become increasingly important with the passing of time. Jesus is, in a mysterious way, the presence of the divine among us. There is distance between Mark's understanding of Jesus' presence as "the rectifying power of the imminent future" (Keck), and the Johannine presentation of Jesus as the incarnation of the divine, preexistent Logos (John 1:1–18). But, despite the subtlety of Mark's association of the life, teaching, death, and resurrection *of Jesus* with the advent of the reigning presence *of God* as king, the Johannine Christology can be seen as a later consequence of the Markan Christology. The shadow of a unique and authoritative presence of "the divine" is to be seen in the Markan Jesus.[7]

The prologue to the Gospel (1:1–13) informs the reader that some of the names and attributes given to God in the Old Testament can now be applied to Jesus. He is described as "Son of God" (1:1, 11), "the Lord" who is to come (vv. 2–3), "the mightier one" (v. 7), the one who will dispense the Holy Spirit (v. 8), and who reestablishes God's original created order (vv. 12–13). This Son of God takes over not only the names of God, but also some of his functions, giving the Spirit and restoring the original order of creation. Mark does not *identify* Jesus with God, but, as Joel Marcus comments, "where Jesus is acting, God is acting."[8] The authority of God lies behind his healing of the sick, his authority over the demonic, and even over death itself. This notion is well caught when, after the cure of the Gerasene demoniac, Jesus instructs the cured man to return to his home town and his friends, "and tell them how much *the Lord* (ὁ κύριος; *ho kyrios*) has done for you" (5:19). The man does as he is instructed, but "began to proclaim in the Decapolis how much *Jesus* had done for him" (v. 20). The actions of God are identified with the actions of Jesus.

On one occasion Jesus uses OT language used to indicate a theophany: "I am he" (6:50b: ἐγώ εἰμι; *egō eimi*). This formula is regularly adopted in the OT to refer to the presence of the living God (see Gen 15:1; 26:24; 46:3; Isa 41:13–14; 43:1, 3), a God who has authority over the terror of the sea (see Exod 14–15; Deut 7:2–7; Job 9:8; 38:16; Pss 29:3; 65:8; 77:20; 89:10; 93:3–4; Isa 43:1–5; 51:9–10). In Mark 6:48–50, Jesus comes across the stormy waters to his disciples. They think they are seeing a ghost, and cry out in fear (6:48–50a). The formula "I am he" is often associated with the OT exhortation not to fear, and this is also found in Mark 6:50b: "Take heart, it is I; *have no fear*" (μὴ φοβεῖσθε; *mē phobeisthe*).[9]

These indications of the presence, already in the Gospel of Mark, of what might be called a "high Christology" should not be forgotten. In the end, the Gospel of Mark tells of what God does for the human situation by means of the life, teaching, death, and resurrection of his beloved Son (see 1:1, 11; 9:7; 15:39). God may not appear as an active character in Mark's Gospel, but God's design lies behind every turn in the story.

# Jesus as the Christ

Mark the interpreter makes it clear from the first line of the gospel that he regards Jesus of Nazareth as "the Christ." Indeed, the story he is about to tell will proclaim that this truth is "good news" (εὐαγγέλιον; *euangelion*). But the proclamation of the good news that Jesus is the Christ, so taken for granted by later Christians down through the centuries, is a major interpretative action on the part of Mark. The expression "the Christ," as we have come to understand it, was not at all common in the world that produced Christianity. Yet, for Mark, it is a word he uses to open his story of Jesus of Nazareth. The Greek ὁ χριστός *(ho christos)* renders a Hebrew/Aramaic word "Messiah" that literally means "the anointed one."

## The Christ

It probably comes as a surprise to the modern reader of the Gospel of Mark that there was no fixed idea of what "the Christ" meant in first-century Judaism, within which the Christian movement was born. It is not as if Mark took over a ready-made title of honor for Jesus, containing everything he wanted to say about Jesus. A close identification between "Jesus" and "Christ" developed quickly in the early Church. It had already been forged into a proper name for Jesus of Nazareth ("Jesus Christ") by the time of the Apostle Paul.[10] This leads us to think that "the Christ" was a long-awaited figure who would restore God's design for Israel and the chosen people. It was not quite like that. The idea of a "messiah" circulated at the time of Jesus, but it was not universally held, and there were many ways in which the figure was expected to act. For the Essenes at Qumran, for example, although the expression "the messiah" is not widely found in the scrolls they left behind, there were several understandings of the coming Messiah: a conquering military

figure, a more spiritual figure who would restore Israel to a right relationship with God, or a combination of both.[11] "Thus, postexilic Jews as
a whole did not expect 'the messiah,' and those that did held divergent
opinions about the anointed one or anointed ones. The New Testament
proclamations about Jesus the Messiah . . . need to be read in this context."[12] Therefore, in our reflections on Mark's designation of Jesus as
"the Christ" (1:1), we need to be aware that Mark was acting as an interpreter, and not simply claiming that Jesus fulfilled a commonly held
messianic expectation. Some did speak of a Christ figure, but many did
not, and those who did had different ideas of what the expression
meant, or how the figure would restore Israel's fortunes. In the light
of this, we recognize Mark's interpretation of Jesus' being "the Christ"
as the creative theological activity of an early Christian thinker and
writer.[13]

## The good news: Jesus is the Christ

Within the first line of the gospel, so clear in its affirmation that
Jesus is the Christ, and that his being the Christ is "good news," there
*may be* a qualification of this description of Jesus. It is not altogether
certain that the words "Son of God" (υἱοῦ θεοῦ; *huiou theou*) in Mark
1:1 are original,[14] but as the gospel proceeds, it will soon become clear
that Mark wishes the reader to understand that these two designations
belong together.[15] Whether or not the expression "Son of God" was
originally present in Mark 1:1, the prologue to the gospel (vv. 1–13)
quickly associates the two expressions. Jesus is not named as the Messiah
across the rest of the passage, but a number of other significant expressions are used to describe him: "the Lord" (v. 3), "the mightier one"
(v. 7), the one who will "baptize with the Holy Spirit" (v. 8), and, as a climax: "My beloved Son, with you I am well pleased" (v. 11). There are no
doubts about Jesus' being called "Son" by the divine voice from heaven
in v. 11. Thus, the association made in v. 1 between "the Christ" and
"Son of God" is entirely appropriate. The close association between "the
Christ" and "the Son" will become clearer to the reader as the story
unfolds.[16]

But the piling up of these titles of honor, almost overwhelming the
reader, fades as the story itself begins to unfold. Indeed, it is not until Peter's confession in 8:29 that the expression "the Christ" reappears in the
story.[17] Mark certainly interprets Jesus of Nazareth as the Christ, but
there is more to Mark's understanding of Jesus' messianic status than
may, at first, meet the eye. The further descriptions of Jesus across

1:1–13, and the promise that Jesus' being the Christ will also lead to his being the Son in whom the Father is well pleased, indicate to the reader that the Markan portrait of Jesus as the Christ may contain some surprises. As we saw in our reading of the story as a whole, there can be no doubt that Mark wanted to insist *that* Jesus is the Christ, but what calls for further investigation is *how* Jesus acted out his messianic role. How does Jesus the Messiah act as a Son in whom the Father is well pleased?

## Who is this man?

Across the first half of the story (1:14–8:30) Jesus acts with authority. He calls others to follow him, and they do, without question (1:16–20; 2:13–14; 3:13). He performs actions indicating that the reigning presence of God is with him, overcoming the evils of sickness, taboo, demons, the threat of nature gone wild, and death itself (1:21–28, 29–31, 40–45; 2:1–11; 3:1–6; 4:35–41; 5:1–20, 21–43; 6:31–44; 7:24–30, 31–37; 8:1–9, 22–26).[18] He teaches authoritatively of the mysterious inbreak of the imminent yet impinging presence of God as king (1:14–15), especially by means of his teaching in parables, summoning his listeners to repentance and a fullness of life (4:1–34). Even his actions are seen as an authoritative teaching (see 1:27). It is not as if any single one of these actions could be pointed to as proof that the Christ had appeared in Jesus of Nazareth, but questions are asked, and an aura of wonder surrounds him: Who can this man be? (See 1:27, 37; 2:2, 12; 3:7–9, 20; 4:1; 6:14–16, 33–34, 53–56; 7:37; 8:1–2.)

Toward the end of the first half of the story, after two miracles worked in Gentile lands, for the Syrophoenician woman and the deaf man who had difficulty in speaking (7:24–37; see the indications that Jesus is always in Gentile territory in vv. 24 and 31), there emerges a first suggestion that Jesus might be the Christ. The man's ears are opened, and he begins to speak clearly, but Jesus charges the crowd to tell no one (vv. 35–36). The response of the crowd, however, is hardly silence: "And they were astonished beyond measure, saying, 'He has done all things well; he even makes the deaf hear and the dumb speak'" (v. 37). Ironically, Mark places on the lips of a Gentile crowd words that make a clear allusion to Isa 35:5–6. Speaking of the coming of God for the restoration of Jerusalem, over against all her enemies, the prophet announces: "Then the eyes of the blind will be opened, the ears of the deaf unsealed . . . and the tongue of the dumb sing for joy." This passage was already used in pre-Christian times to announce the Messiah,[19] and rapidly became part of the Christian adaptation of the Old Testament to describe Jesus (see Matt 11:5//Luke 7:22; Acts 26:18).[20]

However, again with reference to 7:36, accompanying this wonder and excited questioning, Jesus repeatedly insists that news of his miraculous deeds is not to be spread abroad (see 1:44; 3:12; 5:43; 7:36; 8:26). These commands to silence led Wilhelm Wrede to suggest that the idea developed in the early church that Jesus was the Messiah, but that he never made any such claim.[21] Since that time, the so-called "messianic secret" has been often used as the key to unlock the interpretation of the Gospel of Mark.[22] But this must have been the worst-kept secret in the history of secrecy. After the first command to secrecy (1:44), Mark reports: "But he went out and began to talk freely about it, and to spread the news so that Jesus could no longer openly enter a town, but was out in the country. And people came to him from every quarter" (1:45). The same could be said for his command that no one report that Jairus's daughter had been raised from the dead (5:43). Furthermore why does Jesus command the Gerasene demoniac to announce what *the Lord* had done for him, with the result that the ex-demoniac announces what *Jesus* did for him (5:19–20)?[23]

The regular command to silence certainly is important for Mark the interpreter's presentation of Jesus as the Messiah, but the secret is not kept. It simply points the reader elsewhere. The origin of the command may well lie with Jesus, but for Mark it is a technique to make sure that the reader does not think that Jesus' messianic status is to be understood in terms of his being a miracle worker. Miracles are important. They demonstrate the reigning presence of God in Jesus as he sweeps away the evils of sickness, demon possession, taboo, angry nature, and untimely death. The miracles are a means to an end, not an end in themselves. To understand Jesus as a miracle worker is to misunderstand Jesus—and Jesus' commands to silence regularly remind the reader that, however badly the secret is kept, miracles do not explain who he is. But if they do not, then what does?

The narrative has already provided hints that Jesus' presence arouses opposition. While the powers of evil collapse before the authority of his word and person, opposition mounts. This has been systematically presented in the conflicts between Jesus and the leaders of Israel in 2:1–3:6. At the heart of the passage Jesus warns: "The days will come when the bridegroom is taken away from them" (2:20), and it concludes with the ominous remark from the narrator: "The Pharisees went out and immediately held counsel with the Herodians against him, how to destroy him" (3:6). Similar anger and opposition appear in 7:1–13, where Jesus questions attachment to human traditions that threatens the designs of God. But the answer to the question concerning Jesus' messianic status emerges more clearly as the first half of the gospel draws to a close and opens the door upon the second half of the story.

Our description of the plot of the Gospel of Mark showed that 8:22–26, the curing of the blind man at Bethsaida, opens a section of the narrative that closes with the miracle of the curing of blind Barti-maeus in 10:46–52.[24] Between the two miracles where blind men are cured, Jesus announces his forthcoming passion three times (8:31; 9:31; 10:32–34). At Caesarea Philippi, after the total blindness of those who think that Jesus is a precursor to the Messiah (8:27–28; see v. 22), Peter is the first character in the story to confess: "You are the Christ" (8:29). In this confession he repeats the partial sight of the man who could see human beings that looked like walking trees (see vv. 23–24). Jesus commands that no one say anything of this (8:30). Jesus is the Messiah (see 1:1), but it is possible to misunderstand the implications of the truth of Peter's words. As will become obvious as one follows the disciples through the gospel, they struggle to accept that Jesus' being the Messiah means he must suffer and die on the cross, and on the third day rise again. For that reason, as the second half of the gospel opens, Jesus announces his forthcoming suffering, death, and resurrection (8:31). Jesus is the Messiah, but only in so far as he is the suffering and vindicated Son of Man (see also 9:31; 10:32–34).

## The crucified Christ

There are four references to "the Christ" in the second half of the gospel (12:35; 13:21–22; 14:61; 15:32). Each is carefully plotted and used by Mark the storyteller and interpreter to instruct the reader on the correct understanding of Jesus, the Messiah. Interestingly, two references indicate *false understandings* of the Messiah. The first discussion, found in 12:35–37, is one of the most singular elements in Mark's interpretation of Jesus' messianic status. The early church always regarded the Old Testament as part of its sacred Scriptures, and explained Jesus in the light of the hopes of Israel. It was thus accepted that Jesus was the fulfillment of the messianic hopes of Israel associated with the line of David. The Messiah was to be a "Son of David." For example, both Matthew (see Matt 1:1–17) and Paul (see Rom 1:1–4) make the claim quite explicitly. Mark appears to be unhappy with this identification. When Jesus is being welcomed into Jerusalem with the acclamation, "Blessed is the kingdom of our father David that is coming!" (11:10), Jesus' response is to enter Jerusalem, go to the temple, gaze ominously at all the surroundings, and withdraw to Bethany. There is no indication that he accepts the Davidic acclamation. In discussing the scribal tradition that the Christ was to be the Son of David (12:35), he shows, by means of a subtle explanation of Ps 110:1, that this cannot be correct. In the Psalm, David, inspired by the Holy Spirit, announces that God (the Lord) says to David's Lord (the Messiah), that he is to sit at God's right hand, so that all his enemies can be subjugated (Mark 12:36). Jesus thus concludes: "David himself calls him (the Messiah) Lord; so how can he be his son?" (v. 37). Whatever other early Christian interpreters (e.g. Matthew and Paul) made of Jesus as the Son of David, for Mark, Jesus the Christ must not be identified with the tradition of a Son of David. Jesus' messianic status had nothing to do with his coming in splendor to restore the political and majestic authority of a royal dynasty.[25]

A similar negative use of "the Christ" appears in Jesus' final discourse on the Mount of Olives. The first half of Jesus' final discourse, delivered on the Mount of Olives (13:5–23) is strongly shaped by the events surrounding the fall and the destruction of Jerusalem and its temple in 70 C.E. (13:5–23).[26] During this section of the discourse, Jesus warns against those false "messiahs" who will arrive at the time of this terrible destruction, announcing that these events mark the end of time. They must be ignored, and recognized for what they are, "false christs" who only lead people astray (v. 23).[27] Jesus has already told his disciples (and the readers of the gospel) that the events surrounding the end of Jerusalem do not mark this moment as the end of the world. If false christs arrive, announcing that this is the end of time, they are to be ignored because, "the gospel must first be preached to all the nations" (v. 10). Only after all the nations have heard the gospel will the end time come, and the elect will be summoned from the four winds, from the ends of the earth to the ends of heaven (see v. 27).

The remaining uses of "the Christ," within the context of Jesus' suffering and death (14:61; 15:32), point the reader firmly toward Mark's interpretation of Jesus' messianic status. They form the climax to the Markan interpretation of Jesus as the Christ. During the Jewish trial of Jesus, after a series of contradictory and false charges, the high priest asks Jesus directly: "Are you the Christ, the Son of the Blessed" (14:61). Here, as in 1:1, there is an association made between Jesus' being the Messiah and the Son of God. The expression "Son of the Blessed" is a respectful Jewish way of avoiding the use of the name "God." What is surprising, however, is that Jesus accepts this description. He responds: "I am; and you will see the Son of Man seated at the right hand of power, and coming with the clouds of heaven" (v. 62). These words associate "the Christ," "the Son of God," and "the Son of Man." In doing so, Jesus articulates the basis of Markan Christology.[28] "These are perhaps the most condensed christological statements in Mark and represent the culmination of motifs that run the length of the Gospel."[29]

The final use of "the Christ" is found on the lips of those who insult Jesus as he hangs on the cross. Markan irony is present here. In words that are hurled against Jesus as an *insult,* the opposite is proclaimed: the truth about Jesus. The chief priests and the scribes abuse the falsely accused and unjustly crucified Messiah. They have been responsible for the persuasion of the Romans to execute Jesus (see 15:1, 10). As he hangs on the cross, they cry out: "He saved others; he cannot save himself. Let the Christ, the king of Israel, come down from the cross, that we may see and believe" (15:31–32). But Mark the interpreter has skillfully led the reader to a point of recognizing that it is *on the cross* that Jesus is the Christ. His opponents have completely misunderstood his messianic status. If Jesus, the Christ, were to *come down from the cross,* he would show that he was *not* the Christ.[30]

## Conclusion

Mark makes it clear in the first verse of the gospel that he has no doubt that Jesus is the Christ. However, Mark's understanding of Jesus' messianic status is entirely determined by the historical fact that Jesus of Nazareth was unjustly crucified. It is *on the cross* that Jesus is the Christ. Not only is this impossible for his opponents to understand (see 15:31–32), but within the story of the Gospel of Mark, it was also impossible for his disciples to understand. He saves others, only because he perfects his messianic role on the cross. This remains one of the enigmas of the Christian tradition, solidly founded in the Markan interpretation of Jesus as the Christ. The messianic function of Jesus of Nazareth has been best summarized by Jesus himself, as he explained to his disciples: "For the Son of Man also came, not to be served, but to serve, and to give his life as a ransom for many" (10:45). Here we see the blurring of distinctions between the designation of Jesus as "the Christ" and "the Son of Man." But they are distinctions rightfully blurred, as they point to the single saving event of the crucifixion.

# Jesus as the Son of God

The plotting of the use of "the Christ" to speak of Jesus so that the reader would look forward to the crucifixion is repeated in Mark's presentation of Jesus as "the Son (of God)."[31] The expression is found in the prologue (1:1, 11), it returns at the center of the gospel, at the scene of the transfiguration (9:7), and forms a christological climax to the account of the crucifixion. The Roman centurion, on seeing the death of Jesus, exclaims, " Truly, this man was the Son of God" (15:39).[32]

## The Son (of God)

The identification of Jesus as the Son of God is a fundamental expression of Christian belief in Jesus. As the centuries passed, and the doctrines of Christianity emerged from the great ecumenical councils, Jesus' being the Son of God developed as a crucial expression of the Christian faith, especially in relationship to the Father and the Spirit in the articulation of the doctrine of the Trinity (325 C.E.: Council of Nicea), and later in the further development of an understanding of Mary as "Mother of God" (431 C.E.: Council of Ephesus). The Markan interpretation of Jesus as the Son of God must be understood in terms of its use by an early Christian storyteller, and not in the light of important doctrines that developed later.

The most likely *background* for Mark's use of the expression to speak of Jesus comes from Jewish thought, but an important *foreground* can also be found in the Greco-Roman world. Certain great figures from Hellenism (for example, Alexander the Great, who died in 323 B.C.E.) were regarded as an earthly presence of the divine.[33] In the Roman world Caesar came to be called *divi filius* (son of God). Notice, however, I am suggesting that these notions provided *foreground* for Mark's interpretation of Jesus as the Son of God. Having its origins in Judaism, the description of Jesus as "the Son of God" would have appealed to early Greco-Roman converts. The expression may have had its origins within Judaism, but it was a familiar term for new non-Jewish converts to Christianity.[34]

However, the Jewish world provided Mark with the elements from which he forged his interpretation of Jesus. It is impossible to review here all the streams of pre-Christian thought that led Mark, and Christianity prior to Mark (e.g., Paul), to speak of Jesus as the Son of God.[35] Fundamental to the Jewish idea of a human "son of God" was the use of sonship language in such texts as 2 Sam 7:14 and Ps 2:7. The prophet Nathan tells David that he will not build a temple to house the ark of the covenant, but his son will. However, in announcing this "son," speaking in the name of God, Nathan prophesies of the son of David: "I shall be a father to him and he a son to me" (2 Sam 7:14). Psalm 2 is probably a psalm that has its background in the enthronement of a king in Israel. During the proclamation of that psalm, the decree of God is announced:

"You are my son; this day I have begotten you" (v. 7). Both of these "sonship" texts are associated with royalty, but in their original setting they did not look forward to a future messianic or eschatological era. Nevertheless, they provided material for later messianic expectations, especially those associated with the Davidic line.[36] There are also numerous places in the Old Testament where the people of God are called "son," the most famous of these being the one used by Matthew to speak of Jesus' exodus from Egypt (Matt 2:15). In its original setting (Hos 11:1), it refers to God's people, rescued from slavery in Egypt by means of the gracious action of God: "Out of Egypt I have called my son."

What most needs noticing about these Old Testament texts, which led to the use of the expression "son of God" as a messianic term in pre-Christian times, is that there is no suggestion that God in some way generated a divine son. Here the Jewish understanding of "son of God" differs from many of the Greco-Roman myths. The Jewish son of God is a human being who comes into the world via human parents, but who has a *unique relationship with God*. To use language foreign to the New Testament, one might say that the Jewish idea of "son of God" was an ideal king or people. This ideal king or people *behaved* or *functioned* as a child should relate to a parent. The later expression of the church's Christology uses the title "Son of God" to claim that Jesus *is* metaphysically the Son of God. The link between Jesus and *the Jewish background* for "son of God" provided Mark the interpreter with his language. Mark has no infancy narrative that suggests a divine parenting by means of a virgin mother (see Matt 1–2; Luke 1–2), much less the idea of Jesus as the only begotten Son of God, as one finds in the Gospel of John (see John 1:14). No doubt the early church also knew of the genuine historical memory, passed on by Jesus' contemporaries. They recalled his remarkable oneness with the will of God, expressed in the use of the expression "Abba" on the lips of Jesus in Mark 14:36, and regarded as one of the privileges of the Spirit-filled believers by Paul. They, too, like Jesus, can call out, "Abba, Father!" (see Rom 8:15; Gal 4:6). This memory of Jesus' acceptance of all that the God of Israel called him to was fundamental to the rapid application of the expression "the Son of God" to Jesus in the earliest preaching of the Christian church.

## My beloved Son

The prologue to the Markan story is a resounding affirmation of Jesus' relationship to the God of Israel as his Son. The first verse of the gospel announced the good news that Jesus was the Son of God (1:1), and this good news is affirmed as Jesus rises from the waters of John's baptism. The Baptist had already announced that Jesus would baptize with the Holy Spirit (v. 8), and at the baptism of Jesus the Spirit descends upon and takes possession of him. The Spirit continues to direct Jesus' actions as it "drove" him into the wilderness for his encounter with Satan, and his restoration of God's original order of creation (vv. 12–13). However, other signs accompany Jesus' rising from the waters of John's baptism. The heavens are split open. This is a traditional sign in the Jewish world, and also in other ancient cultures, that the heavenly is about to communicate with earth (see Gen 7:11; Isa 24:18; 64:1; Ezek 1:1; John 1:51; Rev 4:1; 11:19). Earth is below, but God resides on the other side of the firmament. The glow of the sun and the twinkling of the stars are hints of the divine splendor that lies behind the firmament of the heavens. Thus, the sign of the tearing apart of the heavens indicates that God from on high is communicating with the earth below. In 1:11 the voice of the God of Israel comes from above, addresses Jesus as his beloved Son, and indicates—already at the beginning of the story—that he is well pleased with this Son.

These words from heaven recall Ps 2:7, "You are my son," and there may also be a reminiscence of the relationship of love that existed between Abraham and Isaac, his beloved son (see LXX Gen 22:2, 12, 16; *T. Levi* 18). Perhaps this suggestion of the love between Abraham and Isaac, whom he was asked to sacrifice as a sign of his allegiance to God, is a first hint of Jesus' destiny, in his unconditional self-gift to the will of his Father. As you have seen, in the prologue to the gospel God announces that he is well pleased with his Son (1:11). The following story of the Son will show that God's pleasure works itself out in unexpected ways. What Jesus will say, do, and suffer is in accord with God's design and God's good pleasure, and thus there may also be hints of the famous words of the first chapter of Genesis. As God completed the creative action of each perfect day, he saw that "it was good."[37] God has no doubts about the allegiance of his Son.

## Listen to my beloved Son

On three occasions demonic powers show that they recognize who Jesus is. In 1:24, as Jesus performs his first expulsion of a demon, in the synagogue at Capernaum (vv. 21–28), the unclean spirit recognizes that "Jesus of Nazareth" is "the holy one of God." In the summary of Jesus' power over unclean spirits in 3:11–12, Mark reports that they fell down and cried out, "You are the Son of God" (v. 11), and the legion of demons possessing the man at Gerasa also cries out, "What have you to do with me, Jesus, Son of the Most High God" (5:7). These are important indications that the spiritual world, the world that knows more than can be understood by human means and measures, can recognize Jesus. In each case, the demons call Jesus by his correct name in order to usurp his authority. In the ancient world, to "name" someone was to claim authority over that individual.[38] The reader of the story is aware that the demons are correct, but their aggressive recognition of Jesus does nothing for the characters in the story. Indeed, in the first two of these episodes Jesus commands the evil spirits to silence (1:25; 3:12) and in the third, he destroys them by expelling them into the unclean swine and plunging them to destruction in the abyss of the sea (5:13).

But the evil spirits are correct: Jesus is the Son of God. With this in mind the reader arrives at the turning point of the narrative: Peter's confession of Jesus as the Christ, and Jesus' warning not to spread this awareness abroad (8:29–30), followed immediately by the first prediction of Jesus' forthcoming death and resurrection, and Peter's refusal to accept these words (8:31–32). Peter must keep his place *behind* Jesus, and all the disciples and the crowd must now be instructed on the need to lose their lives if they wish to save them. The messianic question has been raised and answered (8:27–30), but its consequences are yet to be spelled out in full. All who wish to be followers of Jesus are asked to take up their cross. That is what it means *to follow* Jesus, both physically and spiritually. It is by means of this form of following that they will join in the glory Jesus will share with his Father and the holy angels (8:34–9:1).

God's design for Jesus is now clear: He must suffer many things, be rejected, put to death, and on the third day rise again (8:31).[39] This comes as a shock to Peter and the disciples, but what is even more difficult for them to accept is that if they wish to be his followers, they must be prepared to accept the same destiny: suffering, rejection, death, and ultimate victory with God and the holy angels. An urgent question emerges at this stage of the gospel. Both the characters in the narrative (especially the disciples) and the readers of the story can justifiably ask by what authority this man summons others to follow him to a cross, and promises victory on the other side of such an unconditional giving of one's life for the sake of Jesus and for the Gospel.

The account of the transfiguration (9:2–8) responds to that question.[40] As Jesus turns toward Jerusalem, the cross, and the resurrection (8:31), he strains to draw his disciples with him. He urges them to join him "on the way," but they are frightened, and full of wonder (see 10:32). Taking on a divine appearance, he converses with two great figures who had been transported to heaven, Elijah and Moses. Jesus' divine authority and promise of ultimate victory cannot be questioned (9:2–4). The disciples stumble in their fear and misunderstanding (vv. 5–6). The visual manifestation of Jesus' authority to call people to suffering and death, that they might join him in glory, is not enough. Thus, a heavenly voice, as in 1:11, commands the fragile disciples: "This is my beloved Son, *listen to him*" (v. 7). Looking round, they see only Jesus, as they have always known him (v. 8). His turning toward Jerusalem, death, and resurrection, *must* take place (8:31). Those who wish to regard themselves as his disciples *must* follow him down the same path (8:34–9:1). The voice of God has announced that the man Jesus is also his beloved Son (9:7): they *must* listen to his voice! As Jesus *must* suffer, so *must* his disciples listen to his voice. No less a figure than God commands this listening to what Jesus has asked of his followers in 8:34–9:1. A new element is added to the Markan interpretation of Jesus as the Son of God. The *fact* of his sonship was announced in 1:1 and 1:11, but its *consequences* have been further clarified in 9:2–13. In close association with his exercising of his messianic role on the cross, Jesus, the Son of God, will manifest his unconditional allegiance to the Father *on the cross*. This "way of Jesus," the fulfillment of God's good pleasure in his Son (1:11; 9:7), must also be the way of the disciple.

## This man was the Son of God

As Jesus moves toward Jerusalem, Mark uses two further occasions to inform the reader of Jesus' destiny as a suffering Son of God, and a Son who depends totally on the Father. In the parable of the wicked tenants (12:1–12), there is a blending of the Old Testament symbol of a vine and its fruit (see Isa 5:1–2; Ps 80:8–13; Jer 2:21), the rejection of the prophets (Jer 7:25; 25:4; Amos 3:7; Zech 1:7; 1QpHab 2:9; 7:5), and the story of Jesus. The owner's beloved son is the final figure to be sent to the wicked tenants. The link with Jesus as the beloved Son of God in 1:11 and 9:7 is unmistakable. The beloved son is slain and his body thrown out of the vineyard. These violent actions look forward to the events that will take place at Golgotha. Jesus' final warning to his audience, however, is to tell them that the rejected stone, the slain beloved son, will become the cornerstone of a new temple (see 12:8, 10). During the discourse on the end of Jerusalem and the end of the world (13:1–37), Jesus responds to questions posed by the disciples (see v. 4). One of the questions concerns the timing of the events that bring about the end of all time (v. 4a: "When will this be?"). Such knowledge is outside the ken of the Son. The Son depends entirely on the Father, does his will, announces his word, and waits for whatever the Father may decide. Thus he can frankly state: "But of that day or that hour no one knows, not even the angels in heaven, nor the Son, but only the Father" (13:32).

Hence, the climax of the Markan interpretation of Jesus as the Son of God, as with his interpretation of his messianic status, comes during the account of his passion and death. The two interpretations lie side by side as the high priest asks Jesus, during the Jewish trial: "Are you the Christ, the Son of the Blessed?" (14:61). Jesus accepts this double designation of Christ and Son of God, and in doing so is unjustly condemned to death on the basis of his own witness. He informs his corrupt judges, however, that the death penalty they are about to mete out will not be the end of the story. He will return as the vindicated and judging Son of Man (v. 62). In the end, Jesus' sonship and his messianic status come together in 14:61–62. He is both Christ and Son of God on the cross. Only at the end of the story does a human being, ironically a Roman soldier, see the events of Jesus' crucifixion, and identify the crucified one with the Son of God (15:39).[41]

## Conclusion

Mark has focused intensely on the death of Jesus as the place where he reveals himself as both the Christ and the Son of God. Yet, he began his Gospel by claiming that this was "good news." How is that possible? Is there no sign of a victorious Messiah, as one might get in some Jewish streams of thought (Psalms of Solomon, Dead Sea Scrolls), or the return of the Son of God to his Father, as one finds in other places in the New Testament (Paul, Luke, and John)? No such signs of ultimate victory for the Christ and the Son of God appear in the Markan interpretation of Jesus. He is the Christ and the Son of God as the crucified one. This is a matter of major importance for Mark: Jesus is the crucified Christ and the crucified Son of God. It is in and through crucifixion that Jesus fulfills God's messianic design, and shows that he is the beloved Son of God, in whom the Father is well pleased (1:11; 9:7). However, the tragic end of Jesus' life is not a dreadful fate that simply falls unjustly upon him. Mark associates the categories of Messiah and Son of God with Jesus' death because he wants his readers and hearers to be aware that the crucifixion of God's Son and Messiah are part of God's larger design. This aspect of the Christology of the Gospel of Mark is a sign of the originality of the author's interpretative activity.

But there is a further designation used of Jesus throughout the Gospel of Mark that does look beyond the cross: the Son of Man. This designation for Jesus appears in close association with the Markan presentation of Jesus as Messiah and Son, for example, in 8:29–31, and especially in 14:61–62. Perhaps the most enigmatic of all the expressions used in the gospels to speak of Jesus, the Son of Man is therefore crucial to the Markan interpretation of Jesus.

## Jesus as the Son of Man

In the Gospel of Mark (and in the other gospels) "the Son of Man" is the only expression Jesus uses to speak of himself. He uses it when one would expect him to say "I." For example, he does not say: "*I* will be delivered into the hands of men, and they will kill *me*," but rather: "*The Son of Man* will be delivered into the hands of men and they will kill *him*" (see 9:31). Frequently used across all the gospels, the expression was long regarded as the key to the discovery of Jesus' own understanding of himself. It was so revered by the early church as Jesus' preferred self-designation, that the Fourth Evangelist continued to use it at the end of the first century.[42] If the gospels recorded Jesus' repeated self-identification with "the Son of Man," then an understanding of what he meant by the expression could lead to a better appreciation of his self-understanding. Jesus *never* explained to his listeners what he meant by "the Son of Man." It was taken for granted that they knew what he meant.

The discussion that follows, however, will not be concerned with the possibility that the pre-Easter Jesus spoke of himself in this way, nor will it attempt to identify Jesus' self-understanding by tracing the meaning of the expression.[43] We are concerned with Mark the interpreter. Across the Gospel of Mark, the expression appears fourteen times, always on the lips of Jesus, and always at crucial moments in the development of the plot, and in the development of Mark's interpretation of Jesus of Nazareth. After our study of Mark's interpretation of Jesus as the Christ and the Son of God, it comes as no surprise that Mark did not invent the expression "the Son of Man," and apply it to Jesus. It had a long and complicated pre-Christian Jewish background, and scholars suggest that the expression may have had its roots in ancient, and then later (perhaps gnostic) reflections on a primal or heavenly man figure.[44] Again, Mark took traditions that came to him from the Jewish origins of Christianity, and used them creatively to complete his presentation of Jesus of Nazareth, the Christ, the Son of God, and the Son of Man in whose word and person the reigning presence of God enters the world.

## The Son of Man

Pre-Christian biblical traditions provided the expression "son of man."[45] On numerous occasions in the encounters between God and his prophet Ezekiel, the prophet is reminded of his lowly human condition by the address "son of man." This is the primary meaning of the Hebrew *ben 'ādām* (and the Aramaic *bar nashā'* [or variations on that expression]). The words simply mean that the person addressed is a frail human being, a person whose existence is the result of being born of human stock. Thus, God can say to his prophet: "Son of man, get to your feet; I will speak to you" (Ezek 2:1), or "Son of man, eat what you see; eat this scroll, then go and speak to the house of Israel" (3:1). An immense distance exists between the God who commands and the prophet who is entrusted with the task of announcing the word of God (see, for example, 2:3; 3:4, 17; 6:2; 7:2; 8:5–6; 11:4; 13:2; 16:2; 17:2; 21:14, etc.).[46] This form of address "expresses . . . the weakness of the creature to whom the mighty Lord shows such condescension."[47] Although not of major formative influence in the development of the use of "the Son of Man" by Jesus in the Gospel of Mark, Ezekiel should not be entirely ignored. The same sense of wonder is found in Ps 8:5, where the psalmist asks how it can be possible that the God of creation demonstrates concern and gives attention to "the son of man." There is a sense in which Jesus' use of "the Son of Man" places him—especially in his suffering—side by side with fragile humankind.[48]

For Mark's interpretation of Jesus as the Son of Man, the most formative Old Testament passage is found in Dan 7. The book of Daniel was written in the early decades of the second century before Christ, at a time when the power of the Hellenistic empires, especially the Seleucids, based in present-day Syria and Turkey, attempted to destroy the traditional religious practices of Israel. Under the powerful rule of King Antiochus IV, those who would not follow the newly imposed pagan cults were persecuted and slain (see the description of the situation in 1 Macc 1:1–64). Two responses to this situation are recorded in the books of the Bible.[49] The two books of Maccabees (especially 1 Macc) tell of the *military revolt*, led by the Maccabee family. By means of a remarkable series of events, the Jewish forces overcame the powerful Seleucids and reestablished Jewish sacred places and practices. The second response, found in Daniel, is a more *theological* reaction to the crisis. The author does not tell of the victory of human armies, but of the ultimate victory of God.[50] Daniel 7 is the heart of the book. There, Daniel the visionary (see v. 1) sees the traditional enemies of Israel (Babylonians, Medes, Persians) as horrible animal forms emerging from the sea. Last among them, the most terrible enemy emerges (vv. 2–8). This figure, with a mouth full of boasting, represents the Seleucid empire, and especially the figure of Antiochus IV (a small horn who has rooted out three other horns to make its way).[51] But the scene changes. A court is set up, and a divine figure takes the throne, amid a blazing of flames and wheels burning with fire. The appearance of God in Ezek 1:4–28 lies behind this figure who sits in judgment. The books are opened, and all the enemies of Israel are deprived of their power, and the most terrible beast is slain, its body destroyed and consigned to the flames (Dan 7:9–12). God has reversed the situation of vv. 2–8, and in the place of the threatening animals there appears, coming on the clouds of heaven, "one like a son of man." To him is given all power, honor, and kingship. The whole world recognizes him, and his rule is everlasting (vv. 13–14).

As is traditional in apocalyptic texts, the fast-moving and symbolic vision is then explained by an interpreting angel (vv. 15–22).[52] In vv. 23–27 the saga of vv. 2–14 is narrated, but with a special focus on the fourth beast who devastated the kingdoms of the earth, and insulted God ("the Most High"). He persecuted and killed the holy ones of the Most High, those who remained loyal to God, and would not give in to the imposition of a religion that was an insult to God (vv. 22–25). He will be judged and destroyed, and the faithful in Israel, those who have never wavered in their unconditional acceptance of the religion of Israel and the ultimate Lordship of God, will be given kingship and rule, an everlasting authority over every empire (vv. 26–28). The message of the vision in the night (see v. 1) is clear. No matter how much insult, suffering, persecution, pain, and death must be endured, ultimate vindication and victory are promised to those who remain loyal to God and never abandon his ways. They may appear to be humiliated and slain, but in the end, they will reign over all the nations. God will give them all authority and ultimate victory. What is promised to the holy ones of the Most High in v. 27 repeats the promise made to "the one like a son of man" in v. 14. The "one like a son of Man" of v. 13 is the personification of "the holy ones of the Most High," the loyal Israelites of vv. 25–27.[53] As the enemies of Israel are described as beasts, the personification of those loyal to the one true God is described as a human being: "one like a son of man."[54]

This is the source of the use of "the Son of Man" as the self-designation of Jesus in the gospel traditions. It most probably had its beginnings in words that Jesus used to speak of himself, no longer "one like a son of man," but "*the* Son of *the* Man."[55] The majority of interpreters do not read the use of "son of man" in Daniel 7, or the development of its use in the gospels in this way. They look to the use of Daniel 7 in other Jewish texts, especially in the *Similitudes of Enoch* and *Fourth Ezra*.[56] Although very different, both of these early reinterpretations of Daniel 7 regard the Son of Man as the Messiah, hidden by God, who will return at the end of time.[57] Thus, many scholars claim that in the gospels "the Son of Man" originally referred to an end-time figure (perhaps other than Jesus), and that the description of Jesus as a present and suffering Son of Man developed in the Christian tradition. My interpretation runs in the opposite direction. As I have argued above, already in Daniel 7 the figure represents the suffering and ultimately vindicated holy ones of the Most High. The origin of the use of "the Son of Man" (perhaps with Jesus himself) was associated with suffering and vindication. The early church, as with Judaism (the *Similitudes* and *Fourth Ezra*), gradually developed the use of the expression to speak of the return of the Son of Man as judge.[58]

These discussions guide us in the evaluation of Mark the interpreter of Jesus as "the Son of Man." They lie behind our evaluation of how *Mark* used his traditions in a presentation of Jesus of Nazareth, the crucified Christ and Son of God, who is also the suffering, but ultimately vindicated, Son of Man.

## The authority of the Son of Man

The most satisfying way to appreciate Mark's development of his interpretation of Jesus as "the Son of Man" is to follow the strategic use he makes of the expression across the unfolding plot of the gospel.[59] It is surprising that from Mark 1:1 to 8:30 the expression appears on only two occasions, and both have to do with Jesus' authority. Within the context of Jesus' initial series of conflicts with the leaders of Israel (2:1–3:6), on two occasions his authority is questioned. Jesus' surprising words to the paralytic man who is let down through the roof of Jesus' home in Capernaum (2:1–12) are: "My son, your sins are forgiven" (v. 5). This creates the suggestion that Jesus is a blasphemer, as only God can forgive sins (vv. 6–7). Jesus' response to this murmuring is to cure the man, but not simply to effect a cure. Jesus never works miracles just for the sake of it! He informs his questioners that he is performing this miracle "that you may know that the Son of Man has authority to forgive sins" (v. 10). The subsequent curing of the man, who takes up his pallet and goes home (vv. 11–12), is proof of the authority of Jesus as the Son of Man. This is very puzzling for the reader. Why does Jesus speak of the authority of the Son of Man? Even if Mark could presuppose that his readers knew of the OT background to the Son of Man, the appearance of the expression at this stage of the story is surprising. And that is the way Mark wishes it to strike the reader! This earliest use of "the Son of Man" who has authority to forgive sins raises questions—and does not provide answers. It is a moment in the story that cannot be explained by what has gone before, or by its own immediate context.[60] In other words, the reader comes away from 2:1–12 with questions very much like those raised by all who witnessed what had happened: "they were all amazed and glorified God, saying, 'We never saw anything like this!'" (v. 12). On encountering the more systematic presentation of Jesus as the Son of Man in the second half of the gospel (8:31–15:47) the reader will come to recognize Jesus' God-given authority.

The same impression is made on the reader in 2:23–28. Jesus is questioned about the performance of his disciples, plucking the heads of grain on a Sabbath. Accused that his disciples are performing unlawful acts on a Sabbath (v. 24), Jesus' response is to ask his questioners to look beyond the legislation of the minutiae of how one must observe the Sabbath. David, a great hero for Israel, had allowed parallel activities (vv. 25–27), but the ultimate reason for the disciples' behavior reaches outside Jewish history and traditions. It depends on the authority of Jesus, the Son of Man: "The Sabbath was made for man, not man for the Sabbath; so the Son of Man is lord even of the Sabbath" (vv. 27–28).[61] Something about the authority of the presence of Jesus calls for further explanation. It will be provided as the narrative reaches its climax. In the meantime, the people in the story and the reader of the story have been provided with two uses of the expression "the Son of Man" by Jesus (2:10, 28) that can only lead them to ask: "Who, then, is this Son of Man?" (see John 12:34). In all its simplicity, this careful plotting of two unexplained uses by Jesus of the expression "the Son of Man" keeps the reader attentive, awaiting further episodes or words from Jesus that will help to understand the authority of the Son of Man over sin and over the Sabbath.[62]

## The Son of Man must suffer many things ... but he will be vindicated

On three occasions across the center of the story, Jesus speaks of his oncoming death *and resurrection* (8:31; 9:31; 10:33–34). The words of Jesus in 9:31 are stark: "The Son of Man will be given into the hands of men, and they will kill him; and when he is killed, after three days he will rise." But the predictions of his death and resurrection in 8:31 and

10:33–34 have been written in the light of the events of Jesus' suffering, death, and resurrection, as reported in Mark 14–16.[63] Jesus probably did speak of the real possibility of his oncoming death, and may well have used the words "the Son of Man" to do so. Whatever may be the case with that question, for *Mark the interpreter*, Jesus willingly accepts all that God asks of him, and journeys along the way toward Jerusalem (see 8:27; 9:33–34; 10:52), toward insult, suffering, death, *and resurrection*. As Mark wrote the story of Jesus, he *knew* of the events of Calvary, and of the experience of the risen Lord. He could thus adopt "the Son of Man," looking back to its use in Daniel 7, to speak of Jesus, but refer explicitly to what actually happened to Jesus. Despite the cost, nothing less than death itself, Jesus remained loyal to the God of Israel, his mysterious "Father" (see 14:36). However, at no place in the gospel does Mark present "the Son of Man" purely as a suffering figure. He will be vindicated, and, in the passion predictions, the constant reference to the resurrection makes that clear to the reader. This theme of vindication and ultimate victory and universal rule (Dan 7:14, 27) will be developed in the more apocalyptic sayings (Mark 13:26; 14:62). But first and foremost, Jesus is the suffering and vindicated "Son of Man," the personification and perfection of the promise made to suffering Israel in Daniel 7.

The passion predictions of 8:31, 9:31, and 10:33–34, so central to the unfolding story of Jesus,[64] can serve as a key to the other sayings in the gospel where Jesus refers to himself as the suffering and vindicated Son of Man. As he comes down from the mountain of the transfiguration, he explains to his awestruck and puzzled disciples that they are not to speak of their experience until the Son of Man, who "must suffer many things and be treated with contempt" (9:12), has risen from death (9:9). On two occasions Jesus speaks of himself as "the Son of Man" when telling of his future betrayal (14:21), and then when announcing the arrival of the betrayer (14:41). These sayings could be judged as focusing only on the suffering of the Son of Man: "The hour has come; the Son of Man is betrayed into the hands of sinners" (v. 41). But such is not the case. Earlier Jesus has warned: "For the Son of Man goes as it is written of him, but woe to that man by whom the Son of Man is betrayed! It would have been better for that man if he had not been born" (v. 21). The betrayal of the Son of Man into the hands of sinners, unto suffering and death, fulfils the Scriptures, as Jesus lives out the promise made in Daniel 7. What is more, the betrayer will not have the last word; God will. For this purpose Jesus utters his threat: The betrayal is a necessary although paradoxical part of God's design, the fulfillment of what was written about the Son of Man, whose vindication will be matched by disaster for the betrayer.[65]

Two further uses of "the Son of Man" by Jesus stand alone in their association of suffering and vindication. In terms of the flow of the narrative, the first of these is found in 8:38. Often regarded at one and the same time as the most difficult, but the most decisive, of the Markan Son of Man sayings, it must be placed within its context. The passage reads: "For whoever is ashamed of me and my words in this adulterous and sinful generation, of him will the Son of Man also be ashamed, when he comes in the glory of his Father with the holy angels." What are these "words" of Jesus? Mark 8:34–38 is Jesus' invitation to all who would be his followers to take up their cross and follow him (v. 34), to lose their lives for his sake and the sake of the gospel. It is through this process of self-loss that one finds oneself (v. 35). This is the one true way to find one's life, our most treasured possession (vv. 36–37). The first passion prediction (v. 31) made it clear to the disciples and the reader that loss of self to find true life will be the way of Jesus, the Son of Man. They are now called to follow him down that way. It is the association between the call to join the suffering and vindicated Son of Man and the promise of ultimate vindication that is expanded in v. 38.[66] The words of Jesus in vv. 34–37 can cause fear and shame. They must not, or else the finally vindicated suffering Son of Man will be ashamed of those who reject him.

Closely associated with this is the saying found in 10:45: "For the Son of Man also came, not to be served but to serve, and to lay down his life for the ransom of many." This saying serves as a christological conclusion to the central section of the gospel, dedicated to the instruction of the failing disciples (8:22–10:52).[67] The disciples have been called to the cross (8:34–38; 10:35–40) and to humble service (9:33–37; 10:41–44), but they do not go alone. They are followers of the Son of Man whose life and death are dedicated to service and unconditional self-gift unto death, so that others may have life. The themes of suffering and vindication are developed theologically in this saying, and hold the key to a proper understanding of Mark the interpreter. With these words Jesus sums up not only the purpose of his life and death, but also the purpose of the lives and death of all who would claim to be his followers. Contrary to what one might expect, self-gift in service and death does not end in humiliation and nothingness, but brings life to many.[68] An association of the suffering and vindicated "one like a son of man" in Daniel 7 with Jesus "the Son of Man," developed in the experience of Jesus and in the teaching of the early church. Rightly has Vincent Taylor claimed, "This saying is one of the most important in the Gospels."[69]

## The Son of Man will come in glory

Jesus promises a share in the glory of the Father and the holy angels to those who accept, and are not ashamed of his foretelling of his own destiny (8:31) and the destiny of all who would follow him to a cross and loss of self for his sake and for the sake of the gospel (vv. 34–38). On the basis of that saying alone, the reader can begin to understand why, at the beginning of his ministry, Jesus could claim to have authority over sin and over the Sabbath (2:10, 28). Forging even closer links with Dan 7:13–14, the remaining words of Jesus that use "the Son of Man" speak explicitly of the return of the Son of Man "coming in clouds" (13:26), "coming with the clouds of heaven" (14:62) to execute judgment.[70] Within the context of Jesus' discourse on the end of Jerusalem and the end of the world in Mark 13, Jesus has told the disciples that before the end-time "the gospel must be preached to the nations" (13:10). But once that is in place, the Son of Man who has suffered, died, and has been raised, will have the final word. He will appear in power and glory, sending out the angels (see 8:38) to gather the elect "from the four winds, from the ends of the earth to the ends of heaven" (13:26–27). The one who has been insulted, offended, and slain has been raised. The Christian community now continues its missionary task, suffering as Jesus suffered (vv. 9–13), knowing that God will have the last word in and through the appearance of this same Son of Man.

The climax of Mark's interpretation of Jesus as the Son of Man is found in the final appearance of the expression, in 14:62. As we have already seen, Jesus' self-revelation as the Christ and the Son of God appears in the same verse. All three expressions run together. Mark holds back this collection of expressions, so central for his interpretation of Jesus for the last few pages of the story. "Yes," Jesus replies to the question of the high priest; he is the Christ, the Son of the Blessed (14:61). Soon in the narrative he will show that he exercises his messianic role and his sonship *on the cross* (see especially 15:32, 39). What is remarkable about this interpretation is Mark's focus on the cross when presenting Jesus as Messiah and Son of God, a focus transcended in his interpretation of Jesus as the Son of Man. Jesus is Christ and Son of God on the cross (14:61–62; 15:32, 39). Jesus, the Son of Man, is also destined to suffer and die, but he will rise (8:31; 9:31; 10:33–34). More than that: He will gather in glory those who follow his way of the cross, in self-gift and unconditional service (8:38; 10:45). At the end of time, the suffering Son of Man who has risen from the dead will return in glory: "You will see the Son of Man seated at the right hand of Power, and coming with the clouds of heaven" (14:62). Seated at the right hand of God (see Ps 110:1), Jesus, the suffering Messiah and Son of God, will exercise ultimate authority. Little wonder that Jesus of Nazareth could tell puzzling readers—at the beginning of his ministry—that the Son of Man has authority to forgive sin and over the Sabbath (2:10, 28). Now they have an answer to their unstated question: "Who is this Son of Man?" (see John 12:34). Jesus is the suffering Son of Man whose service and self-gift unto death, the result of unswerving loyalty and obedience to God, leads to the vindication of the resurrection. This same suffering and vindicated Son of Man will return, at the right hand of God, to exercise ultimate authority. The one who was unjustly judged and done to death by crucifixion will return as the final and universal judge.

# Conclusion

The Markan interpretation of Jesus of Nazareth, when considered in the light of the traditions that came to him from the Old Testament, the Judaism of his time, and the Greco-Roman influences of the world within which he was writing his story of Jesus, is highly original. Mark has made it clear, especially by means of his continuation of Jesus' use of "the kingdom of God," that Jesus was the bearer of a divine authority. The story of the gospel is *about Jesus,* but his life, teaching, death, and resurrection established the reigning presence *of God* as king.

Mark's use of titles for Jesus continues the originality of his interpretation. Two expressions, the Christ and the Son of God, could have been used to describe the dignity and authority of Jesus, and to indicate the church's belief that, despite the cross, Jesus' life, teaching, death, and resurrection bore the stamp of God. Mark avoids this assiduously. Jesus is the Christ and the Son of God (1:1), but God is well pleased with a Son and a Messiah who goes to a cross, in unconditional obedience to his Father (1:11; 14:36). Mark, as interpreter, wishes to disassociate all worldly success and honor from his presentation of Jesus of Nazareth. He must be understood as Christ and Son of God insofar as he is the crucified one. Moreover, the crucified one does have the last word. To make this clear, Mark uses the enigmatic expression "the Son of Man," taken from Daniel 7. The Son of Man is also—and above all—a figure who suffers and dies (see 8:31; 9:9, 12, 31; 10:33, 45; 14:21, 41). But, as with the "one like a son of man" in Dan 7:13–14, he is ultimately vindicated by God and all authority is given to him (8:38; 13:26–27; 14:61–62).[71]

Other early Christian traditions (Paul, Matthew, Luke, and John) will devote more attention to Jesus as the Son of God, each with its own nuance. As we have seen, Mark also tells a story of Jesus that systematically insinuates that *in Jesus,* one finds the presence of *the divine.* Jesus' word and presence introduce into the human story the reigning presence of God as king (see 1:14–15). However, Mark relentlessly points to Jesus of Nazareth as abandoned, suffering, and slain. The reader is never allowed to forget that fact, not even in the Markan interpretation of Jesus as the Christ, the Son of God. Mark's use of the expression "the Son of Man" enables him to continue his focus on Jesus' preparedness to accept suffering and death. His unique use of "the Christ" and "the Son of God" never allows a sense of a figure who restores the fortune and former glory of Israel. Looking back to Daniel 7, and perhaps to the way Jesus used the expression, Mark was able to focus initially on a Christ who is a suffering Son of Man (8:29–31), but whose suffering led to the vindication of the resurrection and his ultimate return in glory and with authority. Thus "the Son of Man" emerged as his major expression to communicate his interpretation of Jesus of Nazareth—slain, vindicated, and the apocalyptic judge.

Even with "the Son of Man" there is no suggestion of a royal, military, or priestly figure who restores the hopes of Israel. Jesus, the Son of Man, is handed over to men, and they slay him (9:31). Only the action of God can reverse this situation of unjust suffering and death, through resurrection (8:31; 9:31; 10:32–34) and the final return of the Son of Man at God's right hand (8:38; 13:26–27; 14:62). This is the case because, in the end, the Gospel of Mark is not about Jesus, but about God, the Father of Jesus, and the definitive establishment of God's reigning presence as king by the Son in whom the Father delights (see 1:11; 9:7).

# Notes

1. Classical studies that reflect this approach are O. Cullmann, *The Christology of the New Testament* (London: SCM Press, 1975); F. Hahn, *Christologische Hoheitstitel: Ihre Geschichte im frühen Christentum* (3d ed.; FRLANT 83; Göttingen: Vandenhoeck & Ruprecht, 1966). This study has appeared in an abbreviated English translation: F. Hahn, *The Titles of Jesus in Christology: Their History in Early Christianity* (trans. H. Knight and G. Ogg; London: Lutterworth Press, 1969). See also C. F. D. Moule, *The Origin of Christology* (Cambridge: Cambridge University Press, 1977); W. Kramer, *Christ, Lord, Son of God* (SBT 50; London: SCM Press, 1966).

2. For a through and carefully documented study of Jesus' preaching of the kingdom of God, see J. P. Meier, *A Marginal Jew: Rethinking the Historical Jesus* (3 vols.; ABRL, New York: Doubleday, 1991–2001), 2:237–506. For a briefer, but

very helpful, assessment of Jesus' understanding of the kingdom of God, see L. E. Keck, *Who Is Jesus? History in Perfect Tense* (Studies on Personalities of the New Testament; Columbia: University of South Carolina Press, 2001), 65–112.

3. Keck, *Who Is Jesus?*, 71 (and elsewhere).

4. Rightly, therefore, has Norman Perrin (*Jesus and the Language of the Kingdom* [Philadelphia: Fortress, 1976], 15–34) written on Jesus' use of "the kingdom of God" as a tensive symbol.

5. For this interpretation of 9:1, and the scholarly discussion that surrounds it, see F. J. Moloney, *The Gospel of Mark: A Commentary* (Peabody: Hendrickson, 2002), 176–77.

6. The position taken in these few pages is very different from one of the most important studies of the kingdom in Mark, W. Kelber, *The Kingdom in Mark: A New Place and a New Time* (Philadelphia: Fortress, 1974). This influential study looks beyond the human story for the resolution of the temporal tension in the Markan kingdom sayings. For Kelber, the apocalyptically inspired Markan community still waits, feeling the absence of the risen Jesus (see 16:8), for the establishment of an eschatological kingdom. For an important study of the kingdom, largely supportive of my suggestions, see J. Marcus, *The Mystery of the Kingdom* (SBLDS 90; Atlanta: Scholars Press, 1986).

7. In contrast R. A. Horsley argues, *Hearing the Whole Story: The Politics of Plot in Mark's Gospel* (Louisville: Westminster John Knox, 2001), that Mark had no interest in theology, Christology, or discipleship. For Horsley, the evangelist develops prophetic and messianic "scripts," based mainly on the figures of Elijah and Moses, around the figure of Jesus. These "scripts" serve to restore a true Israel among oppressed Galilean villagers, over against the corruption of the covenant by the powers in Jerusalem. See especially pp. 213–53.

8. J. Marcus, *Mark 1–8* (AB 27: New York: Doubleday, 2000), 148.

9. See H. Zimmerman, "Das absolute *egō eimi* als neutestamentliche Offenbarungsformel," *BZ* 4 (1960): 54–69, 266–76.

10. See, on the Pauline use of the categories of Christ, Lord, and Son of God, Kramer, *Christ, Lord, Son of God.*

11. For a collection of essays that demonstrate the multiplicity of expectations (or lack of them) and understandings of "the Christ" in the period of emerging Christianity, see J. H. Charlesworth, ed., *The Messiah: Developments in Early Judaism and Christianity* (The First Princeton Symposium on Judaism and Christian Origins; Minneapolis: Fortress, 1992). See also J. J. Collins, *The Scepter and the Star. The Messiahs of the Dead Sea Scrolls and Other Ancient Literature* (ABRL; New York: Doubleday, 1995). On the Dead Sea Scrolls, see pp. 1–19. For a briefer, but concise, presentation of the Dead Sea material, see J. A. Fitzmyer, *Responses to 101 Questions on the Dead Sea Scrolls* (Mahwah: Paulist, 1992), 53–56.

12. J. Neusner and W. S. Green (eds.), *Dictionary of Judaism in the Biblical Period 450 B.C.E. to 600 C.E.* (Peabody: Hendrickson, 1999), 426.

13. For an excellent summary of the traditions concerning "the Christ" that Mark received, and his theological interpretation of them, see H.-J. Fabry and K. Scholtissek, *Der Messias* (Die Neue Echter Bibel-Themen 5; Würzburg: Echter, 2002), 57–79.

14. See above, p. 78, note 9.

15. As J. Painter, *Mark's Gospel: Worlds in Conflict* (New Testament Readings; London: Routledge, 1997), 25, remarks, whether or not "Son of God" was

present in the original gospel text (and Painter suspects that it was not), "the title is entirely appropriate."

16. The Markan use of the expressions, "the Christ," "the Son (of God)," and "the Son of Man," are the three major categories used in the interpretation of the life, teaching, suffering, death, and resurrection of Jesus. However, while we divide them in the following analysis, all three categories overlap (see especially 14:61–62).

17. Mark always uses the Greek ὁ χριστός (ho christos), the anointed one, and never the transliteration of the Hebrew/Aramaic word, ὁ Μεσσίας (ho Messias), found in the New Testament only in John 1:41 and 4:25.

18. In this list I am reporting only miracle stories, and not the summaries of Jesus' miraculous activity (see, for example, 1:34; 3:10–11; 6:6b).

19. For references and further discussion, see C. K. Barrett, The Holy Spirit in the Gospel Tradition (London: SPCK, 1970), 70–71.

20. In the New Testament it is often associated with the similar sentiments expressed in Isa 58:6 and 60:1–2. See B. Lindars, New Testament Apologetic: The Doctrinal Significance of the Old Testament Quotations (London: SCM, 1961), 248. Lindars, however, misses Mark 7:37, claiming that it is only used by Q and Luke. Isaiah 35:5–6 is also used in a messianic sense in the rabbinic tradition (see Gen. Rab. 95; Tep. 146.8).

21. See above, pp. 23–25.

22. For a good summary of these discussions, see U. Schnelle, The History and Theology of the New Testament Writings (trans. M. E. Boring; Minneapolis: Fortress, 1998), 210–17.

23. On this change from Jesus' command to announce what "the Lord" (ὁ κύριος; ho kyrios) had done for him to the ex-demoniac's announcing what "Jesus" had done for him, see above, p. 71.

24. After the many miracles reported across 1:14–8:30, only two appear in 8:31–15:47. In 9:14–29 the curing of an epileptic boy is used as the context where disciples fail, while the faith of the boy's father shows his belief. On this, see Moloney, Mark, 182–86. Blind Bartimaeus (10:46–52) closes the cycle begun in 8:22–26, again throwing into relief the limitations of the disciples' belief. See Moloney, Mark, 208–11.

25. Two points need to be made here. In the first place, neither Paul nor Matthew understood Jesus as restoring the Davidic dynasty either. However, Mark wants to avoid even the spiritualizing of that tradition, because of his strong focus on the crucified Christ. Second, in the episode of blind Bartimaeus (10:46–52), Jesus does listen to the appeals of a man who calls to him as "son of David" (vv. 47–48). The context of that miracle, however, indicates that Bartimaeus's appeal is on the basis on his belief that Jesus was a healer, in the tradition of Solomon, the son of David. Thus the title is not associated with Jesus' messianic status. On this, see Moloney, Mark, 208–11, and especially J. H. Charlesworth, "The Son of David: Solomon and Jesus," in The New Testament and Hellenistic Judaism (eds. P. Borgen and S. Giversen; Peabody: Hendrickson, 1997), 72–87.

26. For more detail on the background and structure of Mark 13, see Moloney, Mark, 248–52.

27. For evidence that such figures did appear during the final days of Jerusalem and its temple in 70 C.E., see Josephus, Ant. 19.162; 20.167–172, 188; J.W.

2.258–263; 6.285–286. For further reflections on these false messiahs at the fall of Jerusalem, see Marcus, *Mark 1–8*, 498–99.

28. Some commentators claim that Jesus' response is ambiguous. See, for example, D. E. Nineham, *The Gospel of St. Mark* (Westminster Pelican Commentaries; Philadelphia: Westminster, 1978), 408. This is not the case. Looking back to 1:1, and the development of Jesus' self-identification as "the Son of Man" across the Gospel (see below), these words from Jesus—within the context of his suffering and death—announce the meaning of his messianic status. It is in the unjust crucifixion of the innocent Jesus that he exercises his messianic role. See, for example, R. E. Brown, *The Death of the Messiah: From Gethsemane to the Grave. A Commentary on the Passion Narratives in the Four Gospels* (2 vols; ABRL; New York: Doubleday, 1994), 1:467–89; M. D. Hooker, *The Gospel according to St. Mark* (BNTC; Peabody: Hendrickson, 1991), 360–61.

29. D. Senior, *The Passion of Jesus in the Gospel of Mark* (The Passion Series 2; Wilmington: Michael Glazier, 1984), 94.

30. For further reflection on the irony of the Markan crucifixion account, see Moloney, *Mark*, 317–31. See also, above, pp. 98–111.

31. There is a formal distinction between "the Son" and "the Son of God," but both point to the same Markan understanding of Jesus' unique relationship with the God of Israel, and will be treated together.

32. For the present writer, lack of attention to these details *in the text* spoil the attempt of Horsley, *Hearing the Whole Story*, to read the gospel as an appeal to Galilean peasants to restore Israel's true covenant. The study makes for exciting reading, but its argument depends on unsubstantiated claims concerning social and political issues *outside the text*. Horsley is more interested in "politics" than "plot."

33. On Alexander the Great, see R. D. Milns, "Alexander the Great," *ABD* 1 (1992): 146–50. On his deification, see pp. 148–49.

34. On this, see T. H. Kim, "The Anarthrous υἱὸς θεοῦ in Mark 15:39," *Bib* 79 (1988): 221–41; A. Y. Collins, "Mark and His Readers: The Son of God among Jews," *HTR* 92 (1999): 393–408; A. Y. Collins, "Mark and his Readers: The Son of God among Greeks and Romans," *HTR* 93 (2000): 85–100; C. A. Evans, "Mark's Incipit and the Priene Calendar Inscription: From Jewish Gospel to Greco-Roman Gospel," *Journal of Greco-Roman Christianity and Judaism* 1 (2000): 67–81; C. A. Evans, *Mark 8:27–16:20* (WBC 34B; Nashville: Thomas Nelson, 2001), lxxx–xciii. Kim looks to the lack of the definite article before "Son of God" in 15:39, and Evans points to the same feature in 1:1, as links between the Markan "Son of God" and the Roman *divi filius*. Collins points to the broader Jewish background and Greco-Roman foreground for the expression.

35. For a fundamental study of the data, see B. J. Byrne, *"Sons of God—Seed of Abraham": A Study of the Idea of the Sonship of God of all Christians in Paul against the Jewish Background* (AnBib 83; Rome: Biblical Institute Press, 1979), 9–78. For a more recent and excellent synthesis, see J. J. Collins, *The Scepter and the Star*, 154–72. Collins updates Byrne, devoting attention to "son of God" texts from the Dead Sea Scrolls.

36. See J. J. Collins, *The Scepter and the Star*, 163–65.

37. On the possibilities of this rich Old Testament background to the divine words addressed to Jesus in v. 11, see C. R. Kazmierski, *Jesus the Son of God: A Study of the Marcan Tradition and Its Redaction by the Evangelist* (FB 33; Würzburg: Echter, 1979), 37–61; R. E. Watts, *Isaiah's New Exodus and Mark*

(WUNT 2; Reihe 88; Tübingen: J. C. B. Mohr [Paul Siebeck], 1997), 108–18; J. Marcus, *The Way of the Lord: Christological Exegesis of the Old Testament in the Gospel of Mark* (Louisville: Westminster John Knox, 1992), 48–56.

38. See Marcus, *Mark*, 187.

39. The Greek word δεῖ *(dei)*, meaning "must," is used in Jesus' prediction of his forthcoming suffering to show that it is a divine necessity. This word is used regularly in this way across the New Testament. See W. Grundmann, "δεῖ, δέον, ἐστί," *TDNT* 2 (1964): 21–25.

40. For a detailed analysis of 9:2–13, on which the following few remarks are based, see Moloney, *Mark*, 177–82.

41. Because the expression "Son of God" in 15:39 does not have a "the" (it is called "anarthrous"; see also 1:1), many have claimed that this is not a full confession of the Markan understanding of Jesus as "the Son of God." For a full discussion, concluding (as above) that this is a moment of christological climax for the Gospel of Mark, see Brown, *Death*, 2:1146–50. See, for a full discussion, Moloney, *Mark*, 330, note 282.

42. For a study of the Johannine use of the expression, see F. J. Moloney, *The Johannine Son of Man* (2d ed.; BScRel 14; Rome: Libreria Ateneo Salesiano, 1978).

43. For a survey of this discussion, with further bibliographical indications, see "Excursus 1: The Son of Man Discussion," in Moloney, *Mark*, 212–13.

44. For a thorough survey of this possible background, see A. J. Ferch, *The Son of Man in Daniel Seven* (Andrews University Seminary Doctoral Dissertation Series 6; Berrien Springs: Andrews University Press, 1979), 43–77.

45. I am discounting the *formative* influence of other ancient and gnostic reflections on a "primal man," however much the use of "the Son of Man" may have been *received* by early Christian converts in the Greco-Roman world. For an important study that claims they were important in the development of the use of "the Son of Man" in the New Testament, see F. H. Borsch, *The Son of Man in Myth and History* (London: SCM Press, 1967). For a survey of possible biblical background to "son of man" in Daniel 7, see Ferch, *The Son of Man*, 78–107.

46. The examples provided are but a sample of the ninety-three times in Ezekiel where God addresses his prophet as "son of man." This form of direct address is unique to Ezekiel.

47. W. Eichrodt, *Ezekiel: A Commentary* (trans. C. Quin; Philadelphia: Westminster, 1970), 61. For Eichrodt's further reflections upon the figure of Ezekiel and his sense of frailty in the face of his prophetic mandate, see pp. 22–43.

48. E. Schweizer, "Der Menschensohn," *ZNW* 50 (1950): 185–209; E. Schweizer, *Jesus* (trans. D. E. Green; Atlanta: John Knox, 1971), 19–22; and E. Schweizer, *The Good News according to Mark* (trans. D. H. Madvig; Richmond: John Knox, 1970), 166–71, have consistently—and correctly—drawn Ezekiel's use of "son of man" into the debate.

49. Not all my readers would regard 1 and 2 Maccabees as "books of the Bible." You will, however, find them reproduced in most modern Bibles, listed as "non-canonical" or "apocryphal" in Bibles from the Protestant tradition, and as "deutero-canonical" in Catholic Bibles.

50. In doing this, Daniel resorts to what is known as an "apocalyptic" literary form. When all hope of human self-preservation seems impossible, apocalyptic writings resort to the use of imagery and symbolic language to speak of

the intervention of God. As God is the chief agent in the restoration of right order, only images and symbols can be used. One is dealing with the action of the ineffable!

51. These "horns" represent the violence used by Antiochus IV to come to power, rooting out three other pretenders.

52. Interpreters of Daniel 7 often disregard the function vv. 15–28 within the chapter, and within the book itself. Influenced by the studies in form criticism and the history of religions by Martin Noth and H. Louis Ginsberg, many scholars see the second half of Daniel 7 as a secondary interpretative addition. Thus the identification of "the one like a son of man" with "the holy ones of the Most High" is ignored. I regard the identification as a key to both Daniel 7 and the use of the expression "the Son of Man," initially by Jesus, and then in the New Testament. For a detailed and vigorous defense of the literary and theological unity of Dan 7:1–28, devoting attention to the work of Noth and Ginsberg, see Ferch, *Son of Man*, 108–13.

53. The practice of incorporating the qualities (or defects) of the nation into one symbolic figure is found elsewhere in antiquity, and also in the Old Testament. The figure is called a "corporate personality." See, on this, the important study of H. Wheeler Robinson, *Corporate Personality in Israel* (Facet Books Biblical Series 11; Philadelphia: Fortress, 1964). This booklet contains two earlier essays: "The Hebrew Conception of Corporate Personality" (1935) and "The Group and the Individual in Israel" (1937).

54. See L. Hartman and A. A. di Lella, *The Book of Daniel* (AB 23; Garden City: Doubleday, 1978), 86–87. However, see Ferch, *Son of Man*, 175–80, who defends the unity of Daniel 7, but suggests that "the one like the son of man" of vv. 13–14 is a heavenly being and the "holy ones of the Most High" of vv. 23–27 are earthly. However, they *share* a perpetual kingdom.

55. On Jesus' use of the term, see Moule, *The Origin of Christology*, 11–22; M. D. Hooker, *The Son of Man in Mark* (London: SPCK, 1967), 174–98; F. J. Moloney, "The End of the Son of Man?" *DRev* 98 (1980): 280–90. This clumsy English expression "the Son of the Man" renders the Greek, *ho huios tou anthrōpou*. In order to make clear that the generic "one like a son of man" from Dan 7:13 is focused entirely on the person of Jesus, in Greek two definite articles are used: "the son" of "the man." To catch this intense personalization of a generic term in Jesus, I capitalize "the Son of Man." See C. F. D. Moule, "Neglected Features in the Problem of 'the Son of Man,'" in *Neues Testament und Kirche: Festschrift für Rudolf Schnackenburg* (ed. J. Gnilka; Freiburg: Herder, 1974), 413–28.

56. These texts, and especially the *Similitudes of Enoch*, a section of a larger book, known as *The Book of Enoch*, are difficult to date. However, both show dependence on Daniel 7, and are later than the beginnings of the Jesus movement. See the excellent summary of Collins, *The Scepter and the Star*, 177–89.

57. See Collins, *The Scepter and the Star*, 187–89.

58. This is certainly the way it looks in the Gospel of Mark, where suffering and vindication lie behind ten of the Son of Man sayings (8:31, 38 [!]; 9:9, 12, 31; 10:33, 45; 14:21[twice], 41), the authority of the earthly Son of Man behind two sayings (2:10, 28), and the end-time (apocalyptic) appearance of the Son of Man behind three of them (8:38 [!]; 13:26; 14:62). In 8:38, vindication and final appearance are united.

59. This approach is not widely used. Most studies of "the Son of Man" classify Jesus' sayings into the present Son of Man, the suffering Son of Man, and the Son of Man who will come at the end of time (the apocalyptic Son of Man). This approach imposes categories on a storyteller that probably never occurred to him!

60. Narrative critics call this technique a prolepsis. It creates a "gap," a spot of indeterminacy within the flow of the narrative that is not resolved till later.

61. Mark does not present Jesus as nullifying Sabbath, but as comparing the actions of David and Jesus. The issue is christological. See Moloney, *Mark*, 68–70.

62. See also G. Bilezekian, *The Liberated Gospel: A Comparison of the Gospel of Mark and Greek Tragedy* (Grand Rapids: Baker, 1977), 123: "The reader knows that Jesus is referring to himself, but this identification does not become clear to the personae of the Gospel until the momentous confrontation with the high priest." See, along these lines, R. Fowler, *Loaves and Fishes: The Function of the Feeding Stories in the Gospel of Mark* (SBLDS 54; Chico: Scholars Press, 1981), 162.

63. The history of the development of these predictions in the tradition is an important exegetical question, but is not the concern of this study. See, however, Moloney, *Mark*, 171–72.

64. As we have seen in our study of Mark the storyteller. See above, pp. 83–87.

65. On this passage, see Moloney, *Mark*, 284–85.

66. The saying is important and crucial to many scholars who claim that there was a stage (perhaps on the lips of the historical Jesus) when there was a separation between Jesus ("my words") and the judging Son of Man ("will the Son of Man also be ashamed"). Whatever one makes of the origins of the saying (with Jesus, in the tradition?), for *Mark the interpreter,* the disciple is called to follow the way of Jesus, the suffering Son of Man, to eventually join the vindicated Son of Man in the glory of his Father and the holy angels (8:31–38).

67. See above, p. 86.

68. The expression "many" in Mark 10:45 does not mean that many will be ransomed and others not. It reflects a Semitic way of saying "the multitude" in an inclusive, rather than exclusive, fashion.

69. V. Taylor, *The Gospel according to St. Mark* (2d ed; New York: St. Martin's, 1966), 444. This rich saying has been the subject of much debate, as it appears to be the only place in the gospels where Jesus associates the Son of Man (from Daniel) with the idea of his life given as a ransom (from the Isaian Suffering Servant?). For a full discussion of this question, see "Excursus 2: Son of Man and Suffering Servant in Mark 10:45," in Moloney, *Mark*, 213–14.

70. Much scholarly debate surrounds the nature of this coming. Does the Son of Man ascend or descend with the clouds, or on the clouds? Much depends on the interpretation of Dan 7:13, but the point at issue is that Jesus, the suffering Son of Man, will also be the apocalyptic Son of Man, coming to gather and judge. The use of the image of "the clouds" looks back to Dan 7:13.

71. For a succinct summary of Mark's understanding of Jesus as Messiah, Son of God and Son of Man, see F. J. Matera, *New Testament Christology* (Louisville: Westminster John Knox, 1999), 24–26.

# Mark the Interpreter of the Christian Community

Each gospel was written to proclaim the good news of Jesus Christ (see Mark 1:1; Matt 1:1; Luke 24:44–49; John 20:30–31). But Jesus is never a solitary figure. In each gospel he calls followers and challenges them to learn from him as his disciples.[1] The disciples, present with Jesus at almost every turn, are major players in Mark's story. Jesus is certainly the most important character, but the disciples also play a vital role.[2] Surprisingly, however, the disciples of Jesus, despite a positive start to their relationship with him, fail their master as the story comes to an end. Indeed, unless one accepts the longer ending of Mark 16:9–20, the story closes without any resolution of their increasing fear and failure across the latter part of the gospel. Their last appearance is marked by fear and flight, as they abandon Jesus in the Garden of Gethsemane (14:50–52). Both Paul and the other gospels tell of the presence of the risen Jesus to the disciples (see 1 Cor 15:3–11; Matt 28:16–20; Luke 24:36–49; John 20:18–23). This is not the case in the Gospel of Mark. There is no account of the appearances of the risen Jesus and the reestablishment of discipleship.[3]

We have seen that Mark told a story that interpreted who Jesus was, and the same must be said for his story of the disciples. Mark's presentation of both the performance of the disciples and Jesus' teaching on the nature of discipleship is an *interpretation* that reaches beyond any attempt to report "how it was." Mark tells of disciples and discipleship with an eye to the Christian community, to interpret *their* story of following Jesus. The Markan presentation of Jesus *along with* his description of the role of the disciples sought to address the experience of being a follower of Jesus in his own 70 C.E. Christian community. His message, however, can address all subsequent disciples who read the gospel. While Mark was primarily interested in instructing his own community in the first century, the ongoing reading of the gospel has continued to instruct Christian communities over two millennia.

What is more, the words and the actions of Jesus, along with the participation of the disciples, at two bread miracles (6:31–44; 8:1–9) and at a meal celebrated the night before he died (14:22–25), reflect the fact that Mark's Christian community celebrated a ritual meal. As we will see, many words and actions in these accounts reflect this community ritual. The Markan Christian community's celebration of the table of the Lord looked to the gospel's account of these events from the life of Jesus for a better understanding of the meaning of their ritual celebration. The presentation of the disciples and their meal with Jesus *in the story*, while written for Mark's original readers, continues to address the life situations of succeeding generations of readers *of the story*. Thus, side by side with a reflection on the disciples in the gospel, our study of Mark as the interpreter of his Christian community will consider his careful description of three meals Jesus shared with them.[4]

## The Disciples

Some studies of Mark distinguish between "the Twelve" (οἱ δώδεκα; *hoi dōdeka*) and the more generic description of "the disciples" (οἱ μαθηταί; *hoi mathētai*). In the life of Jesus, his choice of his first followers and the appointment of the inner circle of "the Twelve" was, historically, an important distinction.[5] However, for the purposes of the following reflection, they are considered together. Mark's interpretation of the Christian community depends on the readers' appreciation of his portrait of both "the Twelve" and "the disciples." Another less clearly defined group is simply called "those who follow" (οἱ ἀκολουθοῦντες; *hoi akolouthountes*). All three groups are called to follow, instructed on the requirements of true discipleship, and described as failing to understand and accept Jesus' demands. Though the Twelve were called to exercise a ministry of leadership, nevertheless, they belonged to the larger community, called "disciples" or "followers" of Jesus. Mark instructs his readers on the blessings and challenges of living in a Christian community by means of his interpretation of all "the disciples": the twelve, the disciples, and those who followed.

When one singles out the principal places across the gospel where the disciples play a significant and active role, along with those passages where Jesus instructs them on the demands of discipleship, three themes emerge:

1. Initially disciples are called to follow Jesus and are associated with him (1:16–20; 2:13–14; 3:13–19; 6:7–13).

2. Gradually, the first signs of their inability or unwillingness to be true "followers" of Jesus becomes apparent (4:35–41; 6:30, 45–52; 8:22–10:52).

3. Finally they sink into total failure (14:50–52; 14:66–72; 16:8).

Strange as this movement into failure may at first appear, Mark's story of struggling and fragile disciples conveys his understanding of the role of their relationship with Jesus, and his care for them. Behind this portrayal of the disciples in the story of the gospel lies Mark's teaching to his own community. As we go on reading the Gospel of Mark as part of our inspired Scriptures, this portrait of the disciples continues to instruct all Christian believers and communities.

## The call of the disciples and their sharing in Jesus' mission

Jesus' disciples share in a privileged way in Jesus' own person and mission. Jesus' first action, after his initial appearance and proclamation of the kingdom (1:14–15), is to call disciples to follow him. They respond to his call and take their place behind him. They leave all the signs of their earthly success and join him, to follow him down *his way* (1:16–20). He not only calls fishermen to become fishers of human beings, but he even summons a public sinner, the tax collector Levi, to become his follower. Like the fishermen, Levi also responds without hesitation (2:13–14). Having called his first disciples, Jesus begins his ministry in Galilee. The disciples witness the wonders he does, and also receive private instruction from him (4:11, 34; 7:17). Across the early chapters of the gospel, the disciples do not actually *do* anything, but they are his constant companions. The initial positive presentation of the disciples and their relationship with Jesus must not be lost from view. The disciples are called to follow Jesus, to be with him, and to share in his ministry. However much they may fail as the story proceeds, this understanding of discipleship retains its place in the Markan instruction of his early Christian community, called to be with Jesus and to continue his ministry in both word and deed.

Jesus is portrayed across the Gospel of Mark as often on the move. Almost every episode begins with a verb of motion, generally closely associated with the adverb *immediately* (εὐθύς; *euthys*). He is frequently going, coming, leading, entering, setting out, and so on. This way of telling the story creates the impression of a restless energy in Jesus, responding to a call of his own as he journeys on. While on this journey, Jesus can call his disciples to be fellow pilgrims, to follow him (ἀκολουθεῖν; *akolouthein*). In the second half of the gospel, this movement settles into a more regular pattern, as Jesus and the disciples journey along the way to Jerusalem (see 8:27; 9:33, 34; 10:17, 32, 46, 52; 11:8). Jesus is not the master of his own destiny, and this relentless and energetic movement, eventually leading to Jerusalem and the cross, is an indication of Jesus' unconditional response to the design of God.

After summoning a further larger group, he appoints from among them "the Twelve" (3:13–14). The appointment of "the Twelve" is an important moment in the Markan interpretation of discipleship. He appoints them "to be with him" (v. 14a: ἵνα ὦσιν μετ' αὐτοῦ; *hina ōsin met'autou*).[6] Jesus establishes an intimacy between himself and his disciples, and this intimacy has its consequences. The "being with him" leads to the promise that they will share in Jesus' mission of spreading God's reign. They will be sent out, they will preach, and they will have authority to cast out demons (v. 14b–15). Up to this stage in the gospel, Jesus has burst on the scene; *he* has preached and *he* has cast out demons. What Jesus does, the disciples will now do, but only if they are *with* Jesus (14a). The action of the disciples flows from the disciples' *being with Jesus*. The intimate personal link between the disciple and Jesus must not be broken. Whatever the disciples are as followers of Jesus and what they are able to do as his missionaries, depend on being *with him*. The promise that they would share his ministry (1:17; 3:14b) becomes a fact when the Twelve are formally sent out on a mission (6:7–13). The disciples are to take Jesus as their model for mission; like him they are sent on a wandering mission (6:7–9). They are not to seek comfort and security but to stay in the place where their message finds a home (vv. 10–11). They successfully preach repentance, cast out demons, and heal the sick (vv. 12–13).[7]

These promising initial moments in the Markan use of his traditions are an important part of his interpretation of the role of disciples and the demands of discipleship. Mark presents Jesus' call to the disciples and his close association with them so that they can join his mission: *Disciples are models for all who are called to be followers of Jesus.* Mark wanted his original readers to develop a sense of oneness between the "disciples of Jesus" in the gospel, and the "disciples of Jesus" reading the gospel. The disciples in the gospel formed an original community of "followers of Jesus." They were called by him, associated with him, and granted a share of his mission to preach the gospel to the whole world (see 13:10). The successful creation of followers who left all and shared successfully in Jesus' mission was a fundamental message addressed to the original Markan community in the story of the gospel. It retains its importance for today's Christian communities. However much the original readers, or hearers, of the Gospel of Mark may have been aware of their failure to live up to this summons to share in Jesus' life and mission, the voice of Jesus still issued the invitation: "Follow me" (1:17).

## Signs of failure

What is surprising about the disciples in the Gospel of Mark is that they cut an increasingly poor figure the longer they are associated with Jesus. After the association of the Twelve with his mission (3:14–15), and even before he sends them out (6:7–13), Jesus chastises "those who were about him and the Twelve" (4:10), because they have not understood the parable of the scattered seed (4:3–9), suggesting that they will never be able to understand his teaching in parables (v. 13). After his teaching, Jesus and the disciples (see v. 34) set off in a boat to go to the other side of the lake. In the midst of a storm they are overcome by fear, an emotion that will become increasingly present among them. Rebuking the wind and the sea, as if they were personifications of evil and violence, Jesus calms the storm, but chastises his disciples for their fear and lack of faith (v. 40). But even this rebuke has little effect. The passage closes with his disciples filled with awe, saying to one another: "Who then is this, that even wind and sea obey him?" (v. 41). They are frightened and unable to recognize the presence and authority of God in the one they are following.

The cost of discipleship is first made clear in the report of John the Baptist's fearless commitment to his mission, unto death (6:14–29). However, before this report, the Twelve were sent out on a successful mission (6:7–13). On their return, immediately following the account of the Baptist's death, they are eager to tell Jesus all the things they had said and done (6:30).[8] They are losing the sense of being the "sent ones" (ἀπόστολοι; *apostoloi;* see vv. 7, 30) of Jesus. They have reached a stage where they regard their successful mission as being the result of *their own* authority over sickness and the demonic. They forget that what they *do* depends entirely on their *being with* Jesus (3:14).[9] Despite Jesus' two-fold feeding of the multitudes (6:31–44; 8:1–9), they are unable to understand his walking on the sea after the first miracle (6:51–52), and they do not understand what he means when he speaks of the leaven of the Pharisees and the Herodians after the second miracle (8:11–21). In 6:52 Mark reports, "For they did not understand about the loaves, but their hearts were hardened" (6:52). The same themes return in 8:11–21. Jesus accuses them of hard-heartedness and blindness (vv. 17–18), and in frustration asks them, "Do you not yet understand?" (v. 21).

The disciples' blindness and inability to understand lead directly into the section of the gospel that runs from 8:22 to 10:52, where Jesus predicts his passion and calls the disciples to the cross, to receptivity, and to service. Jesus' challenging words are set between two miracles where blindness is transformed to sight (8:22–26; 10:46–52). These two miracles symbolically portray Jesus' accusation that the disciples may be blind (8:17–18), and their blindness becomes evident in the central section of the gospel. Here, more than anywhere else in the gospel, Mark tells a story that makes clear the demands of discipleship. Repeatedly, Jesus draws his disciples to one side and instructs them (see, for example, 8:34–38; 9:33–50; 10:23–31, 35–45). As Jesus journeys toward Jerusalem, asking his disciples to follow him, he announces three times his forthcoming passion (8:31; 9:31; 10:33–34). After each of these passion predictions the disciples show that they cannot or will not accept Jesus' "way," and are unwilling to follow him. With Peter as their representative they have their own idea of messiahship (8:32–33). They want to set up an exclusive discipleship, and are hostile to others who do not see things their way (9:38–41; 10:13–16). Even after the final passion prediction, full of the gruesome details of what will happen in Jerusalem (10:33–34), the sons of Zebedee are jockeying for positions of authority (10:35–37), and the other disciples are indignant that they might be beaten out of these honors (10:41). Remarkably, however, Jesus never fails the failing disciples. He instructs them on the need for the cross in 8:34–9:1, on the need for service and receptivity in 9:35–37, and draws cross, service, and receptivity together as he instructs them in 10:38–44.

The earlier moments of close association between Jesus and disciples are attractive, and readers of the gospel are prepared to accept the paradigm of the original disciples in their following of Jesus. However, on arrival at Mark 10:45, the fragility of the original disciples is becoming increasingly obvious, and a matter of concern. The disciples will not and cannot accept that to follow Jesus means to commit themselves to the cross (8:34–38; 10:39), to humble service and receptivity (9:33–37; 10:35–44), for the sake of Jesus and the gospel. Despite these signs of failure, Jesus leads the way: "For the Son of Man came not to be served, but to serve, and to give his life as a ransom for many" (10:45).

The first blind man stumbled from total blindness to partial sight to a fullness of vision (8:22–26); blind Bartimeus leaves all, and follows Jesus down his way toward Jerusalem (10:46–52).[10] But in the episodes between these two miracles, the disciples have not succeeded in such self-abandonment and enthusiastic preparedness to follow Jesus "down his way" (v. 52).[11]

What is surprising about this part of the story, as the disciples waver in their attachment to Jesus, is that, despite the fact that they sink deeper into failure and an inability to understand what is being asked of them, Jesus perseveres with his instruction. This is not simply a sign of Jesus' persistence or patience. His teaching and journeying with his disciples "on the way" to Jerusalem is Mark's presentation of one of the central elements of his teaching on disciples and discipleship. *Jesus never abandons the fragile disciples.* He continues to summon his would-be "followers" to the cross (8:34–38; 10:39), to receptivity, and service (9:33–50; 10:35–44). Jesus' message on discipleship still stands, despite the increasing failure of the disciples. The light in the darkness of their failures is the never-failing presence of Jesus to his fragile disciples. Here we are touching the heart of the Markan interpretation of the relationship between Jesus and the Christian community. Jesus' fidelity to failing disciples, originally articulated by this gospel for the Markan community, offers comfort and inspiration to disciples of all time, wherever this gospel is read.

## The ultimate failure

The failure of the disciples comes to a head in the passion story. Judas, "one of the Twelve," betrays Jesus (14:10–11); Peter denies him (14:66–72); and his most intimate followers, Peter, James, and John, sleep through his hour of anguished prayer (14:32–42).[12] The final appearance of the group of disciples is found in 14:50: "And they all forsook him and fled." Following this lapidary statement of the flight of the disciples, Mark interprets their action with a brief parabolic narrative. There was also a young man "following." He, too, at the threat of danger, fled, leaving in the hands of his assailants the only covering that he had on his body, a linen cloth. Like the disciples who have just fled, he is naked in his nothingness (vv. 51–52).[13]

There are no disciples at the cross or at the resurrection of Jesus in Mark's Gospel (15:1–16:8). There are, however, hints of an eventual restoration to their place following Jesus. The flight of the disciples is symbolized by the parallel flight of the young man, who leaves everything behind to forsake Jesus, but at the empty tomb the women find "a young man, sitting on the right side, dressed in a white robe" (16:5). The similarities between the parable of the naked young man, which describes the fleeing disciples in 14:41–52, and the presence of the young man whose clothing is described at the empty tomb at 16:5 are too close to be irrelevant. The reader senses restoration.[14] The women are commissioned: "Go tell his disciples and Peter that he is going before you to Galilee; there you will see him, as he told you" (v. 7). These words from the young man recall earlier words of Jesus. In the midst of his prophecies of their imminent failure Jesus had promised his disciples: "You will all fall away; for it is written, 'I will strike the shepherd, and the sheep will be scattered.' But after I am raised up, I will go before you to Galilee" (14:27–28). Nevertheless, the fear, silence, and flight return in v. 8, the last verse of the gospel: "And they went out and fled from the tomb; for trembling and astonishment had come upon them; and they said nothing to anyone, for they were afraid." The story of failure is pushed to its limits. Mark is relentless in his interpretation of the fragility of the human response to the divine intervention that took place in the person of Jesus. The Father's voice from heaven that demanded disciples to "listen to him" (9:7) seems to have fallen on deaf ears.

## The disciples and the Christian community

Scholars have interpreted this negative portrait of the disciples in the Gospel of Mark in a variety of ways. Many claim that, for Mark, the disciples offer no paradigm for the Markan church or for the Christian community of any age, as they fail so dismally. As one scholar puts it:

> I conclude that Mark is assiduously involved in a vendetta against the disciples. He paints them as obtuse, obdurate, recalcitrant men who at first are unperceptive of Jesus' messiahship, then oppose its style and character, and finally totally reject it. As a *coup de grace*, Mark closes his Gospel without rehabilitating the disciples.[15]

This widely held position throws into relief the failure, but underplays and misunderstands the importance of the positive side of the disciples' story in Mark's attempt to address his own community and, subsequently, the Christian communities down through the centuries who continue to read the Gospel of Mark. What is the reader to make of the earlier part of the narrative? In 10:32, as Jesus approaches Jerusalem, the disciples, despite all their fear and failure, are still called "those who followed" (οἱ δὲ ἀκολουθοῦντες; *hoi de akolouthountes*). The two sides of the disciples' response to Jesus must be held in tension, as there is a need to take into account both the positive and the negative in the story of the disciples, as it is the story of all disciples.[16] The Markan interpretation of the disciples *in the story* would have been strongly influenced by the Markan readers *of the story*. In other words, for Mark, the story of the disciples reached outside the boundaries of the story of the gospel into the story of the Christian community for which he was writing his interpretation of the life of Jesus.[17]

The lived experience of failure and the ongoing presence of Jesus in the lives of the readers in the original Markan community determined Mark's interpretation of disciples and discipleship. There was little or no room for a *human success story* for Jesus, the Christ, the Son of God, and the Son of Man. It appears that the same interpretation is continued into the Markan presentation of the disciples to the Christian community that he was addressing by means of his gospel. Jesus was finally vindicated by God in the resurrection (see 16:6). Similarly, the disciples' experience of the never-failing presence of Jesus, even in their failure, will not be thwarted. He told them he would be struck and they would flee. At the same time, he promised he would go before them into Galilee (14:27–28). The women failed to communicate this Easter promise to the disciples and Peter (see 16:8), joining the other disciples who had fled in fear (see 14:50–52). But the very existence of the Gospel of Mark, read and heard in the original Markan community (and subsequent Christian communities), is proof that the word of Jesus did not fail. The promise of the young man, catching up an original promise of Jesus— "He is going before you into Galilee. There you will see him"—has come true (16:6; see 14:28). The Gospel of Mark tells the members of a struggling Christian community that human beings may fail, but God will not fail them. Failure will be overcome and discipleship restored, not because men or women understand and succeed, but because of God's graciousness.

# The Christian Community at the Table of the Lord

The close relationship between Jesus and the disciples is the focus of the two accounts of the multiplication of the loaves and fish (6:31–44; 8:1–9) and the report of Jesus' final meal with his disciples (14:22–25). In the bread miracles the disciples are called to overcome fears so that they might join Jesus in his mission (6:31–44; 8:1–9). Mark's account of the celebration of the final supper highlights Jesus' unconditional self-gift for his fragile disciples and for the establishment of the new temple, the reigning presence of God as king (14:22–25).[18]

## The bread miracles and the mission of the disciples

The Lord's table, as it was celebrated in the Markan community, lies behind the two accounts of the multiplication of the bread and the feeding of the multitudes (Mark 6:31–44; 8:1–10).[19] At first sight, the two bread miracles appear to be the repetition of an almost identical miracle story. But there are important differences between them. For example, the miracles are set on different sides of the lake, the first in Israel and the second in a Gentile land. In the first, Jesus "blessed" (6:41: εὐλόγησαν; *eulogēsan*) while in the second he "gave thanks" (8:6: εὐχαριστήσας; *eucharistēsas*). The first makes links with the Old Testament and uses expressions applicable to Israel, while the second alters some of these expressions so that the story is more suitable for a Gentile audience.[20]

Despite the differences, after both miracles Mark reports boat trips in which he shows the disciples failed to understand the significance of the miracles.[21] After the first feeding, Jesus comes to them across the stormy waters (6:45–52). They have responded to his call (1:16–20), been with him during his ministry in Galilee (2:1–3:6), witnessed the appointment of the Twelve (3:13–19), been privileged hearers of the parables of the kingdom of God (4:1–34), and been with him during a long series of miracles (4:35–5:43). Yet the disciples fail to grasp the meaning of Jesus' manifestation of himself in the calming of the stormy sea.

> And he got into the boat with them and the wind ceased. And they were utterly astounded, for they did not understand about the loaves, but their hearts were hardened. (6:52)

After the second feeding story that should have deepened their understanding of Jesus, the disciples set out with him across the lake. He speaks to them about "the leaven" of the Pharisees (8:15), but the disciples presume he is making reference to the "one loaf" that they have on board (8:14). Jesus then speaks strongly to them, recalling both the feeding miracles:

> Jesus said to them, "Why do you discuss the fact that you have no bread? Do you not yet perceive or understand? Are your hearts hardened? Having eyes do you not see, and having ears do you not hear? And do you not remember? When I broke the five loaves for

the five thousand, how many baskets full of broken pieces did you take up?" They said to him, "Twelve." "And the seven for the four thousand, how many baskets full of fragments did you collect?" And they said to him, "Seven." And he said to them, "Do you not yet understand?" (8:17–21)

Mark's two accounts of feeding stories of 6:31–44 and 8:1–10, therefore, lead directly into journeys across the lake during which the disciples show that they have not understood the meaning of the bread miracles. They fail to see that the miracles point to the person of Jesus, his mission, and their association with that mission.

Another feature of the two bread miracles is the close contact that Jesus' words and gestures have with the ritual celebration of the table of the Lord in early Christian communities.[22] Jesus' "taking" the loaves, "looking up to heaven," "giving thanks," "breaking bread," and "giving" it to the disciples (see 6:41 and 8:6) reflect the ritual celebration of the Lord's table. The Greek word used for "fragments" (κλάσματα; *klasmata;* see 6:42; 8:9, 20) was an important term in later eucharistic texts.[23] Mark is interpreting the bread miracles in the light of the eucharistic celebrations of the Christian community that he knows, and for which he is writing his story of Jesus. Yet, in 6:32–44 and 8:1–9, Jesus himself does not make the distribution.[24] In the first miracle, seeing the lonely place and the lateness of the hour, the disciples ask Jesus to send the multitude away to the surrounding villages to buy something to eat. Jesus replies: "You give them something to eat" (6:37). After taking, blessing, and breaking the loaves, Jesus "gave them to the disciples to set before the people" (v. 41). The second miracle is inspired by Jesus' compassion for the crowd that has "come a very long way" (8:3). There is no command to the disciples to feed the people, but they are given the task. Again we read that Jesus "gave them (the broken loaves) to his disciples to set before the people; and they set them before the crowd" (v. 6). The bread miracles, therefore, stress the responsibilities of disciples who celebrate the table of the Lord. They are called to nourish all who come to share that table.

The broader narrative setting of the bread miracles (6:6b–8:26) shows that the twice-repeated Markan accounts of the multiplication of the loaves and the fish play an important role *in an unfolding story.* During the accounts of the feeding of the multitudes, the disciples are commissioned by Jesus to nourish them—but which multitudes? The accounts of the miracles are set within a wider context dominated by *the theme of mission.* The first miracle story (6:31–44) follows Jesus' sending out the Twelve on mission (6:7–13). This leads to a lengthy description of the death of John the Baptist (6:14–29) that makes clear that all who are prepared to take the risk of following Jesus down his way and sharing in his mission may have to pay the ultimate price. Like John the Baptist and Jesus, the disciples may lose their lives. After this interlude, the disciples return from the mission, full of their own importance and success (6:30). They have not fully understood the fact that their success depends on their being the *sent ones of Jesus*, as they tell him of all that *they* have said and done. The feeding (6:31–44) follows this initial mission of the Twelve, marked by success but also overshadowed by the possibility of the death of the missionary and the disciples' inability to understand fully that success in the mission does not depend on their skills or eloquence.[25] The first feeding miracle is set within Jewish territory, but what must be noticed is that the issue of *the mission of the disciples* has been seriously raised in all the material that immediately preceded it (vv. 7–30).

The theme of mission continues to play a dominant role in 7:1–30, the narrative placed between the first and the second feeding accounts. This passage opens with a polemical encounter between Jesus and Israel (7:1–13). The point at issue is "eating." The verb "to eat" (ἐσθίω; *esthiō*) and the word for "bread" (ἄρτος; *artos*) highlight the conflict (see 7:2, 3, 4, 5). The Pharisees are critical of the fact that Jesus' disciples do not eat "according to the tradition of the elders" (v. 5). They are trying to instruct Jesus on the correct way of eating. Jesus angrily rejects their complaints. He tells them they are abandoning the commandment of God, and are led astray by the tradition of human beings (vv. 8, 9, 13). He turns away from the leaders of Israel and addresses the people (vv. 14–15), insisting that Israel judges eating by "what is outside," but that the real causes of sinfulness are found elsewhere.

His teaching becomes more precise as he enters the house and speaks to his disciples (vv. 17–23). In the Gospel of Mark these private instructions "in the house" are aimed at those who are specially attached to Jesus. Jesus addresses his community.[26] He lists vices that "come from within" (vv. 21–23). Some of these are to be expected, as they come from the Decalogue. But at the end of the list there are four further vices not found there: envy, slander, pride, and foolishness. These vices also separate people and break down community. Thus, Jesus insists, while Israel uses external criteria for assessing ritual cleanliness, lasting divisions are created by more profound defects. Writing to his own community, Mark warns these early Christians against their propensity to be divided by envy, slander, pride, and foolishness. It is not only the breach of torah (evil thoughts, fornication, theft, murder, adultery, coveting, wickedness, deceit, and licentiousness) that defiles, but also the internal strife created by envy, slander, pride, and foolishness that tears the community apart.[27] Mark accepts the teachings of the torah, but goes further in his warnings against internal strife that might divide the Christian community. As Jesus instructs his disciples (vv. 17–23), a result of his bitter encounter with the leaders of Israel (vv. 1–13), he points beyond the limitations of a nation and its traditions. Deeper issues are to be attended to for the creation of a genuine Christian community.

Having made this point, Jesus sets out for a journey during which he is always in Gentile territory. So that the reader might understand, Mark stresses the geography of Jesus' movements: "And from there he arose and went away to the region of Tyre and Sidon" (7:24). "Then he returned from the region of Tyre and went through Sidon to the Sea of Galilee through the region of the Decapolis" (v. 31). Jesus is journeying through Gentile lands at these times. While he is on this journey he cures a Syrophoenician woman's daughter and thus reverses the established order of those at table and those seeking the crumbs that fall (7:27).[28] In the first bread miracle, Jesus fed a Jewish crowd in the land of Israel. But he moves away from the land of Israel, and on the way, the woman asks that even the Gentile dogs be allowed to feed at the crumbs that fall from the table. The arrogance of a people that attempts to instruct Jesus on table fellowship (7:1–8) is thrown into disarray by the response of a woman who frankly confesses her nothingness. She receives Jesus' gift of life for her daughter because she recognizes the radical nature of her need and nothingness.[29] This "crumb" from the table looks forward to the second feeding miracle (8:1–9). Still in a Gentile land (see 7:31), Jesus cures a deaf mute whose cure generates wonder. This wonder leads Gentiles to describe Jesus in terms that recall the prophet Isaiah's description of the Messiah: "He even makes the deaf hear and the dumb speak" (7:37; see Isaiah 35:5–6).

The second feeding, set in Gentile territory, follows (8:1–9). Jesus has compassion for the crowds that have gathered, as they have been with him three days and have had nothing to eat. All the while Jesus has been in Gentile lands, he has gradually gathered a crowd. He will not send the people away hungry, for "some of them have come a very long way" (vv. 2–3). But the disciples complain. It is impossible to feed such a huge crowd with bread, as they are in a desert (v. 4). As in the first miracle, Jesus takes from their meager resources, and feeds and satisfies the crowd (vv. 5–7). After the meal, the fragments (κλάσματα; *klasmata*) are gathered into seven baskets; as in the first miracle, fragments were gathered into twelve baskets.[30] As Jesus himself journeys from Israel into the Gentile world, and thus within an overall context of mission, he feeds both Jews (6:31–44) and Gentiles (8:1–9).[31]

How do the disciples perform during these feeding miracles? In both accounts they want to send the crowds away (6:35–36; 8:4). Jesus will not allow this, as they have been called to be part of *his mission*, not one that can be determined by their own good sense, or their traditions and practices. He insists that they cross into unknown territory in their acceptance of his mission. He thus commands them: "You give them something to eat" (6:37) and he involves them in the distribution of the loaves (6:41, 8:6). Here, as throughout the gospel, the disciples are called to a privileged participation in the mission of the Lord. Situating these two bread miracles within the broader narrative context of mission, Mark issues a call to the Christian community to feed Jews and Gentiles. The community of Jesus serves both Jew and Gentile, to be nourished by the disciples of Jesus. But the disciples would prefer that the people look after themselves (6:36; 8:4), and they "did not understand about the loaves" (6:52).

As Mark tells of this *past* failure of disciples during the life of Jesus, he warns the members of his own Christian community, lest they too not understand about the loaves. Behind the narrative that runs from 6:6b–8:30 lie the difficulties of the early Christian community over the mission to the Gentiles. Table fellowship of any kind would have called for a new way of understanding the mission of Jesus to both Jew and Gentile. But it would have been keenly felt when the Christian community gathered at the table of the Lord. The use of the two bread miracles (6:31–44; 8:1–9), within this larger section of Mark's gospel devoted to the question of mission, reflects the pain that was felt in the struggles both for and against the opening of the community's eucharistic table to both Jewish Christians and Gentile Christians. The problem of table fellowship in the early church was understandably widespread, and is found in other parts of the New Testament (especially Acts 10–11 and Gal 2:11–21).

The question of an exclusive concept of who should be admitted to the table of the Lord stands behind the two feeding miracles. They are placed strategically within the context of 6:6b–8:30, where the theme of the universal mission of Jesus and of the Christian community has emerged. Mark has told his story of the two miracles of feeding the multitudes to teach the members of his community that they are to share in the universal mission of Jesus, cost what it may (see 6:14–29, which reports the death of John the Baptist). Jesus, taking from the poverty and insufficiency of the disciples' few loaves and fish (6:41 and 8:6), feeds the multitudes on the Jewish and the Gentile sides of the lake. The Markan interpretation of the bread miracles sends the Christian community on a mission that has no boundaries, in which the divisions generated by envy, slander, pride, and foolishness must be abandoned (see 7:22).

## Jesus' last meal with his disciples

Jesus gathers with his disciples for a final meal on the night before he goes to the cross. He breaks bread and shares a cup in a ritual that continues to be remembered and practiced within the Markan community. The account of this final meal (14:22–25) is found at the heart of a long narrative dedicated to Jesus' final moments with his disciples (14:1–72). In our study of Mark the storyteller, we have noticed that he tends to frame stories. We have seen that Mark shaped the story of Jesus' passion (14:1–15:47) as a long series of intercalations.[32] The light of Jesus' presence to the disciples contrasts with the development of a plot to slay Jesus, betrayal by one of the Twelve, denials by another, and the flight of all of them (14:1–72). Jesus goes to his death, totally open to the design of God, cost him what it may (see 15:34, 37), while others bear false witness, give in to unjust accusations, abuse him, crucify him, and bury him (15:1–47). The use of intercalation across 14:1–15:47 shows that Mark's interpretations can be found not only in *what he writes,* but also in *how he writes.*[33] Indeed, the interpreter is best understood by uncovering how he tells his story.

In Mark 14:17–31, Jesus' unconditional surrender of himself to the will of God is surrounded by the darkness of ignorance, betrayal, and denial. Mark interprets Jesus' presence to the disciples across the story of the gospel as a whole, as never failing his fragile and fearful disciples. An attentive reading of 14:17–31 indicates that, at this important moment during Jesus' last night with his disciples, he is present to them in the same way. As Jesus shares intimacy and himself with his disciples, he tells of betrayal, denials, and flight, but this does not lessen the intensity of his self-gift for them. Nor does it cause him to withdraw the promise of his future presence to them, even though they may all fall away.

In vv. 17–21, the scene that serves as the first part of the frame around the account of the meal, Mark indicates that Judas, who will betray Jesus, belongs to the inner circle of his friends. Jesus "came with the Twelve," a group that was appointed in 3:14 "to be with him" in a unique way (v. 17). The setting for Jesus' prediction of his betrayal is the meal table, a place sacred among friends.[34] The tragedy is heightened by the idea that it is someone who shares table fellowship who will betray Jesus. This theme takes us back to the role of the disciples in the feeding miracles of 6:31–44 and 8:1–10 where, *despite the inability of the disciples to understand about the loaves,* Jesus took from their poverty and fed the masses, both Jew and Gentile. There we saw that they wanted to exclude others from the table of the Lord. Now all of them, Judas, Peter, and the others, are about to break their exclusive table fellowship with Jesus. Mark heightens this theme as Jesus explains that the betrayer will be "one who is eating with me" (v. 18). The intimacy is intensified by the words of Jesus that link Judas with the group of "the Twelve" commissioned "to be with him" (3:14): "It is one of the Twelve, one who is dipping bread in the same dish with me" (14:20). Jesus is to be betrayed by a person who has shared the most intimate of experiences with him.[35]

At the center of the frame that addresses the future failure of the disciples comes the account of the meal itself in vv. 22–25. This passage forms not only the centerpiece of vv. 17–31 but also the whole of 14:1–72. In the heart of Mark's account of Jesus' final moments with his disciples (14:1–72), Jesus shares a last meal with the disciples, who have not understood about the loaves (6:52), whose hearts are hardened (6:52; 8:17), and who will betray and abandon him (14:17–21, 26–31). The broader context makes the account of Jesus' last meal with his disciples with its frame in vv. 17–31 even more poignant.[36] The theme of table fellowship with the betrayers opens the passage: "And as they were eating, he took bread, and blessed, and broke it, and gave it to them and said, 'Take . . .'" (v. 22). This theme is continued in the sharing of the cup, where the same recipients are again specified: "And he took the cup, and when he had given thanks, he gave it to them, and they all drank of it" (v. 23). A bond exists between Jesus and the disciples whom he does not abandon: all eat the bread broken (v.22), all drink of the cup (v. 23), and all sing a hymn together (v. 26). Neither Mark nor Matthew have the words "for you" in their reporting of Jesus' words over the bread broken (as do Luke 22:19 ["This is my body, which is given for you"] and 1 Cor 11:24 ["This is my body which is for you"]) or the cup shared (as does Luke 22:20 ["This cup, which is poured out for you"]). Nevertheless, Mark sets up an intimate dialogue between Jesus and the disciples around the table. He commands them, "Take" (14:22), and they do.[37]

For Mark, the words over the bread and the cup point to the cross, a body given in death and blood poured out as the result of a broken body (vv. 22 and 24). Yet they look beyond the day of crucifixion. The blood is to be a covenant, "poured out for many" (v. 24), and Jesus comments that he will not "drink again of the fruit of the vine *until* that day when I drink it new in the kingdom of God" (v. 25). The word "until" (ἕως; *heōs*) has a temporal function within the sentence that forces the readers to look beyond the events of the crucifixion. Jesus' words, in the midst of predictions of betrayal, flight, and denial, ring out a message of trust and hope. This message is associated with Mark's interpretation of Jesus of Nazareth, traced in the preceding chapter. The person and mission of Jesus, and the person and mission of the disciple, are intimately linked. We have seen that, for Mark, Jesus is the Christ and the Son of God on the cross, but he also the suffering Son of Man whose self-gift in unconditional obedience will be vindicated. This death will be for the ransom of many (10:45).

Mark devotes similar attention to the closeness between Jesus and his disciples in vv. 26–31, the passage closing the frame around the account of the meal in vv. 22–25. Jesus predicts that the disciples "will all fall away," but he uses the image of the shepherd and his sheep (v. 27), also found within the context of the bread miracles (see 6:34). His predictions lead to expressions of love and devotion. Peter swears an unfailing loyalty, better than all the others who may fall away (v. 29), and claims he is prepared to lay down his life out of loyalty for his master (v. 31). Peter is not alone in swearing his loyalty. Mark adds: "And they all said the same" (v. 31). By means of vv. 17–21 and vv. 26–31, framing the account of the meal in vv. 22–25, Mark communicates a sense of foreboding. Disciples from Jesus' most intimate circle will betray and abandon him. Themes that emerged around the disciples' hardness of heart and inability to understand about the loaves (6:52) are reaching their climax.

Across the passages we have investigated (6:41–42; 8:7–8; 14:22–25), formulae from the early church's celebrations are used to tell of the eating of the bread and drinking from the cup. Expressions reflecting a ritual have been read back into the story of Jesus' meals beside the lake and with his disciples on the night before he died: take (λαβεῖν; *labein:* 6:41; 8:6; 14:22–23), give thanks (εὐχαριστέω; *eucharisteō* 8:6; 14:23), break (κλάω; *klaō:* 6:41, 8:6; 14:22), give (δίδωμι; *didōmi:* 6:41; 8:7; 14:23), bless (εὐλογέω; *eulogeō:* 6:41; 8:7; 14:22), eat (φάγομαι; *phago-mai:* 6:42; 8:8; 14:22), broken pieces (κλάσματα; *klasmata:* 6:43, 8:8). Mark presents a story of a last meal shared by Jesus and the disciples that has become the first of many subsequent meals "in the kingdom." Mark instructed the members of his own Christian community that they were the recipients of a tradition that began with the life, teaching, death, and resurrection of Jesus, and that had to be repeated and safeguarded in their own celebrations of the table of the Lord. They were privileged participants in a meal, shared with Jesus "in the kingdom," however imperfect and fragile that sense of belonging to the kingdom may have often been.

Another Markan theme that has gained importance as Jesus moved toward his death is Jesus' reference to the establishment of the kingdom of God in 14:25. In the closing section of the public ministry, in bitter polemic with the authorities of Israel, Jesus made his first reference to the new temple founded on the rejected cornerstone (see 12:10–11). The theme became more important through the Jewish trial (14:58) and in the abuse that the passersby hurled at the crucified Jesus (15:29–30). In his death, the old temple is destroyed. The holy of holies, opened through the tearing apart of the dividing veil, is made available to the whole world (15:37–38). Mark instructs his readers that this new temple, founded on the rejected cornerstone (see 12:10–11), is the Christian community, called to mission and to a sharing of their table, where Jesus was present, no matter how seriously they may have failed to respond to his teaching. It is the presence of Jesus in the midst of failure that was recalled when the Markan community broke the bread and shared the cup in their celebrations of the table of the Lord.[38]

## Conclusion

The members of Mark's community knew all too well that the Lord had given himself, and that he continued to give himself to disciples who failed. This is the reason why, when Mark recounted Jesus' presence to them in the meal of the Lord's supper, he told the story in such a striking way. Jesus loved his failing disciples with a love that is in not matched by their love for him (14:17–31). The disciples also knew that the task of taking the table of the Lord into the mission field would not be simple. They had to cross barriers never crossed before, being summoned to share the table of the Lord with both Jew and Gentile, but this mission found them wanting (6:31–44; 8:1–9) and here old prejudices came to the surface. The traditions they had received, and respected, from the religion and ritual practice of Israel were being severely challenged by the birth of a tradition with its roots in the life, teaching, death, and resurrection of Jesus of Nazareth. In their moments of hesitation they were challenged by the words of Jesus: "You give them something to eat" (6:36).

> The evangelist has linked Eucharistic texts with some of the most painful pastoral questions of his church: mission and reconciliation. Both involved deep divisions that may have erupted at the Eucharistic celebration; both involved painful alienations which could only be healed and ultimately reconciled in the table-fellowship of Eucharist. There Jew and Gentile could share one bread; there too, a

sadder-but-wiser church could repent of its failures and once again take up the bond of discipleship. The source of hope in both instances was not to be found in the fragile disciples themselves but in the compassion and strength of the Risen Christ.[39]

Mark's interpretation of the role of the disciples, the subject of the first part of this chapter, and his telling of their sharing the table of the Lord, the subject the latter half of the chapter, are closely related. Together, they point to the Markan understanding of the Christian community. The story of failure that is critical to the portrait of the disciples of Jesus in the Gospel of Mark may have its roots in the historical fact of the limitations of the original disciples. However, the central importance of this theme of failure indicates that—whatever its origins—it is a major part of the author's theological interpretation of the story of Jesus so that he might instruct his own Christian community. Mark addressed a Christian community aware of its own experiences of failure. Indeed, it is to disciples who betray, deny, and flee from Jesus (14:17–21, 27–31) that he gives himself in his broken body and his spilled blood (vv. 22–26). Mark tells a story of the never-failing presence of Jesus to disciples who never love him in the way he loves them. He tells us that such was the case in the life of Jesus, but he did not reject disciples *then*. Nor will he reject his fragile disciples *now* or *ever*.

His theme of the failure of the disciples was not primarily a summons to the members of his community to *reject* the portrait of the disciples in the gospel, and thus become perfect disciples of Jesus.[40] Mark interpreted the reality of their fragility, and the potential for failure, ignorance, denial, and even betrayal to address the community for which he wrote the gospel. However, it also pointed to the central need for radical dependence on the person of Jesus who never fails the failing disciple. Disciples may not succeed in the response to the call to lose themselves in following the way of Jesus (see 8:34–9:1). A journey that involves turning the values of the world upside down often produces fear and failure (see, for example 10:32 and 16:7–8).

The vocation to live through the mystery of failure, depending only on the greater mystery of the love and power of God shown to us in Jesus, stands at the heart of the Markan interpretation of the Christian community.[41] Mark endeavors to reveal disciples for what they are, and consequently, the Christian community for what it is. The failure of the disciples, both in their following of Jesus and their celebration at the table of the Lord, is a message about the overpowering need for dependence on Jesus, and trust in God's saving power through him. Discipleship is a mixture of privilege and egoism, of success and failure. Mark interprets this experience forcefully, addressing the problem of the ambiguity of the Christian community through the portrait of Jesus' own first disciples, the first to follow him, and the first to share in the broken body and the spilled blood of their crucified Lord. For Mark, the apparent failure of Jesus of Nazareth will finally be revealed as victory when he returns at the right hand of God (see 14:61–62). The words of Easter are proclaimed to a community of failing disciples: "He is going before you into Galilee, as he promised" (16:6–8; 14:27–28). As God's action reversed the *apparent* failure of Jesus, God's action reverses the *real* failures of Christians.

## Notes

1. In both Greek and Latin, the root of the word "disciple" means "to learn" (Greek: μαθηταί *[mathētai]*, from the verb μανθάνειν *[manthanein]*, "to learn"; Latin: from the verb "discere," also meaning "to learn").

2. For a survey of a variety of approaches and different interpretations of the role of the disciples in Mark, see C. Clifton Black, *The Disciples according to Mark: Markan Redaction in Current Debate* (JSNTSup 27; Sheffield: Sheffield Academic Press, 1989). For a briefer overview, see F. J. Moloney, "The Vocation of the Disciples in the Gospel of Mark," in *"A Hard Saying": The Gospel and Culture* (Collegeville: Liturgical Press, 2001), 53–63.

3. The tradition of the appearances of Jesus to the disciples (especially in the light of 1 Cor 15:3–7) is older than the Gospel of Mark. Mark's original readers (as well as all subsequent readers) would have been surprised by the ending of Mark's Gospel at 16:8. They would be aware that he was not telling the story *as they knew it.* He is *reinterpreting* an established tradition.

4. R. A. Horsley, *Hearing the Whole Story: The Politics of Plot in Mark's Gospel* (Louisville: Westminster John Knox, 2001), 177–201, rightly insists that Mark is not primarily interested in individual discipleship, but "exhibits considerable concern for community" (p. 178). However, for Horsley the community is being summoned to a popular renewal of Israel's covenant. He rejects the christological foundation of a new community, the basis of my understanding of Mark's interpretation.

5. On the historical "Twelve" and the more general group of followers or disciples of Jesus, see J. P. Meier, *A Marginal Jew: Rethinking the Historical Jesus* (3 vols.; ABRL; New York: Doubleday, 1991–2002), 3:125–97.

6. For a detailed analysis of this passage, and the insistence that what is said of "the Twelve" is to be applied to followers of Jesus in general, especially the readers of the Gospel, see F. J. Moloney, *The Gospel of Mark: A Commentary* (Peabody: Hendrickson, 2002), 76–80. See also the important study of K. Stock, *Boten aus dem Mit-Ihm-Sein: Das Verhältnis zwischen Jesus und den Zwölf nach Markus* (AnBib 70; Rome: Biblical Institute Press, 1975).

7. See F. J. Moloney, "Mark 6:6b–30: Mission, the Baptist, and Failure," *CBQ* 63 (2001): 647–56.

8. The passage that runs from 6:7 to 30 is another example of the Markan practice of intercalation. The disciples are sent out (A: vv. 7–13), the cost of

proclaiming the truth is reported in the death of the Baptist, which foreshadows the death of Jesus (B: vv. 14–29), those who were sent out return to Jesus (A': v. 30).

9. See Moloney, "Mark 6:6b–30," 656–63.

10. For a detailed study of 8:22–10:52 that supports the sketch of the disciples offered in this paragraph, see Moloney, *Mark*, 171–214.

11. See R. A. Culpepper, "Mark 10:50: Why Mention the Garment?" *JBL* 101 (1982): 131–32.

12. Peter, James, and John appear to have a special closeness to Jesus (see 3:16–17; 5:37; 9:2; 13:3).

13. See H. Fleddermann, "The Flight of a Naked Young Man (Mark 14:51–52)," *CBQ* 41 (1979): 412–17; Moloney, *Mark*, 344–48.

14. See N. Q. Hamilton, "Resurrection, Tradition and the Composition of Mark," *JBL* 84 (1965): 415–21; Moloney, *Mark*, 344–52.

15. T. J. Weeden, *Mark—Traditions in Conflict* (Philadelphia: Fortress, 1976), 50–51. For Weeden, the disciples are used in the story as the representatives of a false Christology. A similar negative reading of the role of the disciples is found in Horsley, *Hearing the Whole Story*, 79–97. For Horsley, the issue is not Christology (see p. 269 n. 22), but as the oral performance of Mark presents "unmitigated faithlessness and failure from the middle of the story to the end" (p. 97), interpreters of Mark have missed the point in their concern over disciples. The Markan Jesus addresses the authentic but submerged tradition of the Galilean peasants over against the false but accepted tradition of the Jerusalem scribes and the Pharisees.

16. See especially, R. C. Tannehill, "The Disciples in Mark: The Function of a Narrative Role," *JR* 57 (1977): 386–405. This important study is also available in W. Telford, ed., *The Interpretation of Mark* (IRT 7; Philadelphia: Fortress, 1985), 134–57.

17. See Moloney, *Mark*, 352–54.

18. For a more extended treatment of these passages, see also F. J. Moloney, *A Body Broken for a Broken People. Eucharist in the New Testament* (2d ed.; Peabody: Hendrickson, 1997), 31–56.

19. For a critical assessment of this question, see R. M. Fowler, *Loaves and Fishes: The Function of the Feeding Stories in the Gospel of Mark* (SBLDS 54; Chico: Scholars Press, 1981), 132–47.

20. See above, pp. 74–76.

21. There are many parallels between the two bread miracles and the surrounding material. This relationship was first highlighted by R. H. Lightfoot, *History and Interpretation in the Gospels* (Bantam Lectures 1934; London: Hodder & Stoughton, 1935), 113–17, and often pointed out since. It serves as the basis for my reading of Mark 6:31–8:30. See Moloney, *Mark*, 115–68.

22. On the eucharistic elements in the tradition, see, among many, S. Masuda, "The Good News of the Miracle of the Bread. The Tradition and Its Markan Redaction," *NTS* 28 (1982): 201–3, and especially Moloney, *Mark*, 129–32, 152–56.

23. For a detailed study of the process that led from a feeding miracle in the life of Jesus to the Markan eucharistic refashioning of that story, see J.-M. van Cangh, *La Multiplication des Pains et l'Eucharistie* (LD 86; Paris: Cerf, 1975), 67–109. See also B. van Iersel, "Die wunderbare Speisung und das Abendmahl

in der synoptischen Tradition," *NovT* 7 (1964): 167–94, and Masuda, "The Good News of the Miracle of the Bread," 191–219.

24. In John 6:11, in a passage that *heightens* the eucharistic features in the account of the feeding miracle (the only one in the Gospel of John), Jesus distributes the loaves.

25. See Moloney, "Mark 6:6b–30," 647–63.

26. See F. Manns, "Le thème de la maison dans l'évangile de Marc," *RSR* 66 (1992): 1–17.

27. On this list, see Moloney, *Mark*, 143–44.

28. P. Esler, *Community and Gospel in Luke-Acts: The Social and Political Motivations of Lucan Theology* (SNTSMS 57; Cambridge: Cambridge University Press, 1987), 89–91 analyzes Mark 7:1–30 and its understanding of food laws and table fellowship. He concludes: "We are surely meant to see this image as a justification for the eucharistic fellowship of Jews and Gentiles in the Christian community" (p. 91).

29. See Moloney, *Mark*, 144–48.

30. These details are but some of the indications of the Jewishness of the setting of the first miracle, with the number twelve, and the use of the word for "basket" (κόφινος; *kophinos*), and the Gentile setting of the second, with the number seven, and the use of another word for "basket" (σπύρις; *spuris*). For further detail, see Moloney, *Mark*, 155.

31. On the significance of the Jewish and Gentile feedings, see van Cangh, *La Multiplication des Pains*, 111–31. Although this is a position taken by most interpreters, not all would agree. See, for example, M. D. Hooker, *The Gospel according to St. Mark* (BNTC; Peabody: Hendrickson, 1991), 188; J. Gnilka, *Das Evangelium nach Markus* (5th ed.; EKKNT II/1–2; 2 vols.; Zürich/Neukirchen/Vluyn: Benziger Verlag/Neukirchener Verlag, 1998), 1:304.

32. See above, pp. 98–111.

33. It remains true that for most who originally experienced the Gospel of Mark as their "story of Jesus" would have heard it. It would have been an aural experience. It presumes too much, however, to suggest that there was only an "oral" Gospel—indeed many and varied oral tellings and retellings of this gospel, as Horsley, *Hearing the Whole Story*, 53–78, has suggested.

34. On the importance of meals in the biblical tradition, see, among many, X. Léon-Dufour, *Sharing the Eucharistic Bread: The Witness of the New Testament* (New York: Paulist, 1987), 35–38.

35. See, on this passage, V. K. Robbins, "Last Meal: Preparation, Betrayal, and Absence," in *The Passion in Mark: Studies on Mark 14–16* (ed. W. Kelber; Philadelphia: Fortress, 1976) 29–34. Robbins's study is typical of much contemporary Markan scholarship that understands the disciples as completely negative characters. This approach is also marked by a "corrective Christology." The disciples have it completely wrong, and thus the author uses them as a foil to present a point of view that "corrects" their errors, presumably present in the Markan community. For a critical survey of this scholarship, see J. D. Kingsbury, *The Christology of Mark's Gospel* (Philadelphia: Fortress, 1983), 25–45.

36. On the broader picture, see above, pp. 99–105.

37. Léon-Dufour, *Sharing the Eucharistic Bread*, 60–62, 117–18, 130–32, 195–96, rightly insists on this "dialogic" character of the Markan/Matthean account.

38. See, on this, the fine study of D. Juel, *Messiah and Temple: The Trial of Jesus in the Gospel of Mark* (SBLDS 31; Missoula: Scholars Press, 1977).

39. D. Senior, "The Eucharist in Mark: Mission, Reconciliation, Hope," *BTB* 12 (1982), 71.

40. This claim has been made by a number of redaction critics. Robbins, "Last Meal," and Weeden, *Traditions in Conflict,* are representative of this position.

41. See Moloney, "The Vocation of the Disciples," 83–84.

# PART FOUR

# MARK THE EVANGELIST

# CHAPTER 8

---

# The Good News of the Gospel of Mark

The word "evangelist" has taken on a meaning in contemporary English that is closely associated with certain charismatic figures who have led movements in the churches of the evangelical Protestant tradition. In some sense, Mark can be seen as a forerunner to this meaning of an "evangelist." He looked back to the biblical tradition, and the life of Jesus, in order to revive the flagging spirits of a struggling Christian community. He wrote for a community suffering from persecution, trying to cope with failure among its members, and wondering if the destruction of Jerusalem and its temple was the sign of the end of time. There was not much space for hierarchy and cult in his message, although the celebration of the table of the Lord was certainly in place. But Mark provides his own reason for writing a narrative that reports the life of Jesus.

Mark the evangelist wished to announce "good news" (Mark 1:1: Ἀρχὴ τοῦ εὐαγγελίου; *archē tou euangeliou*),[1] and the English word "evangelist" receives its primary meaning from the Greek word for "good news" (τὸ εὐαγγελίον; *to euangelion*).[2] The good news of the Gospel of Mark cannot become the property of any single Christian tradition, or any single understanding of the challenges of preaching and responding to the word of God. If it remains "good news" as the third millennium opens, it speaks to all Christian believers, regardless of their cultures or their traditions.

A study of Mark *the evangelist* looks to the ongoing relevance of the good news contained within the pages of this particular rendition of the life and teaching, the death and resurrection of Jesus of Nazareth.

However, as the analysis of Mark as a storyteller and as an interpreter has shown, his proclamation of the good news of Jesus, the Christ, and the Son of God takes some surprising turns. He writes in rough Greek, but crafts a narrative that is impressive in its simple profundity. A closer reading of Mark's unique interpretation of Jesus of Nazareth and the Christian community demonstrates the work of a creative and original early Christian thinker. Mark took traditions that came to him, and rewrote them in a way that produced an understanding of Jesus, the Christ, the Son of God, and the Son of Man that addressed the strengths and weaknesses of the Christian community. Is this version of Jesus' life and teaching, death and resurrection, "good news"? It is with this question in mind that we turn to the final section of this study: Is Mark an evangelist? In other words, is the story of the life and teaching, death, and resurrection of Jesus, as it is reported in the Gospel of Mark, "good news"?[3]

## Anonymity

The author of this story never appears, neither as a character nor by the insertion of his name. This fact has puzzled interpreters, and provided them food for hypothesis upon hypothesis about the author of the gospel since the testimony of Papias in the second century. But this anonymity points to another feature of the Gospel of Mark: not only the author remains nameless. Among the many characters who suddenly appear and disappear across the story, only a few have names: Jesus, some of his disciples (see 3:13–19: the Twelve; 2:14: Levi), his mother, Mary, and his brothers James, Joses, Judas, and Simon (6:3), Jairus (5:22), John the Baptist and Herod (1:2–8; 6:14–29), Bartimaeus (10:46), Pilate (15:1), Simon of Cyrene, known because of his sons Alexander and Rufus (15:21), and the women at the cross and the tomb (15:40–41, 47; 16:1). Who are the people possessed by evil spirits (1:21–28; 5:1–20)? Who are the many disciples who do not receive names (see, for example 3:13; 4:10; 10:32)? Who are the people whose lives are touched by Jesus' healing authority (1:29–30, 40–45, 2:1–12; 3:1–6; 5:25–35; 7:24–30, 31–37; 8:22–26; 9:14–29), and whose death he conquers (5:35–43)?[4] What is the function of the anonymous characters he addresses, nourishes, heals, and cares for, but who eventually ask for his death and mock him as he hangs on the cross (see, for example 6:31–44, 53–56; 7:14–23; 8:1–9, 34–38; 15:6–15, 29)? Who is the widow who gives her livelihood (12:41–44), the woman who anoints Jesus' body in preparation for death (14:3–9), and the anonymous young man who refuses to accept Jesus' call to discipleship (10:17–22)?

The named people in the story are there because of their historical importance as active characters during the life of Jesus. This applies especially to Jesus himself, and to the named disciples.[5] The same could be said for John the Baptist, Herod and Pilate, and probably for Mary and the brothers of Jesus.[6] The other names have come to Mark in the tradition, and in some cases, from the fact that the community for which he is writing knew them: Bartimaeus, Jairus, the women at the cross and the tomb, and Simon of Cyrene.[7] If those few named characters in the story can be thus explained, why is there still so much anonymity in the Gospel of Mark? Studies on characterization have shown that authors use anonymous characters in a story to draw the reader or listener more closely into the detail of the action and the point of view of the author expressed by means of the narrative.[8] The medieval moral plays often cast the central character, embodying the virtues that the author wished to communicate to the people attending the performance, as "Everyman." A parallel technique is used by authors who make extensive use of anonymous characters in a narrative. As the reader cannot pin the performance of a particular character to a name and a period of time, that character can transcend such limitations. The author can thus lead the reader to sense a certain identity with an *unidentified* character. The reader may then ask: How would I perform in that situation?

The use of anonymity in the Gospel of Mark has not received the attention it deserves, and the following sketch touches on some possible avenues of interpretation. Anonymous characters in the Gospel of Mark both challenge and encourage the reader, but they might also lead to disappointment. Perhaps more than anywhere else in the gospel, the reader treads carefully before identifying with its anonymous characters. Yet the ambiguity of the performance of the anonymous Markan characters can also address the ambiguous performance of the reader of the gospel.

## Challenge and encouragement

There is encouragement in the freedom that comes from Jesus' victory over the evils that assail unnamed characters. Evil and destructive powers invade the world of two nameless characters, and attempt to overcome Jesus by addressing him by name in the accounts of the possessed man in the synagogue at Capernaum (1:21–28) and the Gerasene demoniac (5:1–20). Drawn into the story by the anonymity of the leading characters, the reader might recognize the occasions when powers larger than themselves seem to violently separate them from the way of Jesus. But the evil powers are not able to control Jesus, despite the fact that they call him by name (1:24; 5:7), or persuade him to allow them to control their victims, or to do as they would like (5:10–12).

The presence of evil and its destructive power is vividly portrayed in the account of the Gerasene demoniac who "lived among the tombs. No one could bind him any more, even with a chain; for he had often been bound with fetters and chains, but the chains he wrenched apart and the chains he broke in pieces; and no one had the strength to subdue him. Night and day among the tombs he was always crying out, and bruising himself with stones" (5:3–5). This is powerful folkloric language, but also a metaphor of the human being trapped by evil, unable to break free from its control.[9] The reader is informed by means of this story that Jesus overcomes the evil forces and the afflicted person once again experiences freedom: "And they came to Jesus, and saw the demoniac sitting there, clothed and in his right mind, the man who had had the legion" (v. 15). Not only does he experience freedom, but he asks that he might be "with Jesus" (v. 18; see 3:14). Jesus, however, must determine the nature of discipleship, and thus he sends the ex-demoniac into the Gentile world of his hometown as a witness to all that "the Lord" has done for him (vv. 19–20). Good reading calls for the use of imagination, and once the reader is drawn into the world of those unnamed people whom Jesus freed from their slavery to the powers of evil, Mark's narrative can address the problem of the slavery imposed by the legions of evil. Mark the evangelist proclaims that the authority of Jesus can free one from such entrapment.

The same metaphor applies to the unnamed characters that Jesus frees from the evil of physical sickness: Simon's mother-in-law (1:29–30), the leper, excluded from society and from his religious culture and practice by his disease (1:40–45), as the woman who was forever impure because of her flow of blood (5:25–34). In each of these accounts, Jesus breaks through the barriers of taboo and accepted ritual practice by allowing a woman to serve him (1:45), and by touching the unclean (1:41; 5:28–33). He restores full health by forgiving sin (2:1–12), and shows his superiority to the limitations of a narrow-minded understanding of the role of the Sabbath by restoring the withered hand of an unnamed man (3:1–6). These miracles, set at the beginning and the end of a series of conflicts between Jesus and the leaders of Israel, lead to a decision that he must be destroyed (3:6). In rapid succession, he heals the daughter of a Gentile woman (7:24–30), restores the speech of a Gentile man (31–37), and cures the epileptic boy, to throw into relief the shallowness of faith of his disciples, and to bless the faith of the father of the boy, who recognizes his need for Jesus' presence (9:14–29).

This overview of Jesus' healing several unnamed characters in the story not only invites the reader to recognize the possibility that Jesus' presence can be found in the midst of physical suffering, but also points to Jesus' preparedness to put himself at risk to assist the afflicted. Indeed, this feature of the miracle stories is at the heart of Mark's use of them to proclaim the "good news." The most telling element in Mark's healing accounts of unnamed people suffering from ailments of many kinds is not so much the fact that they call on Jesus and he restores them to health. Such a reading of the function of the miracle stories in the Gospel of Mark would be superficial in the extreme. The miracles of Jesus are not ultimately about Jesus as a healer, and this was one of the reasons for Mark's use of the so-called messianic secret. Characters in the story and the reader of the story are not to become overfascinated with Jesus as a miracle worker. His response to the design of God, and his establishment of the reigning presence of God, are consummately revealed in his death and resurrection. The healing miracles of Jesus reveal the reigning presence of God to whom Jesus responds without condition.[10] They are not an end in themselves.

These activities of Jesus in favor of the anonymous ailing people in the story summon Christian readers to "go the extra mile" in giving support and bringing healing to those who seek it. In their own turn, they indicate in the "miracles" they perform for the suffering that God, the Father of Jesus, still reigns. Contemporary medical science is able to identify and to heal illness in a way that was foreign to the world of Jesus. But who reaches across the barriers of financially imposed health schemes to bring wholeness to the less privileged, and thus reveal in the twenty-first century the healing presence of Jesus, as he is portrayed in the Gospel of Mark? Jesus was prepared to take a young woman by the hand, to call her in affectionate terms, and rescue her from death (5:35–43). The anonymous people who seek Jesus in their ailments, and are brought healing, no matter how much Jesus had to challenge authority, taboo, ritual practice, and even run the risk of death, announce the "good news" of Jesus, the Christ, the Son of God (1:1). This "good news," however, also meant that the Son of Man had to be slain before his vindication in the resurrection, and his final coming in glory.

The anonymous "crowds" or "people" scattered throughout the story are perhaps the characters with whom the reader can most easily identify. They have no names or places of origin. They are simply part of the story, as is the reader. In a way also similar to the reader, their response to Jesus is mixed. There are times when they enthuse over him (1:27–28), and other times when he is overcome by compassion for them in their need (6:34; 8:2). He nourishes them abundantly by means of meals that cannot be exhausted (6:31–44; 8:1–9). At the end of the two bread miracles, during which Jesus has called on disciples to feed both Jews and Gentiles, the fragments are collected. The meal will continue, as the nourishment generated by Jesus' presence cannot be exhausted (6:32–44; 8:1–9). But the crowd is not simply a vague third party to the Markan story, always outside looking in. The people are instructed on the new criteria for becoming a member of Jesus' new family. They are told: "Whoever does the will of God is my brother, and sister, and mother" (3:35; see vv. 31–35). After the first passion prediction (8:31), and Peter's failure to accept fully what it means to follow Jesus (8:32–33), Jesus calls "the multitude with the disciples" (v. 34), and instructs them on the way of discipleship. In 8:34–38, formal teaching methods are very much in evidence: "If any person would come after me . . ." (v. 34); "For whoever would save his life . . ." (v. 35); "What does it profit a person . . ." (v. 36); "What can a person give . . ." (v. 37); "Whoever is ashamed of me . . ." (v. 38). *Everyone* is a potential disciple, in a way parallel to the "Everyman" of medieval theater.[11]

*Everyone* who reads or hears the proclamation of the "good news" of the Gospel of Mark is summoned to be a disciple of Jesus. But *everyone* is also capable of turning against him, finding that the summons to follow him to resurrection and victory with God only by means of a cross never has and never will make sense to those whose hopes and dreams are determined by the everyday affairs of life. These affairs have their proper and important place, but they must be transcended if one wishes to follow the crucified and risen Christ.

## Disappointment

The crowd, goaded by those who have made up their minds that Jesus must be eliminated (see 3:6; 14:1–2, 43, 53, 61–64; 15:1, 3, 10, 31–32),[12] call for his crucifixion (15:6–15) and hurl abuse at him as he hangs on the cross (vv. 29–30). However, the reader—who has read the prologue of 1:1–13—should be stunned into recognizing that the abuse aimed at Jesus by the passersby is unacceptable: "Save yourself, and come down from the cross" (v. 30). The reader's identification with the anonymous crowds who form the backdrop for much of the Gospel of Mark must cease at this point. The reader *must* recognize that it is *on the cross* that Jesus saves (see 10:45). However, the decision lies with the reader, and this call to decision in favor of the crucified Christ, Son of God, and Son of Man is further Markan good news for the contemporary reader. Resurrection and final vindication are found only on the other side of a life given for the sake of Jesus and the good news (see 8:35).

A variety of responses from among the unnamed individuals also addresses the reader, and Mark the evangelist makes the good news clear in each case. When a certain young man, full of good will, comes to Jesus seeking eternal life, and is summoned to follow Jesus, he fails. The cost of discipleship, to give up everything and follow Jesus, is too much (10:17–22). But Mark has told the reader that Jesus loved this man (v. 21), and it is with pain that he has to comment to his disciples, "How hard it will be for those who have riches to enter the kingdom of God" (v. 23). However, the readers are warned, it is not impossible: "With human beings it is impossible, but not with God; for all things are possible with God" (v. 27), and as the story draws to a close, two anonymous women show the way to disciples. Responding to God's design, a widow gives all she has, and Jesus refers to her as a model for discipleship (12:41–44), and another woman breaks open a precious vase of pure nard to anoint Jesus, much to the horror of the disciples (12:3–9). But, as Jesus points out: "Wherever the 'good news' is preached in the whole world, what she has done will be told in memory of her" (v. 9). This must be the case as what she has done, in unconditional gift of all that she has, like the gift of the poor widow, is good news.

## Conclusion

The reader is invited into the story by anonymous characters. They can join the other unnamed disciples in the narrative: those whom Jesus calls, and who come to him (3:13), the ones described as "those who were about him" (4:10), and those who, even when they are full of amazement and fear, are still described as "those who followed" (10:32). But the problem with identification between the reader of the story with the unnamed disciples in the story is that, in the end—despite some encouraging anonymous performances—it is a story of failure. The unnamed and, *especially,* the named disciples fail (see 14:50–52). Even the named women who persevere with Jesus through the crucifixion to the burial fail at the empty tomb (see 16:7–8). How can this be good news for contemporary disciples of Jesus?

# The Good News of Human Failure

Reflection on Mark's interpretation of Jesus of Nazareth and the Christian community revealed that there was little room for glorious human successes.[13] God's authority shines through the actions and the words of Jesus: He overcomes all forms of evil (1:14–45), but allows human beings the freedom to decide for or against the coming of the reigning presence of God (2:1–3:6). He has authority over nature, and reveals himself to his disciples as "I am he" (6:50: ἐγώ εἰμι; *egō eimi*), a formula used in the Old Testament to refer to the presence of the living God (6:50; see Gen 15:1; 26:24; 46:3; Isa 41:13–14; 43:1, 3), a God who has authority over the terror of the sea (see Exod 14–15; Deut 7:2–7; Job 9:8; 38:16; Pss 29:3; 65:8; 77:20; 89:10; 93:3–4; Isa 43:1–5; 51:9–10). The presence of Jesus brings something new into the human story: the kingdom *of God*. Jesus' person, preaching, and activities are the presence of "the rectifying power of the impinging future" that *only God* can bring.[14] Thus, Jesus is the Son in whom God is pleased (1:11), the one whose voice must be heard (9:7). Jesus' life and teaching, ministry and death, are a manifestation of the design of God because they initiate the rectifying power of the kingdom of God.

But there is no *ultimate victory* for Jesus *within the story*. Although he manifests the presence of God as king in all he says and does, his efforts lead only to crucifixion, a cry of abandonment in his agony, and a final scream as he dies (15:33–38a). It is only *after* his death that God's actions come into recognizable effect. The veil protecting the holy of holies within the temple is rent from top to bottom (v. 38b), a Roman centurion confesses that Jesus was the Son of God (v. 39), women discover an empty tomb (16:1–5) and are informed that Jesus, the crucified one, has been raised. He is no longer lying in the tomb where his executioners had allowed him to be placed (v. 6; see 15:43–47). But even these spectacular events do not fulfill Jesus' promises of ultimate vindication and victory. During his ministry Jesus told of his forthcoming death and resurrection (8:31; 9:31; 10:33–34). Those predictions are fulfilled in the Easter proclamation of 16:6–7. But he also promised that he would return in glory to shame those who have been ashamed of him (8:38), coming on the clouds to gather the elect from the four corners of the earth (13:24–27), to sit at the right hand of God in judgment of those who have unjustly judged him (14:61–62). But none of this takes place *within the story*. We live our Christian lives believing that Jesus' words on his final vindication and victory are "good news." On the basis of the fulfillment of all his other prophecies across the gospel, we place our Christian hope and trust in the fulfillment of these promises, the culmination of Jesus' proclamation of the good news.

The readers of the gospel are part of the ongoing story of the Christian community as they wait upon the fulfillment of Jesus' promises. The Gospel of Mark *provides the word of Jesus, the Son*. And the voice of God from heaven has commanded: "Listen to him" (9:7). The word of Jesus will not be thwarted, and thus the ultimate victory of Jesus, still ahead of the members who are reading the Gospel of Mark, is "good news." This good news announces that the ambiguity and sinfulness that mark the human story will not determine our history. Human history, from as far back as we can trace its records, is marked by violence and arrogance. In the midst of one such period during the history of Israel, it was well symbolized by the description of the fourth beast in Dan 7:7: "fearful, terrifying, very strong; it had great iron teeth and ate its victims, crushed them and trampled their remains underfoot," and its representative Antiochus IV, the emerging small horn, pulling out three other horns, with a mouth full of boasting (v. 8). Human beings cannot usurp the role of God and Father of Jesus. God, at a time that is not known by the angels in heaven, or even the Son (see Mark 13:32), will bring the promises of Jesus to their fulfillment. Heaven and earth will pass away, but the word of Jesus will not pass away (13:31). This is indeed the good news that lies ahead of the readers of the Gospel of Mark, good news made possible by the unconditional self-gift of the Son, so that the design of God may continue to unfold in the new temple built upon the rejected cornerstone (see 12:10–11; 14:58; 15:38).

The story of the disciples is one that began with great promise (1:16–20; 2:13–14; 3:13–19; 6:7–13), but gradually slipped into misunderstanding (4:11–13; 8:32; 10:41), doubt and fear (4:35–41), arrogance (6:30; 9:38–41; 10:35–37), betrayal (14:17–21, 43–45), denial (14:26–31, 53–54, 66–72), and flight (14:50). But what must not be missed in Mark's careful interpretation of the role of the disciples is that however frequently they fail, Jesus *never* abandons them. There are two occasions when he shows his frustration with them. After the second bread miracle, he chides them for their blindness and hardness of heart, and asks, "Do you not yet understand?" (8:21). At the heart of his journey with the disciples to Jerusalem, he teaches them as they follow him down the way (see 9:31). However, after coming down from the mount of the transfiguration, Jesus finds that the disciples continue to lack understanding. After their early success with the sick and their early power over demons (see 6:30), why are they unable to cure the epileptic boy (see 9:28)? Jesus exclaims: "O faithless generation, how long am I to be with you? How long am I to bear with you?" (v. 19).[15] These two rebukes, however, serve to throw into greater relief *the never-failing presence of Jesus to the ever-failing disciples.* However frustratingly Mark portrays blind and hard-hearted disciples (8:21; 9:19), Jesus never abandons them. Indeed, the more they fail, the closer he binds himself to them.

Across the central section of the gospel, running from the curing of the blind man in 8:22–26 to the cure of blind Bartimaeus in 10:46–52,

Jesus insists on his future as the suffering and vindicated Son of Man. The disciples will not and cannot understand that this is the God-willed destiny of Jesus, and thus the destiny of anyone who wants to be his follower (see 8:34–38). After each of the passion predictions (8:31; 9:31; 10:32–34), the disciples fail, but after each failure, Jesus summons them (see 8:34; 9:33–35; 10:42) and continues to instruct them, in 8:34–9:1 on their vocation to the cross, in 9:33–37 on the need for service and receptivity, and in 10:35–44 on both the cross and service.[16] This theme of the never-failing presence of Jesus to his fragile disciples reaches its zenith during Mark's presentation of his final evening with them in 14:1–72 in eleven carefully organized passages. Framing the central sixth scene, in the fifth and seventh scenes Jesus prophesies the betrayal of Judas (vv. 17–21), the flight of all the disciples, and the denials of Peter (vv. 26–31). In the central sixth scene (vv. 22–25), Jesus breaks bread and shares a cup with them, establishing a new covenant that will reach beyond the events of the crucifixion. Jesus gives himself unconditionally to disciples who betray him, abandon him, and deny him. Yet he promises them, "You will all fall away; for it is written 'I will strike the shepherd, and the sheep will be scattered.' But after I am raised up I will go before you into Galilee" (14:27–28).

As was the case with the Markan interpretation of Jesus of Nazareth, this promise of Jesus to the disciples is not fulfilled *within the story of the gospel*. There are a number of signs that the failure of the disciples is overcome by means of the resurrection. Someone other than the women, the first visitors to the tomb, has rolled back the huge stone that covered the opening of the tomb (16:3–4). The presence of the young man at the tomb, dressed in a white robe (16:5), recalls Mark's parabolic use of the flight of the naked young man at Jesus' arrest to comment on the flight of the disciples (14:50–52). The women are told to announce the Easter message to the disciples in words that look back to Jesus' promise of 14:28: "But go, tell his disciples and Peter that he is going before you into Galilee; there you will see him as he told you" (16:7). But all these signs of hope are dashed as the women, joining the fear and flight of the disciples (see 14:50–52), "went out and fled from the tomb; for trembling and astonishment had come upon them; and they said nothing to anyone, for they were afraid" (v. 8). Thus ends the Gospel of Mark. How can this be good news for the disciples *in the story* and all subsequent disciples who are *readers of the story*?

An answer to this question can be found only by looking back to the resolution of the mystery of Jesus' apparent failure. Jesus' ultimate vindication and return in glory does not take place *within the limitations of the narrative of the Gospel of Mark*. In exactly the same way, the restoration of discipleship does not take place *within the limitations of the narrative of the Gospel of Mark.* As with Jesus, so with the disciples, the gospel closes full of unrealized promises. What must be recognized is that, from about 70 C.E. until our present day, disciples of Jesus have continued to read the Gospel of Mark. The good news that Mark wishes to communicate is that no one *in the story* succeeds. As the disciples failed (14:50–52), so do the women fail (16:8). In the end, *human beings fail* . . . but God succeeds. The fact that the Gospel of Mark is read by a community of Christians that continues to celebrate the Lord's Supper, that continues its attempts to follow Jesus' way to life by means of the cross, receptivity, and service, *proclaims* that, as God did not abandon his Son (see 15:34), but raised him from the place where they had laid him (16:6), so he will not abandon his failing disciples. They will see the risen Lord in Galilee. He promised that after he was raised up, he would go before his fragile disciples into Galilee. There, he said, they would see him (14:27–28). The Easter proclamation affirms that this is now about to take place: "He is going before you into Galilee; there you will see him, as he told you" (16:7). The failure of the women in 16:8 cannot thwart the designs of God, made manifest in the words of Jesus (14:28; 16:7).

The realization of Jesus' promises to the disciples is not found *in the text.* The existence of the Markan community and its story of Jesus indicate what took place *among the readers of the text,* in the experience of the original readers and hearers of the gospel of Mark. But that is not the end of the process. The proclamation of the Gospel of Mark in fragile Christian communities, experiencing their own versions of fear and flight, for almost two thousand years, suggests that the accomplishment of the promise of 14:28 and 16:7 continues in the Christian experience of all subsequent readers and hearers of the gospel. What Jesus promised took place, and continues to take place. As Christian disciples continue to fail and flee in fear, they are told that God's action in and through the risen Jesus overcomes all such failure.[17] Jesus is going before them into Galilee. There they will see him. The "Galilee" of 16:7 that overcame the failure of the original disciples, has been endlessly repeated since then. God's saving power has continued and still continues to free fragile disciples from their failure, fear, and flight. The ending of the Gospel of Mark is not a message of failure. It is the proclamation of good news. Indeed it provides the basis for the proclamation of the best possible news. The action of God can and will overcome all imaginable human fear and failure. "This is the end of Mark's story, because it is the beginning of discipleship."[18]

# Conclusion

The prologue to the Gospel of Mark (1:1–13) expressed God's design for his beloved Son (1:11). It was marked by a series of exalted christological claims for Jesus. The story of the gospel that followed indicated how God was well pleased with his beloved Son, whose final words were: "My God, my God, why have you forsaken me?" (15:34). The "good news" according to Mark takes many unexpected twists and turns, between the exalted Christology of the prologue and its tragic ending. The most surprising feature of the story is the dominant role played by Jesus' crucifixion, associated with the total failure of his disciples. John Drury said it well: "Between the understanding given us in its first verse and the radical incomprehension and insecurity of the subsequent tale, Mark's book gets its energy."[19] As the story comes to a close, not only Jesus, but also the reader is forced to ask the question, which comes from Ps. 22:1: "Why have you forsaken me?" (15:34) Is this the way God treats his beloved Son?

This question is answered by the presence of God, through his agents, in 16:1–8. The stone has been rolled away, a messenger from God is found in the empty tomb, and the Easter proclamation announces that Jesus, the crucified Christ and Son of God, the suffering Son of Man, has been vindicated in the resurrection. God has raised Jesus the Nazarene from the dead: "You are seeking Jesus the Nazarene, the crucified one. *He has been raised* (ἠγέρθη; *ēgerthē*). Look at the place where they laid him" (16:6). The main feature of the "good news" of the Gospel of Mark is that, in the end, it is good news about God.[20] Jesus looked forward confidently to the vindication of the Son of Man in the resurrection (see 8:31; 9:31; 10:33–34) and his hopes were not thwarted. God did not abandon Jesus, despite his anguished cry from the cross (15:34). Nor will God thwart Jesus' other promises: he will gather the elect from the four corners of the earth (13:26–27), coming as judge at the right hand of God at the end of time (14:61–62).

The same good news continues to be announced to subsequent disciples of Jesus, Christian readers of the Gospel of Mark. As Christians continue to fail and flee in fear, they are told that God's action in and through the risen Jesus overcomes all such failure. Mark the evangelist provided the Christian tradition with a story that is a resounding affirmation of God's overcoming all imaginable failure (16:1–8), in and through the action of the beloved Son (1:1–13).[21] The God of Israel is the God and Father of Jesus (see 1:2–3). Jesus is God's beloved Son, and he delights in his Son (1:11). Jesus' unconditional self-gift on the cross reveals that he is the Christ, the Son of God (14:61–62). This is the life story that reveals God's design (see 14:36), and lays the foundation for a new temple, not built with human hands (12:10–11; 14:57–58; 15:29, 38). It also looks further, beyond the limitations of human history, and promises the possibility of a new future for all who are prepared to follow the man who came to serve and not to be served, to lay down his life as a ransom for many (10:45). Jesus, the crucified Son of Man, will return and gather the elect from the four corners of the earth (13:26–27). Herein lies the authority of Jesus (see 2:10, 28), who never fails his failing disciples (8:22–10:52; 14:17–31). The words addressed to the struggling disciples at the transfiguration are addressed to all who take up this gospel, and read it as good news: "Listen to him" (9:7).

## Notes

1. For a more detailed study of Mark's first words, "The beginning of the good news," see F. J. Moloney, *The Gospel of Mark: A Commentary* (Peabody: Hendrickson, 2002), 30–31.

2. The English word "gospel" comes from the Old English for "good news": god-spel.

3. An initial hint that Mark may communicate "good news" can be found in the fact that believing Christians still read it. They find guidance and inspiration in that reading experience. Somehow this message of a suffering Son of Man, a crucified Christ and Son of God, addressed to a fragile community was "good news" for the original readers in Mark's community, and remains such for today's readers and listeners as we continue the tradition of turning to the Gospel of Mark. The ongoing practice of reading a text that is now almost two thousand years old says something about the "good news" contained therein.

4. Admittedly, women characters such as Simon's mother-in-law and the daughter of Jairus are identified in terms of their relationship to a significant male. This is a common practice in the patriarchal society of the time.

5. On the historical disciples, the Twelve, and the named individuals among them, see J. P. Meier, *A Marginal Jew: Rethinking the Historical Jesus* (ABRL; New York: Doubleday, 2002), 3:40–285. Levi (2:13–14) presents something of a problem. He is replaced in the Gospel of Matthew by "Matthew" (Matt 9:9). Levi is probably the original (historical) figure called to follow Jesus, and the Evangelist Matthew probably replaced him with "Matthew" so that all the "called" disciples would be found in his list of the Twelve (see Matt 10:2–4), where "Matthew the tax collector" appears (10:3). On this, see the brief remarks of Meier, *A Marginal Jew*, 129–34, 201, and especially R. Pesch, "Levi-Matthäus (Mk 2,14/Mt 9,9; 10,3). Ein Beitrag zur Elösung eines alten Problems," *ZNW* 59 (1968): 40–56.

6. It is hard to imagine that these details would not reach back to the life of Jesus. On the discussions surrounding Jesus, his mother, and his brothers and sisters (Mark 6:3), see Moloney, *Mark*, 112, note 212.

7. The different names of the women in 15:40, 47, and 16:1, along with the unlikely possibility that Roman soldiers would have allowed acquaintances of a condemned criminal to stand by at the execution, makes it likely that the names came to Mark in the pre-Markan tradition. The traditional nature of the names does not mean that women did not witness the event. The names, however, were probably provided by the developing Christian tradition. See the discussion in R. E. Brown, *The Death of the Messiah: From Gethsemane to the Grave. A Commentary on the Passion Narratives of the Four Gospels* (2 vols.; ABRL; New York: Doubleday, 1994), 1:1251. See also E. Schweizer, *The Good News according to Mark* (trans. D. H. Madvig; Richmond: John Knox, 1970), 361.

8. See, for example, T. Docherty, *Reading (Absent) Character: Towards A Theory of Characterization in Fiction* (Oxford: Clarendon Press, 1983), and the application of these suggestions to the Fourth Gospel in D. R. Beck, "The Narrative Function of Anonymity in Fourth Gospel Characterization," *Sem* 63 (1993): 143–58.

9. For a sociopolitical reading of the Gospel of Mark using the metaphor of chains and binding as its fundamental metaphor, see C. Myers, *Binding the Strong Man: A Political Reading of Mark's Story of Jesus* (Maryknoll: Orbis, 1990).

10. See K. Berger, *Identity and Experience in the New Testament: A Historical Psychology* (trans. C. Muenchow; Minneapolis: Fortress, 2003), 85–87. Berger comments: "Christology, both actually and logically, is effectively the presupposition for the miracles of Jesus" (p. 86).

11. For a more detailed analysis of this teaching to both disciples and the multitude, see Moloney, *Mark*, 175–77.

12. In many ways, those who work relentlessly *against* Jesus are anonymous. None of the Sadducees, Pharisees, scribes, chief priests, or elders are ever given a name. Not even the high priest of 14:61–64 is named. There is no Annas or Caiaphas in the Gospel of Mark. The groups, however, can be located in a time, a place, and a religious structure, and the readers recognize them as enemies at all stages of the narrative, with the exception of 12:28–34, where *one scribe* comes close to the kingdom. However, in vv. 35–44, Jesus roundly condemns scribal teaching and practice.

13. See above, Chapters 6 and 7, pp. 125–81.

14. For the expression in quotes, see L. E. Keck, *Who Is Jesus? History in Perfect Tense* (Studies on Personalities of the New Testament; Columbia: University of South Carolina Press, 2001), 71.

15. Not all would accept that these hard words are directed at the disciples. For the position suggested above, see Moloney, *Mark*, 183–84, and the discussion there.

16. See above, pp. 82–87. For simplicity, I am mentioning only the teaching of Jesus that immediately follows the passion predictions and the failures of the disciples. For a reading of 8:22–10:52 that reads all the material following each passion prediction and failure as Jesus' instruction of the disciples, see Moloney, *Mark*, 171–214.

17. For similar suggestions, see T. E. Boomershine, "Mark 16:8 and the Apostolic Commission," *JBL* 100 (1981): 234–39; R. C. Tannehill, "The Gospel of Mark as Narrative Christology," *Sem* 16 (1980): 82–84; S. R. Garrett, *The Temptations of Jesus in Mark's Gospel* (Grand Rapids: Eerdmans, 1998), 137–69.

18. M. D. Hooker, *The Gospel according to St. Mark* (BNTC; Peabody: Hendrickson, 1991), 394. See also J. L. Magness, *Sense and Absence: Structure and Suspension in the Ending of Mark's Gospel* (Society of Biblical Literature Semeia Series; Atlanta: Scholars Press, 186), 107–25; E. S. Malbon, "Texts and Contexts: Interpreting the Disciples in Mark," in *In the Company of Jesus: Characters in Mark's Gospel* (Louisville: Westminster John Knox, 2000), 114–24.

19. J. Drury, "Mark," in *The Literary Guide to the Bible* (ed. R. Alter and F. Kermode; Cambridge, Mass.: The Belknap Press of Harvard University Press, 1987), 405.

20. For studies stressing the centrality of God in the Gospel of Mark, see J. R. Donahue, "A Neglected Factor in the Theology of Mark," *JBL* 101 (1982): 563–94; K. Scholtissek, " 'Er ist nicht ein Gott der Toten, sondern der Lebenden (Mk 12,27): Grundzüge der markanische Theologie," in *Der Lebendige Gott: Studien zur Theologie des Neuen Testaments. Festschrift für Wilhelm Thüsing zum 75. Geburtstag* (ed. T. Söding; NTAbh NF 31; Münster: Aschendorff, 1996), 71–100; J. D. Kingsbury, " 'God' within the Narrative World of Mark," in *The Forgotten God: Perspectives in Biblical Theology* (eds. A. A. Das and F. J. Matera; Louisville: Westminster John Knox, 2002), 75–89.

21. On the literary and theological relationship between Mark's prologue (1:1–13) and his epilogue (16:1–8), see Moloney, *Mark*, 350–54.

# Bibliography

## Commentaries on the Gospel of Mark

Anderson, H. *The Gospel of Mark*. New Century Bible. London: Oliphants, 1976.

Branscomb, B. H. *The Gospel of Mark*. The Moffat New Testament Commentary. London: Hodder and Stoughton, 1937.

Cranfield, C. E. B. *The Gospel according to St. Mark*. Cambridge Greek Testament Commentary. Cambridge: Cambridge University Press, 1959.

Donahue, J. R., and D. J. Harrington. *The Gospel of Mark*. Sacra Pagina 2. Collegeville: Liturgical Press, 2002.

Dowds, S. E. *Reading Mark: A Literary and Theological Commentary on the Second Gospel*. Reading the New Testament Series. Macon: Smyth & Helwys, 2000.

Edwards, J. R., Jr. *The Gospel According to Mark*. Pillar New Testament Commentary Series. Grand Rapids: Eerdmans, 2002.

Ernst, J. *Das Evangelium nach Markus*. Regensburger Neues Testament. Regensburg: Pustet Verlag, 1981.

Evans, C. A. *Mark 8:27–16:20*. Word Biblical Commentary 34B. Nashville: Thomas Nelson, 2001.

France, R. T. *The Gospel of Mark*. New International Greek New Testament Commentary. Grand Rapids: Eerdmans, 2002.

Gnilka, J. *Das Evangelium nach Markus*. 5th ed. 2 vols. Evangelisch-katholischer Kommentar zum Neuen Testament II/1–2. Zürich/Neukirchen/Vluyn: Benziger Verlag/Neukirchener Verlag, 1998.

Grundmann, W. *Das Evangelium nach Markus*. 6th ed. Theologischer Handkommentar zum Neuen Testament 2. Berlin: Evangelische Verlagsanstalt, 1973.

Guelich, R. A. *Mark 1–8:26*. Word Biblical Commentary 34A. Dallas: Word, 1989.

Gundry, R. H. *Mark: A Commentary on His Apology for the Cross*. Grand Rapids: Eerdmans, 1993.

Hooker, M. D. *The Gospel according to St. Mark*. Black's New Testament Commentaries. Peabody: Hendrickson, 1991.

Lagrange, M.-J. *Evangile selon Saint Marc*. Études Bibliques. Paris: Gabalda, 1920.

Lane, W. L. *Commentary on the Gospel of Mark*. The New International Commentary on the New Testament. Grand Rapids: Eerdmans, 1974.

LaVerdiere, E. *The Beginning of the Gospel: Introducing the Gospel According to Mark*. 2 vols. Collegeville: Liturgical Press, 1999.

Lohmeyer, E. *Das Evangelium des Markus*. 17th ed. Meyers Kommentar. Göttingen: Vandenhoeck & Ruprecht, 1967.

Lührmann, D. *Das Markusevangelium*. Handbuch zum Neuen Testament 3. Tübingen: J. C. B. Mohr (Paul Siebeck), 1987.

Marcus, J. *Mark 1–8*. Anchor Bible 27. New York: Doubleday, 2000.

Moloney, F. J. *The Gospel of Mark: A Commentary*. Peabody: Hendrickson, 2002.

Nineham, D. E. *The Gospel of St. Mark*. Westminster Pelican Commentaries. Philadelphia: Westminster, 1978.

Painter, J. *Mark's Gospel: Worlds in Conflict*. New Testament Readings. London: Routledge, 1997.

Pesch, R. *Das Markusevangelium*. 2 vols. Herders theologischer Kommentar zum Neuen Testament II/1–2. Freiburg: Herder, 1976–1977.

Schweizer, E. *The Good News according to Mark*. Translated by Donald H. Madvig. Richmond: John Knox, 1970.

Swete, H. B. *The Gospel according to St. Mark*. London: Macmillan, 1909.

Taylor, V. *The Gospel according to St. Mark*. 2d ed. New York: St. Martin's, 1966.

Thurston, B. B. *Preaching Mark*. Fortress Resources for Preaching; Minneapolis: Fortress, 2002.

van Iersel, B. *Reading Mark*. Translated by W. H. Bisscheroux. Collegeville: Liturgical Press, 1988.

Williamson, L. *Mark*. Interpretation. Atlanta: John Knox, 1983.

Witherington, B., III. *The Gospel of Mark: A Social Rhetorical Commentary*. Grand Rapids: Eerdmans, 2001.

# Other Studies

Abrams, M. H. *A Glossary of Literary Terms.* 5th ed. New York: Holt, Rinehart & Winston, 1985.

Achtemeier, P. *1 Peter.* Hermeneia. Minneapolis: Fortress, 1999.

Alter, R., and F. Kermode. *The Literary Guide to the Bible.* Cambridge, Mass.: The Belknap Press of Harvard University Press, 1987.

Atwood, M. *The Blind Assassin.* London: Virago Press, 2001.

Baird, W. *History of New Testament Research: Volume 1: From Deism to Tübingen.* Minneapolis: Fortress, 1992.

————. *History of New Testament Research: Volume 2: From Jonathan Edwards to Rudolf Bultmann.* Minneapolis: Fortress, 2002.

Balabanski, V. *Eschatology in the Making: Mark, Matthew and the Didache.* Society for New Testament Studies Monograph Series 97. Cambridge: Cambridge University Press, 1998.

Barrett, C. K. *The Holy Spirit in the Gospel Tradition.* London: SPCK, 1970.

Beasley-Murray, G. R. *Jesus and the Last Days: The Interpretation of the Olivet Discourse.* Peabody: Hendrickson, 1993.

Beavis, M. A. *Mark's Audience: The Literary and Social Setting of Mark 4:11–12.* Journal for the Study of the New Testament Supplement Series 33. Sheffield: Sheffield Academic Press, 1989.

Beck, D. R. "The Narrative Function of Anonymity in Fourth Gospel Characterization." *Semeia* 63 (1993): 143–58.

Berger, K. *Identity and Experience in the New Testament. A Historical Psychology.* Translated by C. Muenchow. Minneapolis: Fortress, 2003.

Best, E. *The Temptation and the Passion.* 2d ed. Society for New Testament Studies Monograph Series 2. Cambridge: Cambridge University Press, 1990.

————. *Following Jesus. Discipleship in the Gospel of Mark.* Journal for the Study of the New Testament Supplement Series 4. Sheffield: JSOT Press, 1981.

Bible and Culture Collective. *The Postmodern Bible.* New Haven: Yale University Press, 1995.

Bilezikian, G. *The Liberated Gospel: A Comparison between the Gospel of Mark and Greek Tragedy.* Grand Rapids: Baker, 1977.

Black, C. C. *Mark: Images of an Apostolic Interpreter.* Studies on Personalities of the New Testament. Minneapolis: Fortress, 2001.

————. *The Disciples according to Mark.* Journal for the Study of the New Testament Supplement Series 27. Sheffield: Sheffield Academic Press, 1989.

————. "The Quest of Mark the Redactor: Why Has It Been Pursued, and What Has It Taught Us?" *Journal for the Study of the New Testament* 22 (1989): 19–39.

Boomershine, T. E. "Mark 16:8 and the Apostolic Commission." *Journal of Biblical Literature* 100 (1981): 225–39.

Booth, W. C. *The Rhetoric of Fiction.* 2d ed. Chicago: University of Chicago Press, 1983.

Boring, M. E. "Mark 1:1–15 and the Beginning of the Gospel." *Semeia* 52 (1991): 43–81.

Borsch, F. H. *The Son of Man in Myth and History.* London: SCM, 1967.

Breck, J. *The Shape of Biblical Language: Chiasmus in the Scriptures and Beyond.* New York: St. Vladimir's Seminary Press, 1994.

Brown, R. E. *The Birth of the Messiah: A Commentary on the Infancy Narratives of Matthew and Luke.* New York: Doubleday, 1977.

————. *The Death of the Messiah: From Gethsemane to the Grave. A Commentary on the Passion Narratives in the Four Gospels.* 2 vols. Anchor Bible Reference Library. New York: Doubleday, 1994.

Bultmann, R. *History of the Synoptic Tradition.* Translated by J. Marsh. Oxford: Basil Blackwell, 1968.

Byrne, B. J. *"Sons of God—Seed of Abraham": A Study of the Idea of the Sonship of God of All Christians in Paul against the Jewish Background.* Analecta Biblica 83. Rome: Biblical Institute Press, 1979.

Camery-Hoggatt, J. *Irony in Mark's Gospel: Text and Subtext.* Society for New Testament Studies Monograph Series 72. Cambridge: Cambridge University Press, 1992.

Carr, E. H. *What Is History?* New York: Knopf, 1962.

Carter, W. *Matthew: Storyteller, Interpreter, Evangelist.* Peabody: Hendrickson, 1996.

Charlesworth, J. H. "The Son of David, Solomon and Jesus." Pages 72–87 in *The New Testament and Hellenistic Judaism.* Edited by P. Borgen and S. Giversen. Peabody: Hendrickson, 1997.

————, ed. *The Messiah: Developments in Early Judaism and Christianity.* The First Princeton Symposium on Judaism and Christian Origins. Minneapolis: Fortress, 1992.

Chatman, S. *Story and Discourse: Narrative Structure in Fiction and Film.* Ithaca: Cornell University Press, 1978.

Collins, A. Y. "Mark and His Readers: The Son of God among Greeks and Romans." *Harvard Theological Review* 93 (2000): 85–100.

————. "Mark and His Readers: The Son of God among Jews." *Harvard Theological Review* 92 (1999): 393–408.

————. "Narrative, History and Gospel." *Semeia* 43 (1988): 145–53.

Collins, J. J. *The Scepter and the Star: The Messiahs of the Dead Sea Scrolls and Other Ancient Literature*. Anchor Bible Reference Library. New York: Doubleday, 1995.

Conzelmann, H. *The Theology of St. Luke*. Translated by G. Buswell. London: Faber & Faber, 1961.

Cross, F. L., and E. A. Livingstone, eds. *The Oxford Dictionary of the Christian Church*. 3d ed. Oxford: Clarendon Press, 1997.

Cullman, O. *The Christology of the New Testament*. London: SCM Press, 1975.

Culpepper, R. A. "Mark 10:50: Why Mention the Garment?" *Journal of Biblical Literature* 101 (1982): 131–32.

Davies, W. D., and D. C. Allison. *A Critical and Exegetical Commentary on the Gospel according to Saint Matthew*. 3 vols. International Critical Commentary. Edinburgh: T&T Clark, 1988–1998.

de Balzac, H. *Old Goriot*. Penguin Classics. Harmondsworth: Penguin, 1951.

Dewey, J. "Mark as Interwoven Tapestry: Forecasts and Echoes for a Listening Audience." *Catholic Biblical Quarterly* 53 (1991): 225–36.

———. *Markan Public Debate. Literary Technique, Concentric Structure, and Theology in Mark 2:1–3:6*. Society of Biblical Literature Dissertation Series 48. Chico: Scholars Press, 1980.

———. "The Literary Structure of the Controversy Stories in Mark 2:1–3:6." *Journal of Biblical Literature* 92 (1973): 394–401.

Dibelius, M. *From Tradition to Gospel*. Translated by B. L. Woolf. Library of Theological Translations. Cambridge & London: James Clarke, 1971.

Docherty, T. *Reading (Absent) Characters: Towards a Theory of Characterization in Fiction*. Oxford: Clarendon Press, 1983.

Donahue, J. R. "A Neglected Factor in the Theology of Mark." *Journal of Biblical Literature* 101 (1982): 563–94.

———. "*Are You the Christ?*" *The Trial Narrative in the Gospel of Mark*. Society of Biblical Literature Dissertation Series 10. Missoula: Scholars Press, 1973.

Dowd, S. E. *Prayer, Power and the Problem of Suffering: Mark 11:22–25 in the Context of Markan Theology*. Society of Biblical Literature Dissertation Series 105. Atlanta: Scholars Press, 1988.

Drury, J. "Mark." Pages 401–17 in *The Literary Guide to the Bible*. Edited by R. Alter and F. Kermode. Cambridge, Mass.: The Belknap Press of Harvard University Press, 1987.

Duke, P. D. *Irony in the Fourth Gospel*. Atlanta: John Knox, 1985.

Dyer, K. D. *The Prophecy on the Mount: Mark 13 and the Gathering of the New Community*. International Theological Studies 2. Bern: Peter Lang, 1998.

Edwards, J. R. "Marcan Sandwiches: The Significance of Interpolations in Marcan Narratives." *Novum Testamentum* 31 (1989): 193–216.

Eichrodt, W. *Ezekiel: A Commentary.* Translated by Cosslett Quin. Philadelphia: Westminster, 1970.

Elliott, J. *1 Peter: A New Translation with Introduction and Commentary.* Anchor Bible 37B. New York: Doubleday, 2000.

Esler, P. *Community and Gospel in Luke-Acts. The Social and Political Motivations of Lucan Theology.* Society for New Testament Studies Monograph Series 57. Cambridge: Cambridge University Press, 1987.

Evans, C. A. "Mark's Incipit and the Priene Calendar Inscription: From Jewish Gospel to Greco-Roman Gospel." *Journal of Greco-Roman Christianity and Judaism* 1 (2000): 67–81.

Fabry, H.-J., and K. Scholtissek. *Der Messias.* Die Neue Echter Bibel-Themen 5. Würzburg: Echter Verlag, 2002.

Feldmeier, R. *Die Krisis der Gottessohnes: Die Gethsemaneerzählung als Schlüssel der Markuspassion.* Wissenschaftliche Untersuchungen zum Neuen Testament 2. Reihe 21. Tübingen: J. C. B. Mohr (Paul Siebeck), 1987.

Ferch, A. J. *The Son of Man in Daniel Seven.* Andrews University Seminary Doctoral Dissertation Series 6. Berrien Springs: Andrews University Press, 1979.

Fiorenza, Elisabeth Schüssler. *In Memory of Her: A Feminist Theological Reconstruction of Christian Origins.* New York: Crossroad, 1983.

Fish, S. *Is There a Text in This Class? The Authority of Interpretative Communities.* Cambridge, Mass.: Harvard University Press, 1988.

Fitzmyer, J. A. *Responses to 101 Questions on the Dead Sea Scrolls.* Mahwah: Paulist, 1992.

———. "The Priority of Mark and the 'Q' Source in Luke." Pages 3–40 in *To Advance the Gospel: New Testament Studies.* New York: Crossroad, 1981.

Fledderman, H. "A Warning about the Scribes (Mark 12:37b–40)." *Catholic Biblical Quarterly* (1982): 52–67.

———. "The Flight of the Naked Young Man (Mark 14:51–52)." *Catholic Biblical Quarterly* 41 (1979): 412–17.

Fowler, R. M. *Let the Reader Understand: Reader-Response Criticism and the Gospel of Mark.* Minneapolis: Fortress, 1991.

———. *Loaves and Fishes. The Function of the Feeding Stories in the Gospel of Mark.* Society of Biblical Literature Dissertation Series 54. Chico: Scholars Press, 1981.

Frei, H. *The Eclipse of Biblical Narrative: A Study of Eighteenth and Nineteenth Century Hermeneutics.* New Haven: Yale University Press, 1974.

Garrett, S. R. *The Temptations of Jesus in Mark's Gospel.* Grand Rapids: Eerdmans, 1998.

Geddert, T. J. *Watchwords: Mark 13 in Markan Eschatology.* Journal for the Study of the New Testament Supplement Series 26. Sheffield: Sheffield Academic Press, 1989.

George, A., and P. Grelot, eds. *Introduction à la Bible. Tome III: Nouveau Testament.* 7 vols. Paris: Desclée, 1976–1986.

Grundmann, W. *"dei, deon, esti."* *Theological Dictionary of the New Testament* 2 (1964): 21–27.

Hahn, F. *Christologische Hoheitstitel. Ihre Geschichte im frühen Christentum.* 3d ed. Forshungen zur Religion und Literatur des Alten und Neuen Testament 83. Göttingen: Vandenhoeck & Ruprecht, 1966.

———. *The Titles of Jesus in Christology. Their History in Early Christianity.* Translated by H. Knight and G. Ogg. London: Lutterworth, 1969.

Hamilton, N. Q. "Resurrection, Tradition and the Composition of Mark." *Journal of Biblical Literature* 84 (1965): 415–21.

Hartman, L., and A. A. di Lella. *The Book of Daniel.* Anchor Bible 23. Garden City: Doubleday, 1978.

Hedrick, C. W. "The Role of 'Summary Statements' in the Composition of the Gospel of Mark: A Dialog with Karl Schmidt and Norman Perrin." Pages 121–43 in *The Composition of Mark's Gospel: Selected Studies from* Novum Testamentum. Edited by D. E. Orton. Brill's Readers in Biblical Studies 3. Leiden: E. J. Brill, 1999.

Hengel, M. *Studies in the Gospel of Mark.* Translated by J. Bowden. Philadelphia: Fortress, 1985.

Holtzmann, H. J. *Die synoptischen Evangelien: Ihr Ursprung und geschichtlicher Charakter.* Leipzig: Wilhelm Engelmann, 1863.

Hooker, M. D. *Beginnings: Keys That Open the Gospels.* Valley Forge: Trinity Press International, 1998.

———. "In His Own Image?" Pages 28–44 in *What about the New Testament? Studies in Honour of Christopher Evans.* Edited by M. D. Hooker and C. Hickling. London: SCM, 1975.

———. *The Son of Man in Mark.* London: SPCK, 1967.

Horsley, R. A. *Hearing the Whole Story: The Politics of Plot in Mark's Gospel.* Louisville: Westminster John Knox, 2001.

Iser, W. *The Implied Reader: Patterns of Communication in Prose Fiction from Bunyan to Beckett.* Baltimore: Johns Hopkins University Press, 1978.

Johnson, L. T. *The First and Second Letters to Timothy: A New Translation with Introduction and Commentary.* Anchor Bible 35A. New York: Doubleday, 2001.

Juel, D. H. *Messiah and Temple: The Trial of Jesus in the Gospel of Mark.* Society of Biblical Literature Dissertation Series 31. Missoula: Scholars Press, 1977.

Kazmierski, C. R. *Jesus, the Son of God: A Study in the Marcan Tradition and Its Redaction by the Evangelist.* Forschung zur Bibel 33. Würzburg: Echter Verlag, 1979.

Kealy, S. *Mark's Gospel: A History of Its Interpretation.* New York: Paulist, 1982.

Keck, L. E. "The Introduction to Mark's Gospel." *New Testament Studies* 12 (1965–1966): 352–70.

———. *Who Is Jesus? History in the Perfect Tense.* Studies in Personalities of the New Testament. Columbia: University of South Carolina Press, 2001.

Kee, H. C. *Community of the New Age: Studies in Mark's Gospel.* Philadelphia: Westminster, 1977.

Kelber, W. *Mark's Story of Jesus.* Philadelphia: Fortress, 1979.

———. *The Kingdom in Mark: A New Place and a New Time.* Philadelphia: Fortress, 1974.

———. *The Oral and Written Gospel: The Hermeneutics of Speaking and Writing in the Synoptic Tradition, Mark, Paul and Q.* Philadelphia: Fortress, 1983.

Kermode, F. *The Genesis of Secrecy: On the Interpretation of Narrative.* Cambridge, Mass.: Harvard University Press, 1969.

Kim, T. H. "The Anarthrous υἱὸς θεοῦ in Mark 15:39." *Biblica* 79 (1988): 221–41.

Kingsbury, J. D. *Conflict in Mark: Jesus, Authorities, Disciples.* Minneapolis: Fortress, 1989.

———. " 'God' within the Narrative World of Mark." Pages 75–89 in *The Forgotten God: Perspectives in Biblical Theology.* Edited by A. A. Das and F. J. Matera. Louisville: Westminster John Knox, 2002.

———. *The Christology of Mark's Gospel.* Philadelphia: Fortress, 1983.

Kramer, W. *Christ, Lord, Son of God.* Studies in Biblical Theology 50. London: SCM, 1966.

Kümmel, W. *The New Testament: The History of the Investigation of Its Problems.* Nashville: Abingdon, 1972.

Kürzinger, J. *Papias von Hierapolis und die Evangelien des Neuen Testaments: Gesammelte Aufsätze, Neuausgabe und Übersetzung der Fragmente, Kommentierte Bibliographie.* Eichstätter Materialen 4. Regensburg: Pustet, 1983.

Léon-Dufour, X. *Sharing the Eucharistic Bread: The Witness of the New Testament.* New York: Paulist, 1987.

Lightfoot, R. H. *History and Interpretation in the Gospels.* The Bampton Lectures 1934. London: Hodder and Stoughton, 1935.

―――. *The Gospel Message of St. Mark.* Oxford: Clarendon Press, 1950.

Lindars, B. *New Testament Apologetic: The Doctrinal Significance of the Old Testament Quotations.* London: SCM, 1961.

Lindemann, A. "Die Osterbotschaft des Markus: Zur theologischen Interpretation von Mark 16.1–8." *New Testament Studies* 26 (1979–1980): 298–317.

Magness, J. L. *Sense and Absence: Structure and Suspension in the Ending of Mark's Gospel.* Society of Biblical Literature Semeia Series. Atlanta: Scholars Press, 1986.

Malbon, E. S. "Disciples/Crowds/Whoever: Markan Characters and Readers." Pages 70–99 in *In the Company of Jesus: Characters in Mark's Gospel.* Louisville: Westminster John Knox, 2000.

―――. "Echoes and Foreshadowings in Mark 4–8: Reading and Rereading." *Journal of Biblical Literature* 112 (1993): 211–30.

―――. "Fallible Followers: Women and Men in the Gospel of Mark." Pages 41–69 in *In the Company of Jesus: Characters in Mark's Gospel.* Louisville: Westminster John Knox, 2000.

―――. *Narrative Space and Mythic Meaning in Mark.* New Voices in Biblical Studies. San Francisco: Harper & Row, 1986.

―――. "Texts and Contexts: Interpreting the Disciples in Mark." Pages 100–30 in *In the Company of Jesus: Characters in Mark's Gospel.* Louisville: Westminster John Knox, 2000.

―――. "The Jesus of Mark and the Sea of Galilee." *Journal of Biblical Literature* 103 (1984): 363–77.

―――. "The Jewish Leaders in the Gospel of Mark: A Literary Study of Markan Characterization." Pages 131–65 in *In the Company of Jesus: Characters in Mark's Gospel.* Louisville: Westminster John Knox, 2000.

―――. "The Poor Widow in Mark and Her Poor Rich Readers." Pages 166–88 in *In the Company of Jesus: Characters in Mark's Gospel.* Louisville: Westminster John Knox, 2000.

Malbon, E. S., and E. V. McKnight, eds. *The New Literary Criticism and the New Testament.* Journal for the Study of the New Testament Supplement Series 109. Sheffield: Academic Press, 1994.

Manns, F. "Le thème de la maison dans l'évangile de Marc." *Recherches de science religieuse* 66 (1992): 1–17.

Marcus, J. "The Jewish War and the *Sitz im Leben* of Mark." *Journal of Biblical Literature* 111 (1992): 441–62.

―――. "Mark—Interpreter of Paul." *New Testament Studies* 46 (2000): 473–87.

————. *The Mystery of the Kingdom.* Society of Biblical Literature Dissertation Series 90. Atlanta: Scholars Press, 1986.

————. *The Way of the Lord: Christological Exegesis of the Old Testament in the Gospel of Mark.* Louisville: Westminster John Knox, 1992.

Marshall, C. D. *Faith as a Theme in Mark's Narrative.* Society for New Testament Studies Monograph Series 64. Cambridge: Cambridge University Press, 1989.

Marxsen, W. *Mark the Evangelist: Studies on the Redaction History of the Gospel.* Nashville: Abingdon, 1969.

Masseaux, E. *The Influence of the Gospel of Saint Matthew on Christian Literature before Saint Irenaeus.* Edited by A. J. Bellinzoni. Translated by N. J. Belval and S. Hecht. New Gospel Studies 5. Macon: Mercer, 1993.

Masuda, S. "The Good News of the Miracle of the Bread: The Tradition and Its Marcan Redaction." *New Testament Studies* 28 (1982): 191–219.

Matera, F. J. *New Testament Christology.* Louisville: Westminster John Knox, 1999.

————. *Passion Narratives and Gospel Theologies: Interpreting the Synoptics Through Their Passion Stories.* New York: Paulist, 1986.

————. *The Kingship of Jesus: Composition and Theology in Mark 15.* Society of Biblical Literature Dissertation Series 66. Chico: Scholars Press, 1982.

————. "The Prologue as the Interpretative Key to Mark's Gospel." *Journal for the Study of the New Testament* 34 (1988): 3–20.

Meier, J. P. *A Marginal Jew: Rethinking the Historical Jesus.* 3 vols. Anchor Bible Reference Library. New York: Doubleday, 1991–2001.

Milns, R. D. "Alexander the Great." *Anchor Bible Dictionary* 1 (1992): 146–50.

Moloney, F. J. *A Body Broken for a Broken People: Eucharist in the New Testament.* 2d ed. Peabody: Hendrickson, 1997.

————. "Adventure with Nicodemus: An Exercise in Hermeneutics." Pages 259–79 in *"A Hard Saying": The Gospel and Culture.* Collegeville: Liturgical Press, 2001.

————. *Beginning the Good News: A Narrative Approach.* Collegeville: Liturgical Press, 1993.

————. *Belief in the Word: Reading John 1–4.* Minneapolis: Fortress, 1993.

————. *Glory not Dishonor: Reading John 13–21.* Minneapolis: Fortress, 1998.

————. "Mark 6:6b–30: Mission, the Baptist, and Failure." *Catholic Biblical Quarterly* 63 (2001): 647–63.

————. "Narrative Criticism of the Gospels." Pages 85–105 in *"A Hard Saying": The Gospel and Culture.* Collegeville: Liturgical Press, 2001.
————. "The End of the Son of Man?" *Downside Review* 98 (1980): 280–90.
————. "The Fourth Gospel and the Jesus of History." *New Testament Studies* 46 (2000): 42–58.
————. *The Gospel of John.* Sacra Pagina 4. Collegeville: Liturgical Press, 1998.
————. *The Johannine Son of Man.* 2d ed. *Biblioteca di Scienze Religiose* 14. Rome: Libreria Ateneo Salesiano, 1978.
————. "The Vocation of the Disciples in the Gospel of Mark." Pages 53–84 in *"A Hard Saying": The Gospel and Culture.* Collegeville: Liturgical Press, 2001.
Moo, D. J. *The Old Testament in the Gospel Passion Narratives.* Sheffield: Almond, 1983.
Moule, C. F. D. "Neglected Features in the Problem of the Son of Man." Pages 413–28 in *Neues Testament und Kirche: Festschrift für Rudolf Schnackenburg.* Edited by J. Gnilka. Freiburg: Herder, 1974.
————. *The Origins of Christology.* Cambridge: Cambridge University Press, 1977.
Munro, W. "Women Disciples in Mark?" *Catholic Biblical Quarterly* 44 (1982): 225–41.
Myers, C. *Binding the Strong Man: A Political Reading of Mark's Story of Jesus.* Maryknoll: Orbis, 1990.
Neusner, J., and W. S. Green, eds. *Dictionary of Judaism in the Biblical Period 450 B.C.E. to 600 C.E.* Peabody: Hendrickson, 1999.
Osborne, B. A. E. "Peter: Stumbling Block and Satan." *Novum Testamentum* 15 (1973): 187–90.
Paulsen, H. "Mk XVI 1–8." *Novum Testamentum* 22 (1980): 138–75.
Perrin, N. "The Christology of Mark: A Study in Methodology." *Journal of Religion* 51 (1971): 173–87.
————. *Jesus and the Language of the Kingdom.* Philadelphia: Fortress, 1976.
————. "Towards an Interpretation of the Gospel of Mark." Pages 6–21 in *Christology and a Modern Pilgrimage. A Discussion with Norman Perrin.* Edited by H. D. Betz. Missoula: Scholars Press, 1974.
————. *What Is Redaction Criticism?* Philadelphia: Fortress, 1969.
Pesch, R. "Levi–Matthäus (Mk 2,14/Mt 9,9; 10,3). Ein Beitrag zur Erlösung eines alten Problems." *Zeitschrift für die neutestamentliche Wissenschaft und die Kunde der älteren Kirche* 59 (1968): 40–56.
Petersen, N. *Literary Criticism for New Testament Critics.* Philadelphia: Fortress, 1978.

Powell, M. A. *What Is Narrative Criticism?* Minneapolis: Fortress, 1990.

Prior, M. *Paul the Letter-Writer and the Second Letter to Timothy.* Journal for the Study of the New Testament Supplement Series 23. Sheffield: JSOT Press, 1989.

Quesnell, Q. *The Mind of Mark. Interpretation and Method through the Exegesis of Mark 6,52.* Analecta Biblica 38. Rome: Pontifical Biblical Institute, 1969.

Rhoads, D., J. Dewey, and D. Michie. *Mark as Story: An Introduction to the Narrative of a Gospel.* 2d ed. Minneapolis: Fortress, 1999.

Robbins, V. K. "Last Meal: Preparation, Betrayal, and Absence." Pages 21–40 in *The Passion in Mark. Studies on Mark 14–16.* Edited by W. Kelber. Philadelphia: Fortress, 1976.

——, ed. *The Rhetoric of Pronouncement. Semeia* 64 (1994): i–xvii, 1–301.

Robinson, H. Wheeler. *Corporate Personality in Israel.* Facet Books Biblical Series 11. Philadelphia: Fortress, 1964.

Robinson, J. M., P. Hoffmann, and J. S. Kloppenborg. *The Critical Edition of Q: Synopsis Including the Gospels of Matthew and Luke, Mark and Thomas with English, German, and French Translations of Q and Thomas.* Hermeneia. Minneapolis: Fortress, 2000.

Rohde, J. *Rediscovering the Teaching of the Evangelists.* Translated by D. M. Barton. Philadelphia: Westminster, 1968.

Rohrbach, R. I. "The Social Location of the Markan Audience." *Biblical Theology Bulletin* 23 (1993): 114–27.

Saunderson, B. "Gethsemane: The Missing Witness." *Biblica* 70 (1989): 224–33.

Schildgen, B. D. *Power and Prejudice: The Reception of the Gospel of Mark.* Detroit: Wayne State University Press, 1999.

Schmidt, K. L. *Die Rahmen der Geschichte Jesu: Literarkritische Untersuchungen zu ältesten Jesusüberlieferung.* Darmstadt: Wissenschaftliche Buchgesellschaft, 1964.

Schneiders, S. M. *Interpreting the New Testament as Sacred Scripture.* 2d ed. Collegeville: Liturgical Press, 1999.

Schnelle, U. *The History and Theology of the New Testament Writings.* Translated by M. E. Boring. Minneapolis: Fortress, 1998.

Scholtissek, K. " 'Er ist nicht ein Gott der Toten, sondern der Lebenden (Mk 12,27): Grundzüge der markanische Theologie." Pages 71–100 in *Der Lebendige Gott: Studien zur Theologie des Neuen Testaments. Festschrift für Wilhelm Thüsing zum 75. Geburtstag.* Edited by T. Söding. Neutestamentliche Abhandlungen Neue Folge 31. Münster: Aschendorff, 1996.

Schweizer, A. *The Quest of the Historical Jesus.* First Complete Edition. Edited by J. Bowden. Translated by W. Montgomery, J. R. Coates, S. Cupitt, and J. Bowden. Minneapolis: Fortress, 2001.

———. *The Quest of the Historical Jesus.* Translated by W. Montgomery. London: A. & C. Black, 1910.

———. *Von Reimarus zu Wrede: Eine Geschichte der Leben-Jesu-Forschung.* Tübingen: J. C. B. Mohr (Paul Siebeck), 1906.

Schweizer, E. "Der Menschensohn." *Zeitschrift für die neutestamentliche Wissenschaft und die Kunde der älteren Kirche* 50 (1950): 185–209.

———. *Jesus.* Translated by David E. Green. Atlanta: John Knox, 1971.

———. "Mark's Theological Achievement." Pages 42–63 in *The Interpretation of Mark.* Edited by W. Telford. Issues in Religion and Theology 7. Philadelphia: Fortress, 1985.

Senior, D. "The Eucharist in Mark: Mission, Reconciliation, Hope." *Biblical Theology Bulletin* 12 (1982): 67–72.

———. *The Passion of Jesus in the Gospel of Mark.* The Passion Series 2. Wilmington: Michael Glazier, 1984.

Shepherd, T. "The Narrative Function of Marcan Intercalation." *New Testament Studies* 41 (1995): 522–40.

Sloyan, G. S. *Jesus on Trial: The Development of the Passion Narratives and Their Historical and Ecumenical Implications.* Edited by J. Reumann. Philadelphia: Fortress, 1973.

Smith, D. E. "Narrative Beginnings in Ancient Literature and Theory." *Semeia* 52 (1991): 1–9.

Smith, D. M. *John among the Gospels.* 2d ed. Columbia: University of South Carolina Press, 2001.

Stanley, D. M. *Jesus in Gethsemane: The Early Church Reflects on the Suffering of Jesus.* New York: Paulist, 1980.

Stein, R. H. "The Proper Methodology for Ascertaining a Markan Redaction History." Pages 34–51 in *The Composition of Mark's Gospel: Selected Studies from Novum Testamentum.* Edited by D. Orton. Brill's Readers in Biblical Studies 3. Leiden: Brill, 1999.

Steiner, G. *Real Presences: Is There Anything in What We Say?* Chicago: University of Chicago Press, 1989.

Stock, A. *Call to Discipleship: A Literary Study of Mark's Gospel.* Good News Studies 1. Wilmington: Michael Glazier, 1982.

Stock, K. *Boten aus dem Mit-Ihm-Sein: Das Verhältnis zwischen Jesus und den Zwölf nach Markus.* Analecta biblica 70. Rome: Biblical Institute Press, 1975.

Such, W. A. *The Abomination of Desolation in the Gospel of Mark: Its Historical Reference in Mark 13:14 and Its Impact in the Gospel.* Lanham: University Press of America, 1999.

Talbert, C. H., ed. *Reimarus: Fragments*. Philadelphia: Fortress, 1971.

Tannehill, R. C. "The Disciples in Mark: The Function of a Narrative Role." *Journal of Religion* 57 (1977): 386–405.

———. "The Gospel of Mark as Narrative Christology." *Semeia* 16 (1980): 57–95.

———, ed. *Varieties of Synoptic Pronouncement Stories*. *Semeia* 20 (1981): 1–141.

Telford, W. R. *The Barren Temple and the Withered Tree. A Redaction-Critical Analysis of the Cursing of the Fig-Tree Pericope in Mark's Gospel and Its Relation to the Cleansing of the Temple Tradition.* Journal for the Study of the New Testament Supplement Series 1. Sheffield: JSOT Press, 1980.

———. "The Pre-Markan Traditions in Recent Research." Volume 2, pages 695–723 in *The Four Gospels 1992: Festschrift Frans Neirynck*. Edited by F. van Segbroeck, C. M. Tuckett, G. van Belle, and J. Verheyden. 3 vols. Bibliotheca ephemeridum theologicarum lovaniensium 100. Leuven: Leuven University Press, 1992.

———. *The Theology of the Gospel of Mark*. New Testament Theology. Cambridge: Cambridge University Press, 1999.

———, ed. *The Interpretation of Mark*. Issues in Religion and Theology 7. Philadelphia: Fortress, 1985.

Tracy, D. *The Analogical Imagination: Christian Theology and the Culture of Pluralism*. New York: Crossroad, 1981.

Tuckett, C. M. *Q and the History of Early Christianity: Studies on Q*. Peabody: Hendrickson, 1996.

Updike, J. *The Beauty of the Lilies*. New York: Fawcett Columbine, 1996.

van Cangh, J.-M. *La Multiplication des pains et l'Eucharistie*. Lectio divina 86. Paris: Cerf, 1975.

van Iersel, B. "Die wunderbare Speisung und das Abendmahl in der synoptischen Tradition." *Novum Testamentum* 7 (1964): 167–94.

van Oyen, G. *The Interpretation of the Feeding Miracles in the Gospel of Mark*. Collectanea Biblica et Religiosa Antiqua IV. Brussels: Wetenschappelkijk Comité voor Godsdienstwetenschappen Koninklijke Vlaamse Acadamie van België voor Wetenschappen en Kunsten, 1999.

Waetjen, H. C. *A Reordering of Power. A Socio-Political Reading of Mark's Gospel*. Minneapolis: Fortress, 1989.

Watts, R. E. *Isaiah's New Exodus and Mark*. Wissenschaftliche Untersuchungen zum Neuen Testament 2. Reihe 88. Tübingen: J. C. B. Mohr (Paul Siebeck), 1997.

Weeden, T. J. *Mark—Traditions in Conflict*. Philadelphia: Fortress, 1976.

Wrede, W. *Das Messiasgeheimnis in den Evangelien: Zugleich ein Beitrag zum Verständnis des Markusevangeliums.* Göttingen: Vandenhoeck & Ruprecht, 1901.

————. *The Messianic Secret.* Translated by J. C. G. Grieg. Cambridge & London: James Clarke, 1971.

Wright, A. G. "The Widow's Mite—Praise or Lament?—A Matter of Context." *Catholic Biblical Quarterly* 44 (1982): 256–65.

Zimmerman, H. "Das absolute *egō eimi* als neutestamentliche Offenbarungsformel." *Biblische Zeitschrift* 4 (1960): 54–69, 266–76.

# Index of Modern Authors

# Index of Ancient Sources

Part Two (pp. 47–121) is devoted to a cursive reading of Mark 1:1–16:8. Markan citations are not indexed for those pages.